PIPE FITTINGS

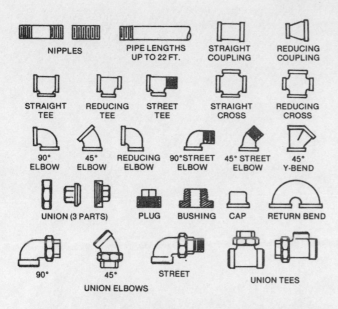

NIPPLES — PIPE LENGTHS UP TO 22 FT. — STRAIGHT COUPLING — REDUCING COUPLING

STRAIGHT TEE — REDUCING TEE — STREET TEE — STRAIGHT CROSS — REDUCING CROSS

90° ELBOW — 45° ELBOW — REDUCING ELBOW — 90° STREET ELBOW — 45° STREET ELBOW — 45° Y-BEND

UNION (3 PARTS) — PLUG — BUSHING — CAP — RETURN BEND

90° — 45° — STREET — UNION TEES
UNION ELBOWS

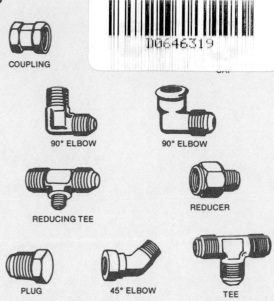

COUPLING — CAP

90° ELBOW — 90° ELBOW

REDUCING TEE — REDUCER

PLUG — 45° ELBOW — TEE

Here are the common steel pipe fittings. Nipples are simply short lengths of pipe threaded on both ends. Reducing fittings join two different sizes of pipe.

Compression fittings of the flared-tube type are the easiest for the novice to handle when working with copper tubing.

STANDARD STEEL PIPE
(All Dimensions in Inches)

Nominal Size	Outside Diameter	Inside Diameter	Nominal Size	Outside Diameter	Inside Diameter
1/8	0.405	0.269	1	1.315	1.049
1/4	0.540	0.364	1 1/4	1.660	1.380
3/8	0.675	0.493	1 1/2	1.900	1.610
1/2	0.840	0.622	2	2.375	2.067
3/4	1.050	0.824	2 1/2	2.875	2.469

SQUARE MEASURE
144 sq in = 1 sq ft
9 sq ft = 1 sq yd
272.25 sq ft = 1 sq rod
160 sq rods = 1 acre

VOLUME MEASURE
1728 cu in = 1 cu ft
27 cu ft = 1 cu yd

MEASURES OF CAPACITY
1 cup = 8 fl oz
2 cups = 1 pint
2 pints = 1 quart
4 quarts = 1 gallon
2 gallons = 1 peck
4 pecks = 1 bushel

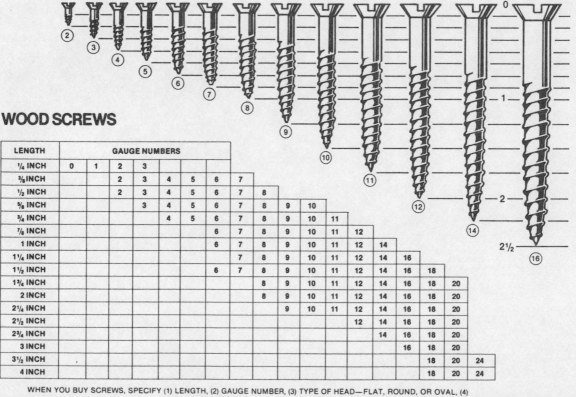

WOOD SCREWS

LENGTH	GAUGE NUMBERS													
	0	1	2	3	4	5	6	7	8	9	10	11	12	14	16	18	20	24
1/4 INCH	0	1	2	3										
3/8 INCH			2	3	4	5	6	7						
1/2 INCH			2	3	4	5	6	7	8					
5/8 INCH				3	4	5	6	7	8	9	10			
3/4 INCH					4	5	6	7	8	9	10	11		
7/8 INCH							6	7	8	9	10	11	12	
1 INCH							6	7	8	9	10	11	12	14
1 1/4 INCH								7	8	9	10	11	12	14	16
1 1/2 INCH							6	7	8	9	10	11	12	14	16	18
1 3/4 INCH									8	9	10	11	12	14	16	18	20
2 INCH									8	9	10	11	12	14	16	18	20
2 1/4 INCH										9	10	11	12	14	16	18	20
2 1/2 INCH													12	14	16	18	20
2 3/4 INCH														14	16	18	20
3 INCH															16	18	20
3 1/2 INCH																18	20	24
4 INCH																18	20	24

WHEN YOU BUY SCREWS, SPECIFY (1) LENGTH, (2) GAUGE NUMBER, (3) TYPE OF HEAD—FLAT, ROUND, OR OVAL, (4) MATERIAL—STEEL, BRASS, BRONZE, ETC., (5) FINISH—BRIGHT, STEEL BLUED, CADMIUM, NICKEL, OR CHROMIUM PLATED.

Popular Mechanics
do-it-yourself yearbook
1983

For your home

- Exciting products for better living
- Projects to improve your home

For the craftsman

- Great craft projects of the year
- Shop projects and expert know-how
- The best of the new tools

For the outdoorsman

- Great new skiing and biking gear
- Know-how tips from the experts

For the photographer

- Professional projects
- What's new in photography

For electronic buffs

- Special projects in electronics
- Newsmakers in electronics

PLUS:

- Great projects just for fun

HEARST BOOKS 224 W. 57th St., New York, NY 10019

EDITOR	Clifford B. Hicks
ASSOCIATE EDITOR	Nancy Dills
ART DIRECTOR	Ralph Leroy Linnenburger
ASSISTANT EDITOR	Tom Balow
PHOTOGRAPHY	Joe Fletcher
ART ASSISTANT	Marian C. Linnenburger
CONTRIBUTING EDITORS	David Paulsen
	Benjamin Lee

**POPULAR MECHANICS
EDITORIAL ADVISORY BOARD**

John A. Linkletter, *Editor-in-Chief*
Joe Oldham, *Executive Editor*
Bill Hartford, *Managing Editor*
Harry Wicks, *Home and Shop Editor*
Ira Herrick, *Art Editor*

Published by Hearst Books
A Division of The Hearst Corporation
224 West 57th Street
New York, N.Y. 10019

ISBN 0-87851-086-9
Library of Congress 75-648427

© 1983 The Hearst Corporation
all rights reserved

CONTENTS

THIS DOLLHOUSE is a toy box, too! The left side, shown here, is for play; the roof of the right side lifts for toy storage. You'll find plans on page 172.

On the following pages

Exciting new products and handsome do-it-yourself projects

LEARN HOW TO MASTER fine wood joinery in the extensive article starting on page 106. In easy steps you'll learn everything from simple butt joints (below left) to cutting edge laps (below right) and how to make strong dowel joints (opposite page). Fine joinery is the touch of a master craftsman.

BUILD HIGH-STYLED "park bench" furniture for your patio or yard. See the plans on page 34.

THIS HANDSOME kitchen organizer takes no space; it hangs on the door. See page 42.

JOIN THE FUN of cycling. Today there are specialty bikes for every interest. See page 142.

IN JUST ONE WEEKEND you can build this handsome harvest table with your chain saw. Find complete plans on page 23.

◆ **THIS TAKE-ME-TO-YOUR-LEADER** look reflects the state of the art in downhill skiing gear. See all the new equipment on page 146.

YOU'LL BE the hero of every kid in the neighborhood if you build this beautiful tower with play equipment. See page 167.

PRACTICAL AND easy-to-set-up beds   turn a bedroom or family room into a guest room.

Twin beds stack into a couch

By ROSARIO CAPOTOSTO

■ THIS ATTRACTIVE FURNITURE is perfect for a teen-ager's room. By day, it can be used for extra seating when the gang is over to listen to records or do homework; at night it becomes the teen-ager's bed. Best of all, it quickly transforms to sleeping for two, should your youngster want to ask a friend over for the night.

This project was developed in conjunction with Georgia-Pacific, the plywood company. The beds were built in the Popular Mechanics' workshop based upon a design idea in a booklet published by Georgia-Pacific. We did vary certain dimensions so that the beds would stand exactly the same height when in the twin-bed attitude. But, the looks remain the same.

The beds are easier to build than you might think. Simple notch and tenon joints are used at the corners, and we include a design for a cutting jig in our plans. You can build the set using basic workshop tools.

A critical point in the construction is the position of the ledger cleats in both of the units. *They are not alike.* The cleats are placed so the beds will fit together properly at a height that is comfortable for sofa-seating, yet stand the same height when they are parked side-by-side. They are built of cabinet-grade birch plywood (lumber-core).

Both beds are made to suit a 6x39x75-in. mattress. For a different size, change the dimensions on our plans to suit.

If the beds are to be painted, you can use fir or MDO plywood. If you want a clear finish, use lumber-core plywood with veneer of your choice. Lumber core gives attractive wood edges instead of plies. Buy domestic plywood to avoid mismatched colors, which are common in imported core materials. You may also avoid interior voids, and knots generally present in the imports.

Use a portable circular saw with a hollow-ground blade to rip the plywood panel into 7⅝-in. widths. The saw shoe should ride against a clamped straightedge guide to ensure straight cuts.

Mark the ends of the boards for notching and indicate the waste area to be cut out to avoid an expensive error.

For accuracy, use the jig shown in the plan to cut notches and tenons on the bed frame. If you have a table saw, set its blade high to make the short end cuts (a high blade minimizes the length of kerf on the underside of the work). Or, you can do all of the cutting with the sabre saw and jig.

Bore a blade-entry hole tangent to the cutting lines to make inside cuts for the notches on the side members. Since it is best to work with the face-side up, use a fine-tooth sabre-saw blade with a slow feed, to avoid splintering the edges.

Bore two 1-in.-diameter holes and make two guided sabre-saw cuts to create the handle holes. Round all exposed corners with a ¼-in.-radius, rounding-over router bit. Be careful when rout-

1 LAY OUT parts for notching with combination square and pencil. Indicate waste with an X.

2 CLEATS nailed to scrap board clamped to drill-press table serve as stops for blade-entry holes.

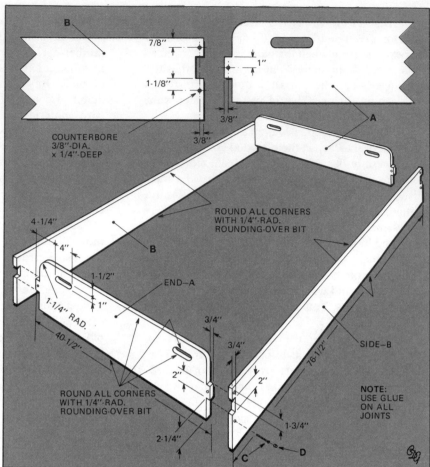

COUNTERBORE
3/8"-DIA.
x 1/4"-DEEP

7/8"

1-1/8"

3/8"

3/8"

1"

B

A

4-1/4"

4"

1-1/2"

1"

1-1/4" RAD.

40.1/2"

ROUND ALL CORNERS
WITH 1/4"-RAD.
ROUNDING-OVER BIT

END—A

B

ROUND ALL CORNERS
WITH 1/4"-RAD.
ROUNDING-OVER BIT

2"

3/4"

3/4"

2"

2-1/4"

1-3/4"

SIDE—B

76-1/2"

NOTE:
USE GLUE
ON ALL
JOINTS

C

D

3 CLEATS nailed to jig also act as stops for accuracy. Cut work face up if using smooth cutting blade.

4 ROTATE jig 90° when making next cuts. Crosspiece on jig is square and supports saw base.

5 START TENONS by making two cuts from the end. Use high blade to achieve minimum undercut.

ing top and bottom edges of the sides and ends not to round over edges in the joint areas.

Assemble the bed components with bar clamps so you can bore pilot holes for the screws accurately. Use a 1/16-in. bit first; then counterbore 1/4-in. deep by 3/8-in. diameter. After you bore the largest hole, drill the shank and body holes.

Use carpenter's glue and 1 1/4-in. common nails to attach the ledger cleats. This is best done be-

fore the sides are assembled. Use glue and No. 10x2-in. flathead screws to join the sides and ends. Cut dowel plugs from solid stock to conceal the recessed screws.

Make certain you bore ventilation holes in the 1/2-in. plywood mattress supports; then glue and nail them into place. Apply stain or finish as desired.

6 MAKE SHOULDER cuts with sabre saw. Square guide cleat with workpiece and attach it with clamps.

7 BORE TWO holes for handles. Then position saw guide so that blade is on line. Use fine-tooth blade.

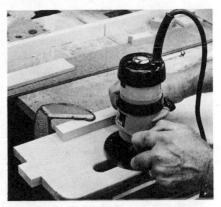

8 ROUND CORNERS of edges with router and rounding-over bit. Do not round edges in area of joints.

9 LASTLY, HOLD bed with bar clamps to bore pilot holes for screws. Counterbore holes first for wood plugs.

MATERIALS LIST—STACKABLE BEDS

Key	No.	Size and Description
A	4	3/4 × 7 5/8 × 40 1/2" plywood
B	4	3/4 × 7 5/8 × 76 1/2" plywood
C	24	2" fh wood screws
D	24	1/4" × 3/8"-dia. dowel plugs
E	4	3/4 × 1 1/8 × 75" ledger-cleat
F	2	1/2 × 38 3/4 × 74 3/4" plywood
G	2	6 × 39 × 75" foam mattress

Misc: carpenter's glue, nails, sandpaper, finishing materials.

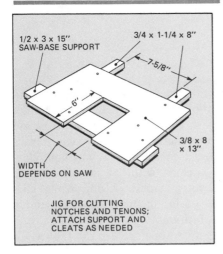

1/2 x 3 x 15"
SAW-BASE SUPPORT

3/4 x 1-1/4 x 8"

7-5/8"

6"

3/8 x 8
x 13"

WIDTH
DEPENDS ON SAW

JIG FOR CUTTING
NOTCHES AND TENONS;
ATTACH SUPPORT AND
CLEATS AS NEEDED

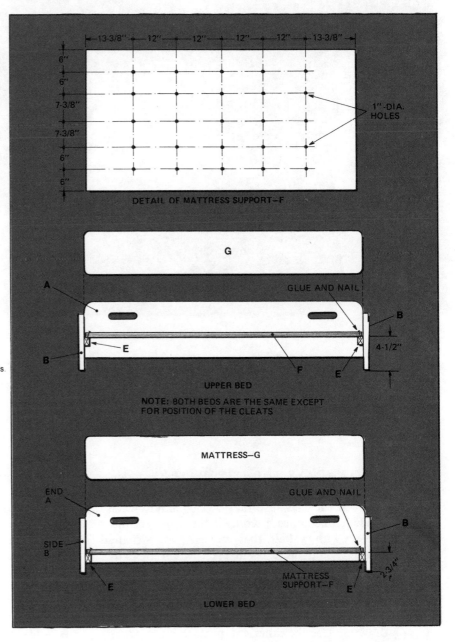

DETAIL OF MATTRESS SUPPORT—F

1"-DIA. HOLES

UPPER BED

NOTE: BOTH BEDS ARE THE SAME EXCEPT FOR POSITION OF THE CLEATS

MATTRESS—G

LOWER BED

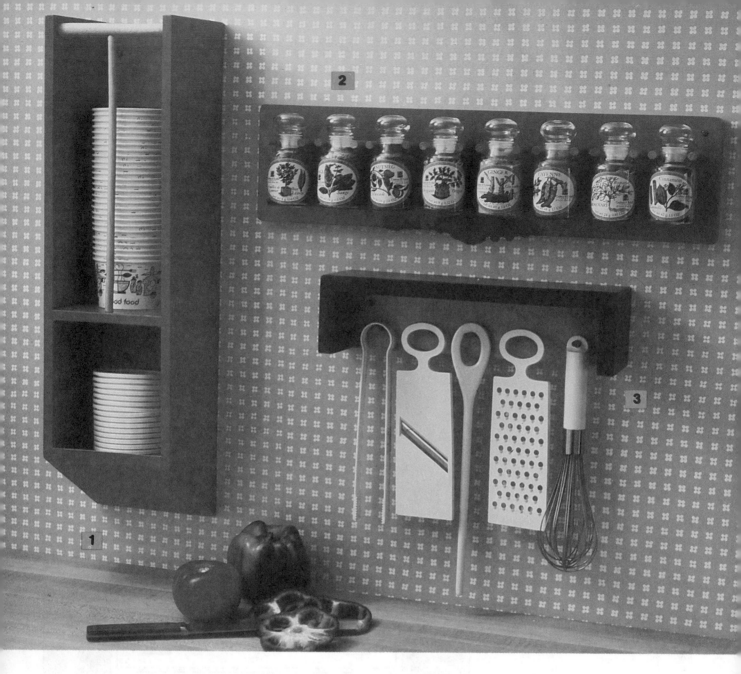

Seven hangups for your house

By HARRY WICKS

■ NOWADAYS THE DECORATING preference seems to be to put functional items on a wall—in full view—so they will be handy when needed. The concept works if the items are displayed with a flair that makes them visually pleasing, and these seven projects designed by Lester Walker do just that.

deli container rack

Lay out and cut all parts as shown in the drawing. Use the miter cut on the bottom of the sides to determine the bevel cut of the front and rear edges of the bottom shelf. Locate the holes for the dowels in the shelf and side pieces and bore them approximately ¼ in. deep. Cut dowels to length and test assemble the rack without glue. When you're satisfied with the fit, disassemble and sand all parts smooth. Using white glue (sparingly) and 1½-in. finishing nails, reassemble the box in this fashion:

■ Attach the back to one side (in the rabbet).
■ Add the middle and bottom shelves.

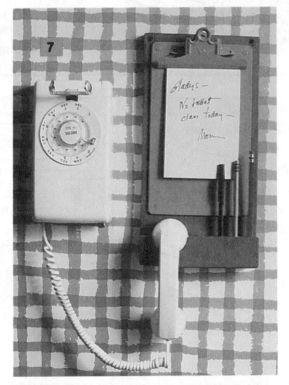

■ Insert the longer dowel into the hole bored at the center of the shorter one, then install this T-configuration as a unit into the partial assembly. (Use *glue only* on the dowels.)

■ Finally, apply glue where required and fasten the second side.

Using your combination square, check the box for square and set it aside to dry overnight.

Next day, wipe the box with a tack rag, and completely protect the dowels with masking tape. Prime-paint the entire box with a pigmented shellac such as Bin, or use flat white spray paint as it comes from the can.

Allow the prime coat to dry completely before spraying with the color of your choice.

When the color has dried completely, peel off the masking tape and spray-paint the entire box—dowels and all—with clear varnish.

DESIGNS BY architect Lester Walker confirm notion that "less is more." All projects shown are built of ½-in. pine using simple construction throughout.

1 Vertical rack holds a healthy supply of deli containers and lids.

2 Eight spice bottles hang from dowels which are inserted in the pine back.

3 Five-piece kitchen-tool set also hangs from dowels glued into pine backboard.

4 Three-board flowerpot shelf simply rests on window's meeting rail.

5 For safety this knife rack keeps blades close to the wall.

6 This hangup lets you park a large roll of paper towels on a convenient kitchen or bath wall; hand towels are displayed below.

7 Clever clipboard sports a pencil keeper, convenient note pad and a place to park the phone when someone's at the door.

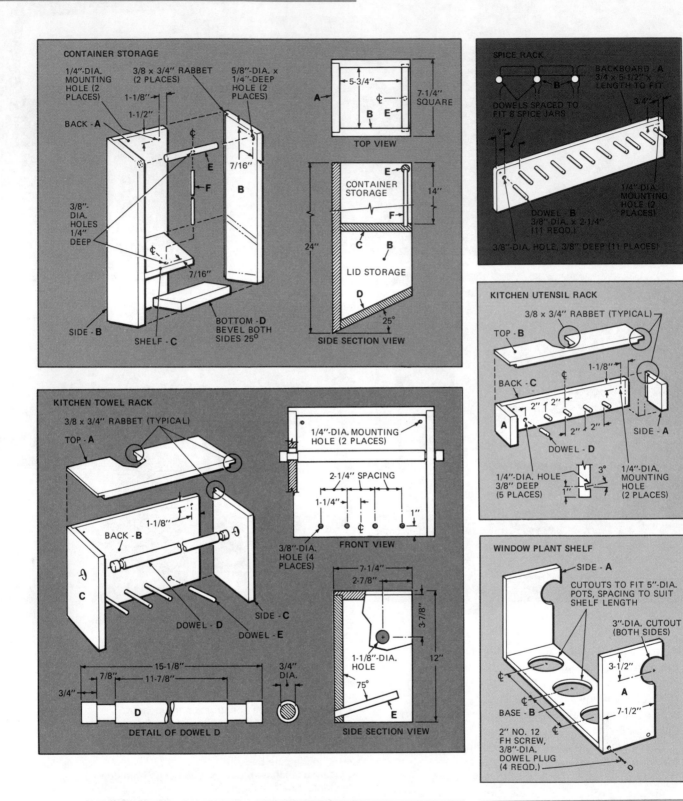

CONTAINER STORAGE

1/4"-DIA. MOUNTING HOLE (2 PLACES)
3/8 x 3/4" RABBET (2 PLACES)
5/8"-DIA. x 1/4"-DEEP HOLE (2 PLACES)
1-1/8"
1-1/2"
BACK - A
3/8"-DIA. HOLES 1/4" DEEP
SIDE - B
SHELF - C
7/16"
7/16"
BOTTOM - D BEVEL BOTH SIDES 25°
E
F
B

5-3/4"
7-1/4" SQUARE
TOP VIEW
A
B
E

E
CONTAINER STORAGE
F
C
B
LID STORAGE
D
14"
24"
25°
SIDE SECTION VIEW

SPICE RACK
BACKBOARD - A 3/4 x 5-1/2" x LENGTH TO FIT
DOWELS SPACED TO FIT 8 SPICE JARS
B
3/4"
1"
DOWEL - B 3/8" DIA. x 2-1/4" (11 REQ'D)
3/8"-DIA. HOLE, 3/8" DEEP (11 PLACES)
1/4"-DIA. MOUNTING HOLE (2 PLACES)

KITCHEN UTENSIL RACK
3/8 x 3/4" RABBET (TYPICAL)
TOP - B
BACK - C
A
2" 2"
2" 2"
1-1/8"
SIDE - A
DOWEL - D
1/4"-DIA. HOLE 3/8" DEEP (5 PLACES)
1"
3°
1/4"-DIA. MOUNTING HOLE (2 PLACES)

KITCHEN TOWEL RACK
3/8 x 3/4" RABBET (TYPICAL)
TOP - A
BACK - B
1-1/8"
C
DOWEL - D
SIDE - C
DOWEL - E

1/4"-DIA. MOUNTING HOLE (2 PLACES)
2-1/4" SPACING
1-1/4"
1"
3/8"-DIA. HOLE (4 PLACES)
FRONT VIEW

7-1/4"
2-7/8"
3-7/8"
12"
1-1/8"-DIA. HOLE
75°
E
SIDE SECTION VIEW

15-1/8"
7/8"
11-7/8"
3/4"
3/4" DIA.
D
DETAIL OF DOWEL D

WINDOW PLANT SHELF
SIDE - A
CUTOUTS TO FIT 5"-DIA. POTS, SPACING TO SUIT SHELF LENGTH
3"-DIA. CUTOUT (BOTH SIDES)
3-1/2"
A
7-1/2"
BASE - B
2" NO. 12 FH SCREW, 3/8"-DIA. DOWEL PLUG (4 REQ'D.)

MATERIALS LIST—CONTAINER

Key	No.	Size and description (use)
A	1	3/4 × 6 1/2 × 24" (back)
B	2	3/4 × 7 1/4 × 24" (sides)
C	1	3/4 × 5 3/4 × 6 1/2" (shelf)
D	1	3/4 × 5 3/4 × 8" approx., trim to fit (bottom)
E	1	5/8"-dia. × 6 1/4" (dowel)
F	1	3/8"-dia. × 13 7/8" (dowel)
	2	3/16 × 3" toggle bolt

MATERIALS LIST—UTENSIL RACK

Key	No.	Size and description (use)
A	2	3/4 × 3 1/8 × 3 1/2" (side)
B	1	3/4 × 3 1/2 × 13 1/2" (top)
C	1	3/4 × 3 1/8 × 12 3/4" (back)
D	1	1/4"-dia. × 1 3/4" dowel
	2	3/16 × 3" toggle bolts

MATERIALS LIST—SPICE RACK

Key	No.	Size and description (use)
A	1	3/4 × 5 1/2" × length to fit, (back board)
B	11	3/8"-dia. × 2 1/4" dowel
	2	3/16 × 3" toggle bolt

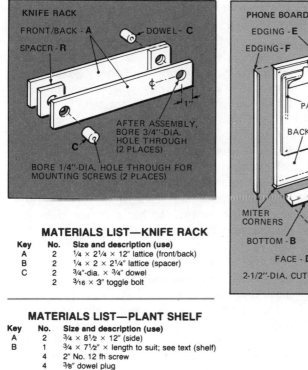

KNIFE RACK

FRONT/BACK - A   DOWEL- C

SPACER - B

¢

1"

AFTER ASSEMBLY, BORE 3/4"-DIA. HOLE THROUGH (2 PLACES)

C

BORE 1/4"-DIA. HOLE THROUGH FOR MOUNTING SCREWS (2 PLACES)

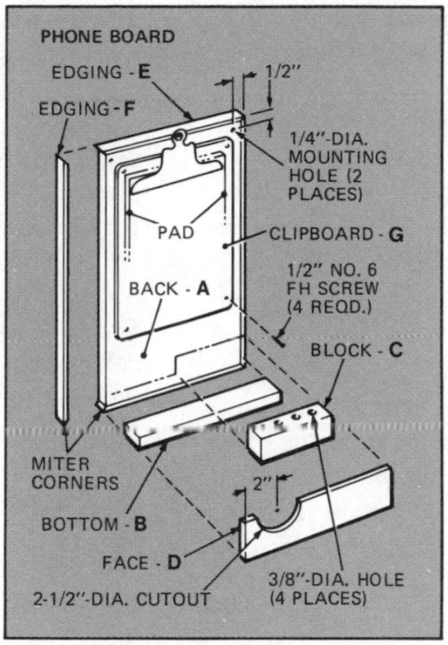

PHONE BOARD

EDGING - E

EDGING - F

1/2"

1/4"-DIA. MOUNTING HOLE (2 PLACES)

PAD

CLIPBOARD - G

BACK - A

1/2" NO. 6 FH SCREW (4 REQD.)

BLOCK - C

MITER CORNERS

BOTTOM - B

FACE - D

2"

3/8"-DIA. HOLE (4 PLACES)

2-1/2"-DIA. CUTOUT

MATERIALS LIST—PHONE BOARD

Key	No.	Size and description (use)
A	1	3/4 × 7½ × 15½" plywood (back)
B	1	3/4 × 1⅛ × 8" (bottom)
C	1	1⅛ × 1⅛ × 4" (block)
D	1	1/4 × 1⅞ × 8" lattice (face)
E	2	1/4 × 3/4 × 8" lattice (edging, top/bottom)
F	2	1/4 × 3/4 × 16" lattice (edging, side)
G	1	1/8 × 6½ × 11" (standard clipboard)
	1	5 × 8" memo pad
	4	1/2" No. 6 fh screw
	2	3/16 × 3" toggle bolt

MATERIALS LIST—TOWEL RACK

Key	No.	Size and description (use)
A	1	3/4 × 7¼ × 13½" (top)
B	1	3/4 × 11⅝ × 12¾" (back)
C	2	3/4 × 7¼ × 11⅝" (side)
D	1	1"-dia. × 15⅛" dowel
E	4	3/8"-dia. × 6" dowel

MATERIALS LIST—KNIFE RACK

Key	No.	Size and description (use)
A	2	1/4 × 2¼ × 12" lattice (front/back)
B	2	1/4 × 2 × 2¼" lattice (spacer)
C	2	3/4"-dia. × 3/4" dowel
	2	3/16 × 3" toggle bolt

MATERIALS LIST—PLANT SHELF

Key	No.	Size and description (use)
A	2	3/4 × 8½ × 12" (side)
B	1	3/4 × 7½" × length to suit; see text (shelf)
	4	2" No. 12 fh screw
	4	3/8" dowel plug

spice rack

Start by selecting the type and number of spice bottles that you want to display. Arrange them so you can verify dimensions for the dowel-hole locations. If necessary, adjust the spacing—and length of the board—to suit. At this time, also check dowel length to see if your bottles need more or less dowel.

Bore the dowel holes through. Change bits and bore the pair of holes for hanging. Sand the pieces smooth, dust and tack off.

This piece is easier to finish before assembly. Before spray-painting, insert short lengths of scrap dowel into the holes to protect the surfaces to be glued.

Prime and paint the board. When it's dry, pull out the waste dowels, apply a small amount of glue to dowels (D) and insert them into the holes. Allow to dry overnight. Finish by spraying the entire piece with satin-finish varnish.

kitchen utensil rack

Cut the four boards to size, as shown in the drawing. Next, set up your saw to cut the 3/8x3/4-in. edge rabbets in the sides and top pieces. Temporarily assemble the pieces and mark where the sidepieces rest on the back (on the inside).

Draw a light pencil line across the front of C (1

in. from the bottom edge) to serve as an aid for locating the dowel holes. To lay out the dowel locations, make a mark at the board's center (L on drawing) and space the dowels 2 in. apart, right and left.

The dowels on the prototype rack were located to suit the equipment to be displayed. To be safe, lay out the actual tools that you plan to hang on the board to check dowel locations. Relocate dowel holes, if necessary.

If you have a steady hand, you can bore the angled blind holes to receive the dowels with your portable drill. Otherwise, tilt your drillpress table 3° and clamp a jig to keep the workpiece from sliding while you bore the row of holes.

Before assembling, sand all pieces smooth.

This project is also easier to paint before assembly. First, test-assemble the box with partially driven nails to make certain you are satisfied with the fit, then disassemble it to apply the finish. Protect all surfaces that will make glue contact by covering them with masking tape.

The dowels can be glued into their holes. Next, board C is wiped with a tack rag and varnished. The board shown received two coats of varnish, with a light sanding between coats.

The sides and top are prime-painted and then sprayed with two coats of a chocolate-brown spray paint.

When the paint is dry, strip off the masking tape and assemble the rack, using white glue (sparingly) and 1½-in. finishing nails. If you assemble in this manner, you will have a mar-free finish: Drive the nails through the back piece into the rabbets in the sides and top. Using wood pads under clamp jaws for protection, clamp the sides into the rabbets at the ends of the top piece.

window plant shelf

Start by checking the window size where you plan to use this shelf. As can be seen in the photograph on page 13, the unit hangs from the "¾-moon" cutouts which simply rest on a double-hung window's meeting rail. The vertical sides bear against the window stiles beneath the meeting rail. So, measure from center to center of the stiles of your window, and use this dimension for the *outside* (overall length) dimension of your shelf.

Cut all three parts to size. Then, using nails in the waste area, tack both sides together. Cut both sides to shape at one time, using either band or sabre saw.

Refer to the actual pots to be displayed to lay out the holes in the shelf. Use a compass to scribe the circle diameters and cut the holes out using a sabre saw. Check all holes for fit with the pots before proceeding.

Assemble the shelf, using 8d (2½-in.) finishing nails and white glue.

When it's dry, mask the shelf (B), using tape and newspapers. Prime and paint the sides with the color of your choice (a burnt orange was used on the prototype). When the paint is dry, remove masking materials and apply two coats of varnish to all surfaces.

knife rack

Before cutting out the four wood pieces, lay out the collection of knives that you intend to display. Adjust rack length if necessary.

Assemble the pieces using glue, and clamp the pieces overnight. Next day, when glue is dry, remove the clamps and secure the joints by driving several ⅜-in. brads through the back and spacer into the front. Do this at both ends. Make certain brads aren't driven where the dowel holes must be bored.

The walnut dowels are actually just for looks. Locate them and bore neat, round holes. Using glue sparingly, install the dowels.

Sand all exposed surfaces smooth, dust and wipe with a tack cloth. Finish with two or three coats of spray varnish.

kitchen towel rack

This case is assembled by using the same construction as for other hanging cases.

First, cut the parts to size. Next, to bore the towel bar holes, clamp the sides together and bore both at one time. Lay out and bore the holes for the dowels and assemble the box.

Insert scrap pieces of dowel into the dowel holes to protect gluing surfaces from the paint. Sand the box smooth, prime and paint with the color of your choice. We used blue spray paint on the case shown.

Cut the towel bar to length and mark for the grooves upon which the bar rides the sides. To cut the grooves, use your miter gauge and table saw.

Raise the saw blade to cut to a depth of ⅛ in. and, slowly and carefully, rotate the dowel to make the cuts.

You can use a conventional blade and make a series of overlapping cuts. Or you can install the dado head, set up to cut a ⅞-in.-wide groove. The first method takes longer, but you might feel more comfortable doing it.

Test the bar for fit; when you're satisfied, apply two coats of varnish to it.

Glue the ⅜-in. dowels in place and set the unit aside to dry overnight. Next day, apply one or two coats of varnish. Sand the first coat lightly when dry, then dust with a tack cloth before applying the second.

phone board

For this project, start by buying the clipboard and memo pad because the backup board (A) is sized to suit the clipboard.

Cut the three parts that make up the tray at bottom, and drill all the pencil holes in C. Sand these parts before fastening them to the backup board.

Miter-cut the edging and fasten it to the plywood board, using white glue (sparingly) and brads.

Locate the clipboard on A and bore pilot holes through for the screws. Countersink the holes in the clipboard and remove it from the phone board.

Dust all pieces and wipe with a tack cloth. Apply prime paint to all surfaces. (*Note:* If you use spray paint, plug the pencil holes first.) Paint the phone and clipboards in the colors of your choice. When the paint is dry, mount the clipboard, using flathead brass screws, or apply dabs of paint to the screwheads.

OUTSIDE THE decorative rosemaling, distinguishing feature of a skammel is fingerhole slot, by which the stool can be easily carried.

Skammel stool

By WILLARD AND ELMA WALTNER

■ THIS NORWEGIAN milk stool, known as a skammel, is decorated with colorful rosemaling: a traditional style of painting flowers, scrolls and leaf shapes. First cut all parts, then sand them with 120-grit abrasive paper, dust and wipe with a tack cloth. Rout the decorative edge on sides (C). Cut finger slot in top (A).

Cut blind dadoes at an 80° angle in the top to create the mortises for the legs. Bevel cut one edge of each cleat (D) at 80°. Square the round dado ends with a chisel.

Glue legs in their grooves. Bore holes in cleats and attach with glue and screws to the top and legs. Glue aprons (C) in place; clamp until dry. Apply a prime coat of paint or pigmented shellac such as Bin. Sand with 150-grit paper, dust and tack off. Favored colors for rosemaling are blues, greens, rusts and off-white—blended with a touch of ochre or umber from a tube of artist's pigment. Apply two coats of background paint: rust with brown added. Use 220-grit paper between coats. Enlarge the rosemaling pattern full size and transfer it by rubbing the back with chalk or soft pencil, placing this chalked side on the wood and retracing the pattern. You can paint over chalklines. Use acrylic paints thinned to flow without dripping. Apply paints with fine-pointed artist's brushes.

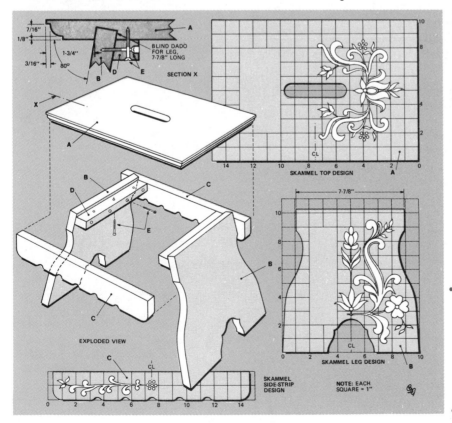

SECTION X

SKAMMEL TOP DESIGN

EXPLODED VIEW

SKAMMEL SIDE-STRIP DESIGN

SKAMMEL LEG DESIGN

NOTE: EACH SQUARE = 1"

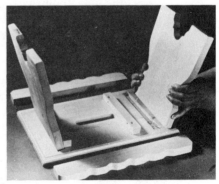

GLUE LEGS into blind dadoes cut at 80° angle for outward slant. Reinforce legs with beveled cleats (D).

MATERIALS LIST—SKAMMEL

Key	No.	Size and description (use)
A	1	3/4 × 10 × 15" pine (top)
B	2	3/4 × 10 × 10 1/4" pine (leg)
C	2	3/4 × 2 × 14 1/4" pine (apron)
D	2	3/4 × 1 × 7 7/8" pine (cleat)
E	14	No. 7 × 1 1/4" fh brass wood screws

Misc.: Glue, primer or pigmented shellac; acrylic paints; artist's brushes.

Three projects from Scandinavia

Functional Scandinavian furniture incorporates economy of materials and clean lines that will fit into a variety of decorating schemes

■ THIS DISTINCTIVE HIGH DESK is built of solid pine using edge-joined boards. But if you plan to paint your desk, you can substitute lumber-core plywood and save yourself the doweling job.

Start by cutting the boards that are to be joined an inch longer than indicated in the materials list. This precaution will allow you to trim the pieces square after the glue has dried. Then lay out the boards and join them with dowels and glue as shown in the section-view drawing.

A few points to remember when using glue with soft wood: Apply glue sparingly, but coat both surfaces. Use scraps of wood between the clamp pads and workpiece to protect the latter from clamp marks. Immediately wipe off excess glue with a clean, damp cloth. Take extra care in this step if you plan to stain the wood; the slightest trace of glue on the surface will prevent the wood beneath it from absorbing the stain. Allow joined work to dry overnight. Sand surfaces smooth with 120-grit sandpaper, then cut the boards to exact size.

Study the plans carefully, remembering that

DESK IS LARGE enough to hold thick reference book like dictionary or phone directory but it's also sufficiently sleek to be used in a foyer.

YOUNGSTERS will love this bench. Its hinged seat lifts for storage space for clothing or lots of favored dolls and toys.

THINGS AREN'T always as they seem: This smart-looking coffee table also is a dining table and stand-up work table. Secret is in way legs work.

MATERIALS LIST—HIGH DESK

Key	No.	Size and description (use)
A	1	3/4 × 6 × 24" pine (front)
B	1	3/4 × 10 × 24" pine (back)
C	2	3/4 × 10 × 16" pine (sides)
D	1	3/4 × 11 3/4 × 25 1/2" pine (lid)
E	1	3/4 × 8 1/4 × 25 1/2" pine (top)
F	4	3/4 × 1 1/2 × 44" pine (outer leg piece)
G	4	3/4 × 1 1/2 × 40" pine (inner leg piece)
H	1	3/4 × 1 1/2 × 14 1/4" pine (rail)
I	1	3/4 × 1 1/2 × 23 1/4" pine (stretcher)
J	1	1/2 × 16 × 22 1/2" plywood (bottom)
K	1	1/4 × 1 1/4 × 25 1/2" pine (lip)
L	2	3/4 × 2" butt hinge
M	(as reqd.)	6d finishing nails
N	2	2" No. 12 fh screws
O	8	1 1/4" No. 10 fh screws

Misc.: Carpenter's glue, dowels.
Note: Parts A, B, C, D and E are all made from 1×4 pine edge-joined with dowels and glue.

THREE-WAY TABLE

Key	No.	Size and description (use)
A	1	3/4 × 31 1/2 × 47" plywood (top)
B	2	3/4 × 2 3/4 × 47 1/4" redwood (leg)
C	2	3/4 × 2 3/4 × 46 1/2" redwood (leg)
D	2	3/4 × 2 3/4 × 29 1/2" redwood (stretcher)
E	2	3/4 × 2 3/4 × 27 1/2" redwood (stretcher)
F	3	3/4 × 1 1/2 × 31 1/2" redwood or pine (stops)
G	2	1/2 × 3 × 32 1/2" redwood (end skirt)
H	2	1/2 × 3 × 47" redwood (skirt)
I	2	5/16 × 2 3/4" rh bolt
	8	5/16" i.d. washer

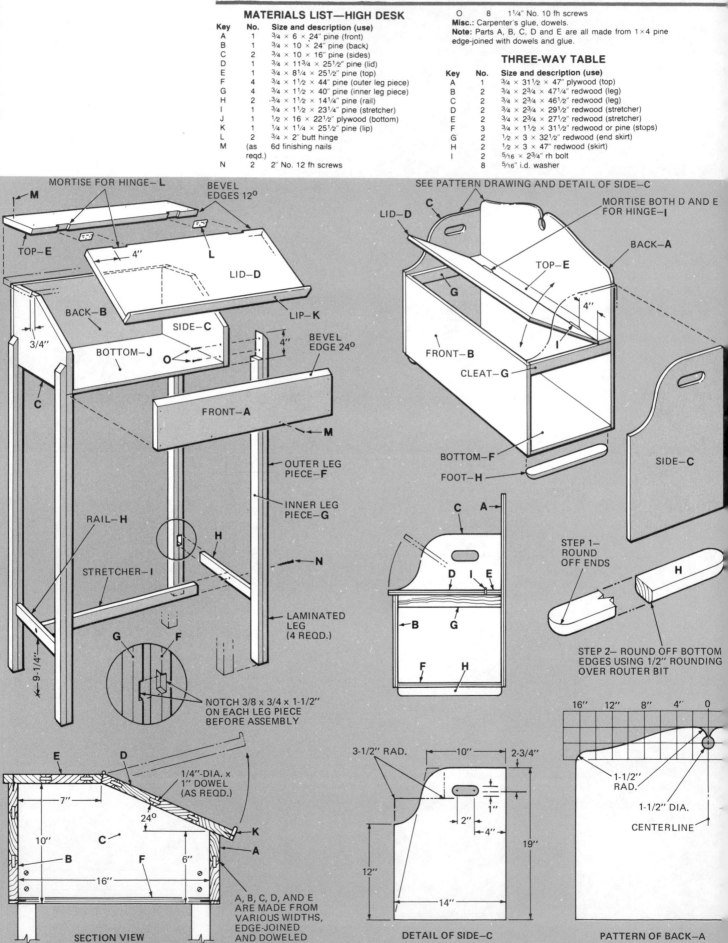

	2	5/16" hex nut
J	12	3/4 × 2" butt hinge, 3/4" fh screws
K	18	2" No. 8 fh screws
L	28	2" No. 12 fh screws

Misc.: Carpenter's glue, 100-grit sandpaper.

SMALL BENCH

Key	No.	Size and description (use)
A	1	1/2 × 24 × 33" plywood (back)
B	1	1/2 × 11 1/2 × 33" plywood (front)
C	2	1/2 × 14 × 19" plywood (side)
D	1	1/2 × 12 × 33" plywood (lid)
E	1	1/2 × 2 × 33" plywood (cleat)
F	1	1/2 × 13 × 33" plywood (bottom)
G	2	3/4 × 1 1/2 × 13" pine (cleat)
H	2	3/4 × 1 1/2 × 13" pine or hardwood (foot)
I	2	1/2 × 2" butt hinge

Misc:. 8d finishing nails, carpenter's glue and paint.

Scandinavian projects, continued →

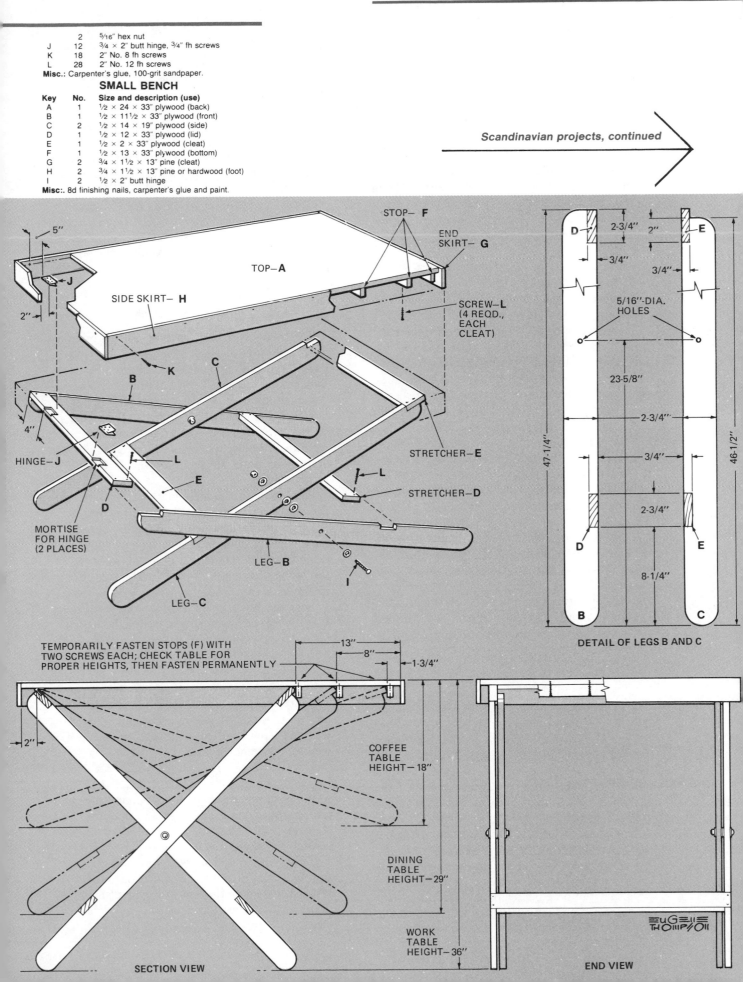

STOP— **F**

END SKIRT— **G**

TOP—**A**

SIDE SKIRT— **H**

5"

2"

J

K

B

C

4"

HINGE— **J**

L

D

E

MORTISE FOR HINGE (2 PLACES)

LEG—**B**

LEG—**C**

I

SCREW—**L** (4 REQD., EACH CLEAT)

STRETCHER—**E**

STRETCHER—**D**

DETAIL OF LEGS B AND C

2-3/4"   2"

D   **E**

3/4"

3/4"

5/16"-DIA. HOLES

23-5/8"

2-3/4"

3/4"

2-3/4"

D   **E**

8-1/4"

47-1/4"

46-1/2"

B   **C**

TEMPORARILY FASTEN STOPS (F) WITH TWO SCREWS EACH; CHECK TABLE FOR PROPER HEIGHTS, THEN FASTEN PERMANENTLY

13"

8"

1-3/4"

2"

COFFEE TABLE HEIGHT— 18"

DINING TABLE HEIGHT— 29"

WORK TABLE HEIGHT— 36"

SECTION VIEW

END VIEW

construction of any square shape is impossible without square parts. Check for square with a framing square. Also check the length of all parts and be sure to make bevel cuts on A and E before construction begins. Cut the diagonal line on sidepieces (C).

Assemble the box, using nails and carpenter's glue. Work in an upright position and, once you have begun assembly, avoid excessive movement. Check again for square with your framing square, then hold the box square, using a pair of diagonal braces temporarily tacked across the opposite corners. Use lattice strips or scrap for the braces.

Allow the glue to dry overnight, then set the nails and fill the holes with wood putty.

Finish the box by mortising for the hinges and installing the lid hardware.

Cut notches in the leg members to receive the rails. Insert the rails in the notches and glue the rails and laminated leg members together. To prevent the chance of twisted leg assemblies, sandwich each assembly between large pieces of ¾-in. plywood. Be sure that the legs and rails are at 90° before clamp pressure is applied.

After the leg assemblies have dried thoroughly, attach them to the desk as shown, using screws and glue. The final step is attaching the stretcher to the legs with screws and glue. If all parts have been cut accurately, the assembly should produce a square desk.

To finish, sand with 120-grit paper, dust off, then finish-sand with 180-grit paper. Dust off, wipe with a tack cloth and apply the stain of your choice, following the manufacturer's directions on the can. Allow stain to dry overnight, then apply the finish. The desk shown was finished with two coats of varnish for durability.

building the small bench

Designed for a child's room, this bench can be built in a weekend or two.

Start by cutting all pieces to the dimensions that are specified in the materials list. Lay out the pattern grid as shown in the drawing and, using a sabre saw, make cuts for the scrollwork on the back and sides. Bore the 1½-in. hole in the back with a hole saw before cutting scrolls.

The handle slots are also made with a sabre saw and drill. Using the measurements in the detail drawing for side C, locate the center points and bore two 1-in. entry holes for each handle. Note that the hole center points are 2 in. apart. Clamp a straightedge to the sides to make straight cuts between holes to complete the handle cutout.

Using carpenter's glue and 8d finishing nails, assemble the front, back, bottom and sides of the box. Work on a flat surface with the box in the upright position. Use a water-dampened cloth to wipe off all glue squeeze-out.

Next, attach the feet and install the seat cleats. Mortise for the hinges and attach them to the lid and hinge cleat. Then attach the hinge cleat to the box.

To finish the bench, round all edges slightly with 120-grit paper, dust and apply a coat of primer, then finish in desired color, using semi-gloss latex paint.

the three-way table

The three-level, multipurpose table is practical and saves lots of space. In the photograph on page 19, it is used as a 13-in.-high coffee table. You can elevate it to 29 in. for dining and also to a conventional work-table height of 36 in.

This table is built of plywood and redwood strips. Although the design is uncomplicated, measure carefully to ensure proper fitting of legs and leg supports. If you don't, the table will not stand firmly.

Starting with the legs, mark and cut notches for the stretchers. Attach the stretchers with countersunk flathead screws and glue. Because of the difference in the length of the legs, stretcher E extends beyond the length of legs C—see leg detail in the drawing. Mortise for and attach hinges to stretcher D.

Bore the holes in the legs for the pivot bolts. Bolt the leg sections together, noting the locations for the four washers used with each nut and bolt. The two washers between the legs eliminate friction and ensure easy pivoting.

To make the tabletop, first accurately locate and attach the leg stops. Use countersunk screws and glue. Attach the skirt using glue and counterbored screws and dowel plugs. Or use glue and well-set 6d finishing nails.

The last step is to attach the hinged leg assembly to the underside of the table. Place the hinges in the position shown in the drawing. Make certain that stretcher E aligns with each of the three stops (F). The hinges may be adjusted to compensate for alignment if necessary.

Finish with a light sanding with 120-grit paper to round-over the edges. If you plan to paint the table, disassemble the legs at the pivot bolts and then paint with the legs apart.

Build a harvest table with your chain saw

One weekend session is all it takes to build this handsome yard set. It's set permanently into the ground for stability. You cut the parts with a chain saw

■ ALTHOUGH THE rough-hewn features of this handsome table and bench set give an impression of stability and agelessness, you can actually build it in a weekend work session, if you organize your work schedule. The sturdy furniture will withstand years of use and weather in your backyard and retain the same timeless appeal that it has today.

This rustic furniture is a joint project developed by Homelite and *Popular Mechanics*. Cut-

WHEN CROSSCUTTING a heavy overhang, make two cuts from opposite sides to prevent splitting.

MAKE FOUR or five kerf cuts to notch out the post top. Use a wood strip as a depth guide.

YOU CAN BREAK out the waste slices by hand. If some pieces are stubborn, use a chisel or pinch bar.

IN ORDER TO LEVEL the bottom safely, you can easily make use of the chain saw itself.

MAKE A SHORT crosscut at the end; then make an angle cut to avoid splitting the wood.

LINE UP the 2x4s with their best surfaces on the top. Identify each piece in order of assembly.

IF YOU MUST bore the holes with a portable drill, a drill guide like this is invaluable.

HOLD SAW at a 45° angle to trim off excess. Keep your body to the left of the chain line.

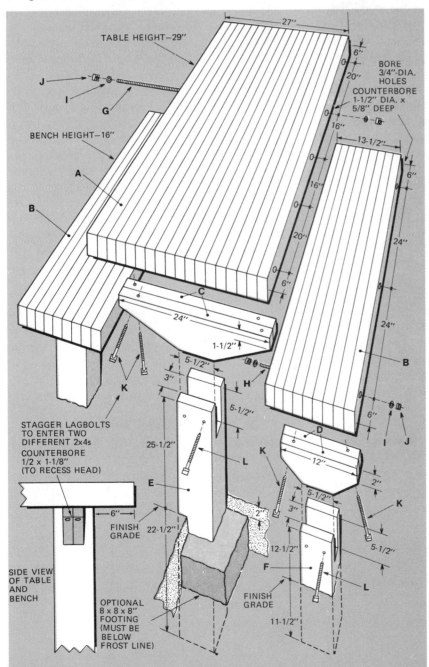

TABLE HEIGHT—29"

BENCH HEIGHT—16"

27"

6"

20"

BORE
3/4"-DIA.
HOLES
COUNTERBORE
1-1/2" DIA. x
5/8" DEEP

16"

13-1/2"

6"

16"

20"

24"

6"

24"

A

B

J
I
G

C

24"

1-1/2"

5-1/2"

3"

H

5-1/2"

B

K

STAGGER LAGBOLTS
TO ENTER TWO
DIFFERENT 2x4s
COUNTERBORE
1/2 x 1-1/8"
(TO RECESS HEAD)

25-1/2"

L

E

22-1/2"

6"

FINISH
GRADE

SIDE VIEW
OF TABLE
AND
BENCH

OPTIONAL
8 x 8 x 8"
FOOTING
(MUST BE
BELOW
FROST LINE)

D

K

12"

2"

5-1/2"

3"

K

2"

12-1/2"

F

L

FINISH
GRADE

11-1/2"

6"

I
J

USE A BELT sander on edges. Assemble top carefully so it won't need sanding. Use same procedure for seats.

MATERIALS LIST—TABLE, BENCHES

Key	No.	Size and description (use)
A	18	2×4" × 7' Wolmanized lumber (tabletop pieces)
B	18	2×4" × 5' Wolmanized lumber (benchtop pieces)
C	4	2×6×24" Wolmanized lumber (tabletop supports)
D	8	2×6×12" Wolmanized lumber (benchtop supports)
E	2	6×6×48" Wolmanized lumber (table legs)
F	4	6×6×24" Wolmanized lumber (bench legs)
G	5	1/2"-dia. × 27" threaded rod (tabletop rods)
H	6	1/2"-dia. × 13½" threaded rod (benchtop rods)
I	22	1/2"-i.d. washers
J	22	1/2"-i.d. nuts
K	16	3/8"-dia. × 6" lagscrews (top fasteners)
L	12	3/8"-dia. × 5" lagscrews (leg fasteners)

continued on the next page →

ting the large wood members that give the furniture its rugged look is made easier with a heavy-duty saw such as a Homelite or other chain saw. The construction design is by Rosario Capotosto based on a drawing by David Stiles.

Legs on the benches and table are of 6x6 Wolmanized lumber notched at the top to receive doubled 2x6 supports for the top and seats. Both the table and benchtops are 2x4s laid on edge and bolted together with a threaded rod.

Begin work by cutting the posts (E and F, see drawing and materials list). Post stock is usually available in 6-, 8- and 12-ft. lengths. *Be sure to wear safety goggles at all times while you're working with the chain saw.*

To avoid tearing the ends of the wood when crosscutting, first make a partial cut from one edge of the wood. Then turn the stock over and complete the cut by sawing through from the opposite side.

The tops of the posts are notched to accommodate the supports for the furniture tops. Before you make the notches, set the posts in the ground. However, the posts must be placed accurately or you will have alignment problems later. You may find it easier to construct and assemble the units out of the ground, and then plant them.

Begin work on the notches by cutting a series of saw kerfs. To make these cuts the post must be rigid. So, if it is not in the ground, first clamp the post to a sturdy support such as a sawbuck. Mark the outline of the notch and tack-nail a strip of wood across the post to serve as a visual guide for the depth of the cut. Start the cut with the chain bar pointing slightly upward. Level the bar off as the cut progresses; continue until you reach the guide stick.

After you've made several side-by-side kerf cuts, you may be tempted to tilt the saw sideways to nibble away at the bottoms of the waste slices. *Don't do it*—you could easily lose control of the saw and experience a kickback, as the teeth at the top of the bar strike wood and cut in the opposite direction. It's much safer to break away the waste slices by hand or with a chisel. Then you can use the saw to level off the remaining stubs at the notch bottom.

cutting the top supports

Next, cut the angled supports (C) for the tabletop, and the supports (D) for the benchtops. Clamp a 2x6 support board to a pair of sawhorses and make a partial crosscut to establish the end.

Then make the angled cut to meet it. In this way, the piece will make a clean break from the waste without splitting. Nail two supports together and smooth the edges with a belt sander. As an alternative, you can join the two pieces of 2x6 together first, and then make the cuts in one pass.

Insert the supports into the posts, clamp them if necessary, and bore the holes for the lag bolts. Put these aside.

making the furniture tops

Align the 2x4s (A and B) for the table and benchtops on their edges. Select the best surfaces for the face sides. Arrange the 2x4s so that any slightly warped ones are positioned in alternate directions to counteract each other. Severely warped or twisted stock should not be used.

Mark the pieces so the tops can be reassembled later, in the same order. Use a T-square to mark the locations for the threaded rod holes.

If you have a drill press, clamp a stop to the table to simplify centering across the width. Otherwise, use a drill guide such as the Portalign to bore all holes perpendicular. First, counterbore the holes on the two outside members to recess the nuts and washers. Bore the larger hole first, otherwise, the drill center will be lost.

Cut the ½-in.-dia. threaded rod to length and grind off the burrs. Assemble the pieces and clamp strips of wood across the top and bottom at both ends and in the center to obtain a good surface alignment. Insert the threaded rods and washers. Then secure the nuts at both ends, using a pair of socket wrenches.

If you use stock size 2x4 lumber, you'll have to trim off the waste at one end. You can easily do this with the chain saw. However, the resulting edge will be rough and will need smoothing with a belt sander and 80-grit paper.

assembling the pieces

You can use the same procedure to assemble both the table and the benches. Begin by turning one of the tops face down on the ground. Bore holes for the lag screws through the supports and into the top. Assemble and place the unit into the holes that have been dug for it. Repeat for the other furniture pieces.

Back-fill and tamp the earth firmly. You can top off the holes with 6 or 8 in. of cement for extra stability if you wish. For added permanency, consider pouring concrete collars around the posts.

SHOWN ABOVE is our reproduction of the mahogany clock that was in the Butler family home, where Lincoln stayed while starting his Springfield law practice. The original clock (top) is now in the Lincoln home.

A Lincoln legacy:
Two mantel clocks you can build

By DAVID A. WARREN

clocks continued on next page

■ WE'VE GONE BACK into history to bring you two clocks that Abraham Lincoln must have checked time by during his early days as an aspiring young lawyer, and later as a U.S. statesman. The mahogany clock was in the Butler home where Lincoln stayed when opening his law practice in Springfield. Today, it is in the sitting room of the Lincoln Home National Historic Site in Springfield, Ill.

The back of the illustration in the pine clock bears an inscription by Lincoln's son Tad. To help you make your reproduction a faithful one, we've reproduced both this inscription and the decorative drawing. Complete plans for duplicating both clocks are on the following pages.

There are minor differences between the original clocks (in the smaller photos) and the reproductions: The originals have 30-hour movements, while ours are eight-day clocks. The original movements are screwed to the backs of the cases. In the reproductions, we've mounted the movements on a sheet-metal faceplate. The winding arbors on the reproductions are at 6 o'clock, whereas on the originals they are at 3:00 and 11:00.

For both clocks, we selected an Urgo eight-day, spring-wound, pendulum movement available from the source given in the materials lists. Modern hands come with the mechanism, but for more authenticity you'll probably want the older styles we've specified. These hands, plus the appropriate paper dial faces, are available from the same source. You merely glue the paper dial to the metal backing plate.

There are, however, many other types of clock movements that you might wish to consider, such as quartz, electric or battery models. For your convenience, we've listed additional sources for clock movements and parts in the box on page 32.

building the pine clock

Tad's pine clock has a fairly straightforward rectangular cabinet. Rip the base stock in one piece and cut the bevel before dividing it into the three parts. Then cut the grooves in the two sidepieces. Next, rip the sides for the case and cut the rabbets, using a table saw, router or jointer.

Glue and nail the bottom and base pieces so the assembly is square. Clamp if needed. Sand the exposed edges of the remaining pieces with 100-grit paper. Glue and clamp the sides to the base, making sure the sides are square. Cut and attach the back, then the top.

Rip stock for the door and make the rabbet to hold the glass. Sand the inside edges with 100-grit paper. Glue up the door; when it's dry, cut the crosspieces and glue them in place. Sand the upper and lower door edges at a 2° or 3° inward angle (bevel) so the door will close smoothly.

Sand all parts, breaking the corners, dust and wipe with a tack cloth. We applied a dark walnut stain to the wood. When the stain is thoroughly dry, rub on several coats of French polish (20 percent boiled linseed oil and 80 percent orange shellac), using 4/0 steel wool. Next, buff with carnauba wax.

You can make pin hinges from 20-ga. brass to mount the door. Cut two hinges as shown in the drawing. Bore a hole for a small brass nail. File the hinges smooth and bend to shape. Use a No. 60 bit to bore hinge-mounting holes in the door. Bend the lower hinge upward slightly, so that the door doesn't rub on the base.

Carefully cut the paper face to fit the opening. Cut the sheet metal to fit the face. Bore holes for the hands, winding arbor and mounting screws in the metal. Apply the paper face to the metal with rubber cement.

Paint flowers at four corners of the dial with light green paint to create the decorative tole design shown on the original. File the paper away from the arbor holes with a round file. Mount the movement to the metal faceplate and screw the assembly into the case. Cut wood strips to hold glass. Attach glass with epoxy resin, glue train art and cement wood strips.

Finally, shape the door catch of 20-ga. brass and attach it with a ⅜-in. brass brad. Nail another brad to the door to receive the catch. Marks on the original indicate that the clock was hung on the wall at one time. If you wish, snip a brass hanger to shape, bore holes as needed and fasten with brads to the case back.

building the Butler clock

Before you begin construction on the mahogany clock, study the drawing carefully. Start by ripping the stock for the sides and top. Round the front edges as shown in the drawing with a spokeshave or other shaping tool.

Cut the bottom to size. Then rip base stock and round its edge as shown before cutting individual lengths. Cut the rabbets and the miters for the front corners. Assemble the sides to the base with glue; when dry, glue and nail the base to the bottom. Bore pilot holes before driving any nails to prevent splitting the hardwood. Miter the three top pieces, and glue and nail them in place. To complete the case, cut the backpiece, and glue and nail it in place.

To construct the door, rip stock and cut the pieces to size, carefully trimming the ends to the correct angles. Then cut grooves for the splines. Notch the door catch on the left sidepiece, and cut panel J (see art) to size.

Dry-assemble and test-fit the door before you glue all of the parts. After gluing, sand with 120-grit paper, beveling the edges to a slight inward angle so the door will close easily.

Next, glue a filler strip (L) on the inside of the front at the bottom, and glue in the mounting blocks (E). You can make the small quarter-round molding in front of the mirror by ripping a ½-in. dowel in half, then the halves into quarters. Paint the quarter-round with gilding.

We finished the case by dipping it and the door (not yet attached) in a solution of 1 tablespoon of

PRIMITIVE but handsome pine mantel clock features the train drawing below. The drawing is actual size (see original clock in the photo on the left), so you can clip it from this page.

EDGE RABBETS for sides, bottom and door frame can be cut with table saw, router or router in overhead arm.

GLUE AND CLAMP mitered door-frame pieces. When dry, bore pilot holes in corners to reinforce with 3d nails.

PIN HINGES for door are reproduced from thin, polished brass. See text and drawing for installation.

PAPER CLOCK FACE is glued to metal backing plate, and plate is fastened into rabbets in case with small screws.

MATERIALS LIST—TAD'S PINE CLOCK

Key	Amt.	Size and description (use)
A	1	$1/2 \times 3^{1/2} \times 6^{5/8}$" pine (top)
B	2	$1/2 \times 2^{5/8} \times 10^{1/8}$" pine (side)
C	2	$1/2 \times 2 \times 3^{1/2}$" pine (base side)
D	1	$1/2 \times 2 \times 7$" pine (base front)
E	1	$3/8 \times 2^{3/4} \times 6^{1/2}$" pine (bottom)
F	1	$1/4 \times 5^{1/2} \times 10^{1/2}$" pine (back)
G	2	$9/16 \times {}^{11/16} \times 6$" pine (door top/bottom)
H	2	$9/16 \times {}^{11/16} \times 10^{1/8}$" pine (door side)
I	1	$7/16 \times 1/2 \times 5$" pine (crosspiece)
J	1	$1/8 \times 5/8 \times 4^{5/8}$" pine (crosspiece)
K	2	$1/8 \times 1/4 \times 4^{15/16}$" (glass retainer)
L	1	$1/8 \times 1/4 \times 4^{15/16}$" (glass retainer)
M	1	$4^{5/16} \times 4^{5/16}$" single-strength glass (for clock)
N	1	$1^{5/16} \times 4^{5/16}$" single-strength glass (for picture)
O	2	$1/4 \times 1$" 20-gauge brass (hinge)
P	1	1×2" 20-gauge brass (door catch)
Q	1	$5/8 \times 3/4$" 20-gauge brass (hanger)
R	1	2×5" (picture, clip from magazine)
S	1	$4^{1/4}$-dia. dial with $5/8$" Roman numerals (paper clock dial; see note below)
T	1	$5^{11/16} \times 5^{11/16}$" 20-gauge sheet metal (metal backing for clock dial)
U	1	Urgo 8-day pendulum clock movement (see note below)
V	2	$1^{3/8}$" and $2^{1/8}$" serpentine clock hands (see note below)

Misc. $1/2$" No. 4 fh brass screws (4); $1/2$" brass brads; epoxy cement; 3d finishing nails; stain; French polish (80% orange shellac and 20% boiled linseed oil).

Note: The 8-day Urgo clock movement (Model 567982) is about $30 from Marshall-Swartchild & Co., 2040 North Milwaukee Ave., Chicago, Ill. 60647; hands and paper dial face can also be ordered from this company or obtained locally. There is no brass bezel on this clock style. Also, on the original, there is no brass grommet in the winding-arbor hole, but one can be added if you wish to protect the face from being scratched by the key.

lye to 1 gal. of water. *Note:* Use extreme caution when working with lye. Wear goggles, gloves and long sleeves.

The lye acts as a bleach, lightening the tone of the wood and helping to get rid of the purplish tinge that mahogany often has. When the wood reaches the desired shade, wash the case off with water and wipe it dry. When completely dry,

apply French polish, a mixture of 20-percent boiled linseed oil and 80-percent orange shellac, rubbed in with 4/0 steel wool.

Fill in the nail holes with the appropriate shade of wax stick and buff with carnauba wax.

Cut a latch from 20-ga. brass and attach it to the knob with epoxy cement. Cut a slot in the case for the catch. Mark and cut the paper dial

INSCRIPTION by Lincoln's son Tad, can be clipped out and pasted behind the door.

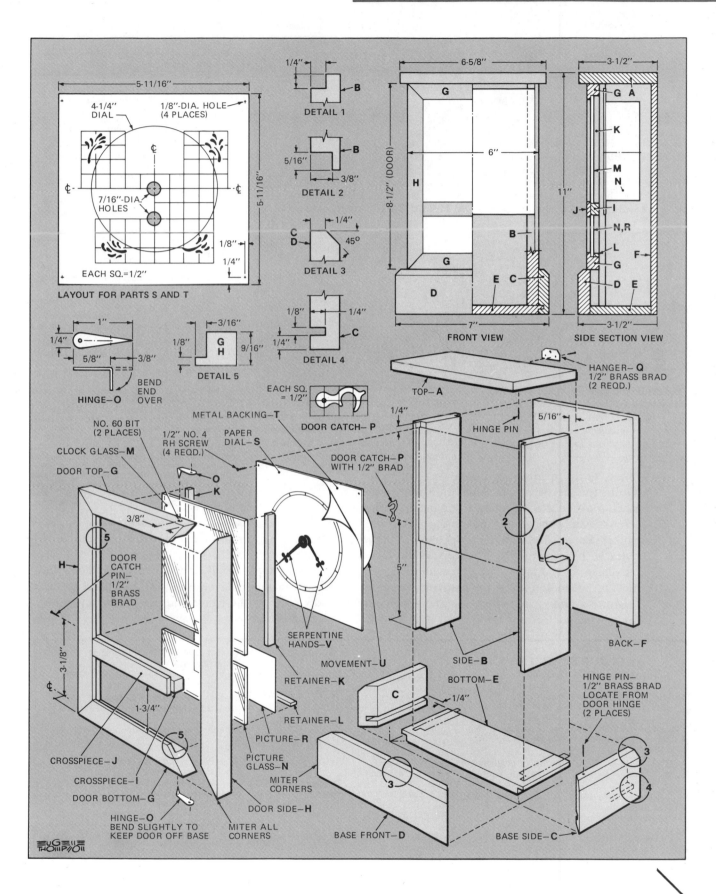

LAYOUT FOR PARTS S AND T

5-11/16"
4-1/4" DIAL
1/8"-DIA. HOLE (4 PLACES)
7/16"-DIA. HOLES
5-11/16"
1/8"
1/4"
EACH SQ.=1/2"

DETAIL 1
1/4"
B

DETAIL 2
5/16"
3/8"
B

DETAIL 3
1/4"
C
D
45°

DETAIL 4
1/8"
1/4"
1/8"
1/4"
C

DETAIL 5
3/16"
1/8"
G
H
9/16"

6-5/8"
G
6"
H
B
G
E C
D
7"
FRONT VIEW
8-1/2" (DOOR)

3-1/2"
G A
K
M
N
J
I
N,R
L
G F
D E
11"
3-1/2"
SIDE SECTION VIEW

HINGE—O
1"
1/4"
5/8"
3/8"
BEND END OVER

NO. 60 BIT (2 PLACES)
CLOCK GLASS—M
DOOR TOP—G
1/2" NO. 4 RH SCREW (4 REQD.)
PAPER DIAL—S
METAL BACKING—T
EACH SQ. = 1/2"
DOOR CATCH—P

TOP—A
HANGER—Q
1/2" BRASS BRAD (2 REQD.)
1/4"
HINGE PIN
5/16"

O
K
3/8"
5
H
DOOR CATCH PIN—1/2" BRASS BRAD
3-1/8"
1-3/4"
CROSSPIECE—J
CROSSPIECE—I
DOOR BOTTOM—G
HINGE—O BEND SLIGHTLY TO KEEP DOOR OFF BASE
MITER ALL CORNERS
DOOR SIDE—H
PICTURE GLASS—N
PICTURE—R
RETAINER—L
RETAINER—K
SERPENTINE HANDS—V
MOVEMENT—U
DOOR CATCH—P WITH 1/2" BRAD
5"
2
1
SIDE—B
BOTTOM—E
C
1/4"
MITER CORNERS
3
BASE FRONT—D
BASE SIDE—C
BACK—F
HINGE PIN—1/2" BRASS BRAD LOCATE FROM DOOR HINGE (2 PLACES)
3
4

please turn the page

CUT GROOVES for splines in door-frame pieces. To prevent narrow wood from slipping through blade slot, run scrap of ⅛-in. hardboard partway through saw to make a temporary surface.

TO FINISH the mahogany clock, wood was immersed in a lye solution. When dry, it was polished, using 4/0 steel wool and a mixture of one part boiled linseed oil with four parts orange shellac.

AFTER CUTTING and grooving door-frame pieces, rout out recess for catch.

FIRST, CUT paper clock face to fit the case, then use paper cutout to transfer shape onto sheet metal. Cut and bore metal and glue paper to it. Movement mounts on back with brass nuts.

MATERIALS LIST—BUTLER CLOCK

Key	Amt.	Size and description (use)
A	2	⅝ × 1⅝ × 3⅝" mahogany (base side)
B	1	⅝ × 1⅝ × 7" mahogany (base front)
C	2	½ × 3 × 7¼" mahogany (side)
D	3	½ × 3 × 2½" mahogany (top)
E	2	½ × ¾ × 4" (mounting block)
F	1	⅜ × 2¾ × 6¼" (bottom)
G	2	⅜ × ¹¹⁄₁₆ × 5¾" mahogany (door side)
H	1	⅜ × ¹¹⁄₁₆ × 5" mahogany (door bottom)
I	1	⅜ × ¹¹⁄₁₆ × 2¹⁄₁₆" mahogany (door top)
J	1	⅜ × 2 × 3⅝" mahogany (door panel)
K	1	¼ × 5½ × 9⅛" (back)
L	1	¼ × 1¼ × 5" (filler)
M	2	⅛ × ¾ × ¾" (spline)
N	3	⅛ × ⁵⁄₁₆ × 3" (spline, trim to fit)
O	2	3⅝" quarter-round molding for top/bottom (cut quarter rounds from ½"-dia. dowel × 6")
P	2	1¼" quarter-round molding for sides (cut from dowel as above)
Q	2	¾ × ¾ × 1½" (glue block)
R	1	⅛ × 1¼ × 3⅝" mirror
S	1	3⁷⁄₁₆"-dia. single-strength glass (for clock)
T	1	4"-dia. brass clock bezel (see note below)
U	3	¼ × ⅝" 20-gauge brass (retainer)
V	2	½ × ¾" brass butt hinge
W	1	½ × ½" brass knob
X	1	⁵⁄₁₆ × ⅝" 20-gauge brass (door latch)
Y	1	Urgo 8-day pendulum clock movement (see note below)
Z	1	3½"-dia. paper dial face (see note below)
AA	1	5×5" 20-gauge sheet metal (metal backing for clock dial)
BB	1	1¾" and 1½" spade clock hands (see note below)

Misc.: ¼" No. 4 rh screws (4); 3d finishing nails; ⅜" brads; extra grommet for winding-arbor hole; gold gilding.

Note: The brass bezel is available from C & R Clock Shop, 11906 Q Drive North, Battle Creek, Mich. 49017 ($9 postpaid). C & R Clock Shop also stocks antique clock movements; write for information. The 8-day Urgo clock movement (Model 567982) is about $30 from Marshall-Swartchild & Co., 2040 North Milwaukee Ave., Chicago, Ill. 60647; hands, paper dial face, circular glass and extra grommet can also be ordered from this company or obtained locally. Mahogany, if not available locally, can be purchased from mail-order suppliers, such as Craftsman Wood Service, 1735 West Cortland Ct., Addison, Ill. 60101 and Constantine, 2050 Eastchester Rd., Bronx, N.Y. 10461.

face to fit the opening, then use it as a pattern for cutting the sheet-metal backing. Bore holes in the metal for the hands, winding arbor and mounting screws. Apply the paper dial to the metal with rubber cement, and trim the paper away from the holes with a round file. Then fasten the clock movement to the metal faceplate with the grommets provided and screw the plate into the case.

Mortise hinges into the door and fasten the door in place. Cement the quarter-round molding to the mirror and the mirror into the door with epoxy.

Also apply small dabs of epoxy to hold the glass in the brass bezel. Install the bezel in the door, attach the hands and pendulum, and your clock is finished.

CLOCK SOURCES

Clock building is an absorbing leisure activity that's easy to get hooked on. The National Assn. of Watch and Clock Collectors Inc., Box 33, 514 Poplar St., Columbia, PA 17512, provides hobbyists with a bimonthly bulletin, lending library and other benefits. Membership fee is $20 per year.

The Antique Nook Inc., 6226 Waterloo Rd., Atwater, OH 44201 (clock parts).

C & R Clock Shop, 11906 Q Drive North, Battle Creek MI 49017 (bezel for PM reproduction and antique movements).

Caldwell Industries, Box 591, Luling, TX 78468 (Arrow Electric Ball Clock kit).

Campbell Tools Co., 1424 Barclay Rd., Springfield OH 45505 (clock parts).

Clock Crafts, 1215 Springfield Pike, Cincinnati, OH 45246 (clock parts).

Craft Products, 2200 Dean St., St. Charles, IL 60174 (kits and parts).

Constantine, 2050 Eastchester Rd.,

Bronx, NY 10461 (kits, parts and fine hardwoods).

Craftsman Wood Service, 1735 West Cortland Ct., Addison, IL 60101 (kits, parts and fine hardwoods).

Crown Clock Co., 756 Nicholas Ave., Drawer G, Fairhope, AL 36532 (kits and parts).

Devore's Antiques, 57 Canton Rd., Akron, OH 44312 (clock parts).

Emperor Clock Co., Industrial Park, Fairhope, AL 36532 (clock kits).

Empire Clock Co Inc., 1295 Rice St., St. Paul, MN 55117 (clock parts).

Heinz Jauch Clock Co., Box 1150, 200 West Fremont St., Burgaw, NC 28425 (clock parts).

Klockit, Box 629, Lake Geneva, WI 53147 (clock parts).

S. La Rose Inc., 234 Commerce Pl., Greensboro, NC 27420 (kits and parts).

Marshall-Swartchild Co., 2040 North Milwaukee Ave., Chicago, IL 60647 (clock parts).

Mason & Sullivan Co., 39 Blossom Ave., Osterville, MA 02655 (kits and parts).

Merritt's Antiques, Rte. 2, Douglassville, PA 19518 (clock parts).

Modern Technical Tool & Supply Co., 211 Nevada St., Hicksville, NY 11801 (clock parts).

Southwest Clock Supply Inc., 2442 Walnut Ridge St., Dallas, TX 75229 (clock parts).

E & J Swigart Co., 34 East Sixth St., Cincinnati, OH 45202 (clock parts).

Swisscraft, 224 West Eighth St., Holland, MI 49423 (clock parts).

The Tiny Clock Shop, 1354 Old Northern Blvd., Roslyn, NY 11576 (clock parts).

Turncraft Clock Imports, 611 Winnetka Ave. N., Golden Valley, MN 55427 (clock parts).

Versage Antiques, Cuddebackville, NY 32729 (clock parts).

Westwood Clocks 'N Kits, 3210 Airport Way, Long Beach, CA 90806 (kits and parts).

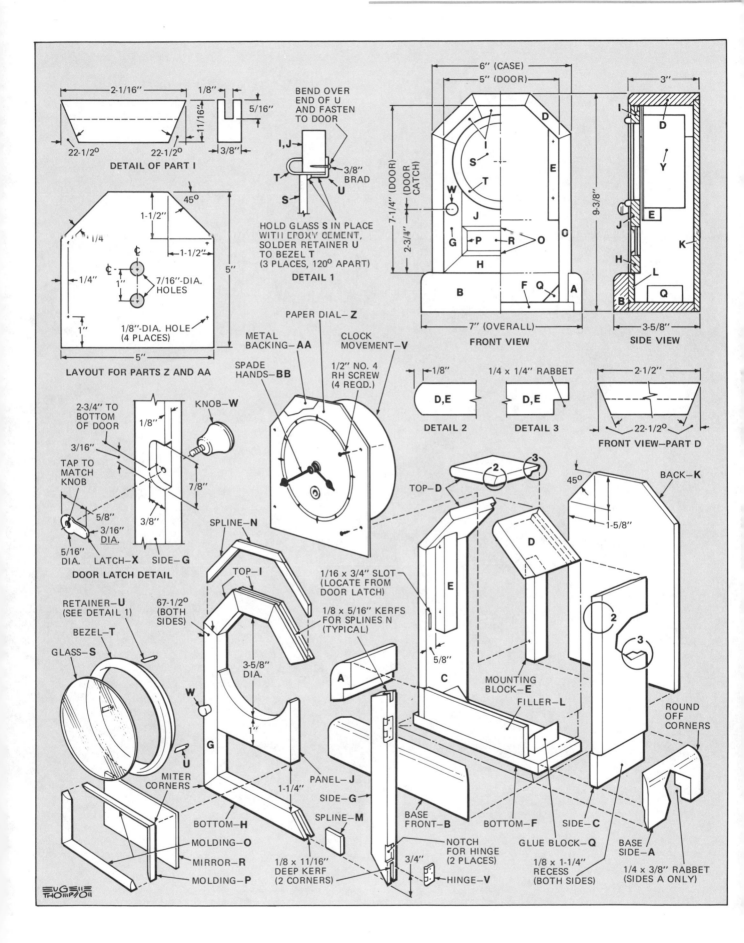

DETAIL OF PART I

2-1/16"   1/8"   11/16"   5/16"   3/8"   22-1/2°   22-1/2°

BEND OVER END OF U AND FASTEN TO DOOR

I,J   T   S   U   3/8" BRAD

HOLD GLASS S IN PLACE WITH EPOXY CEMENT, SOLDER RETAINER U TO BEZEL T (3 PLACES, 120° APART)

DETAIL 1

LAYOUT FOR PARTS Z AND AA

45°   1-1/2"   1-1/2"   1/4   1/4   1"   5"   1"   1"   5"
7/16"-DIA. HOLES
1/8"-DIA. HOLE (4 PLACES)

6" (CASE)   5" (DOOR)   3"
D   I   S   T   E   W   J   G   P   R   O   H   B   F   Q   A
7-1/4" (DOOR)   2-3/4" (DOOR CATCH)   7" (OVERALL)   9-3/8"
FRONT VIEW

I   D   Y   E   J   H   L   K   Q   B   3-5/8"
SIDE VIEW

PAPER DIAL—Z
METAL BACKING—AA
SPADE HANDS—BB
CLOCK MOVEMENT—V
1/2" NO. 4 RH SCREW (4 REQD.)

D,E   1/8   **DETAIL 2**
D,E   1/4 x 1/4" RABBET   **DETAIL 3**
2-1/2"   22-1/2°   **FRONT VIEW—PART D**

KNOB—W
2-3/4" TO BOTTOM OF DOOR
1/8"
3/16"
TAP TO MATCH KNOB
5/8"   7/8"   3/8"
3/16" DIA.
5/16" DIA.   LATCH—X   SIDE—G
DOOR LATCH DETAIL

RETAINER—U (SEE DETAIL 1)
BEZEL—T
GLASS—S
SPLINE—N
TOP—I
67-1/2° (BOTH SIDES)
3-5/8" DIA.
1"
W
G
U
MITER CORNERS
BOTTOM—H
MOLDING—O
MIRROR—R
MOLDING—P
PANEL—J
SPLINE—M
SIDE—G
1-1/4"
1/8 x 11/16" DEEP KERF (2 CORNERS)
NOTCH FOR HINGE (2 PLACES)
3/4"
HINGE—V

TOP—D
1/16 x 3/4" SLOT (LOCATE FROM DOOR LATCH)
1/8 x 5/16" KERFS FOR SPLINES N (TYPICAL)
5/8"
A
C
E
D
2
3
45°
1-5/8"
BACK—K
2
3
MOUNTING BLOCK—E
FILLER—L
ROUND OFF CORNERS
BASE FRONT—B
BOTTOM—F
SIDE—C
GLUE BLOCK—Q
1/8 x 1-1/4" RECESS (BOTH SIDES)
BASE SIDE—A
1/4 x 3/8" RABBET (SIDES A ONLY)

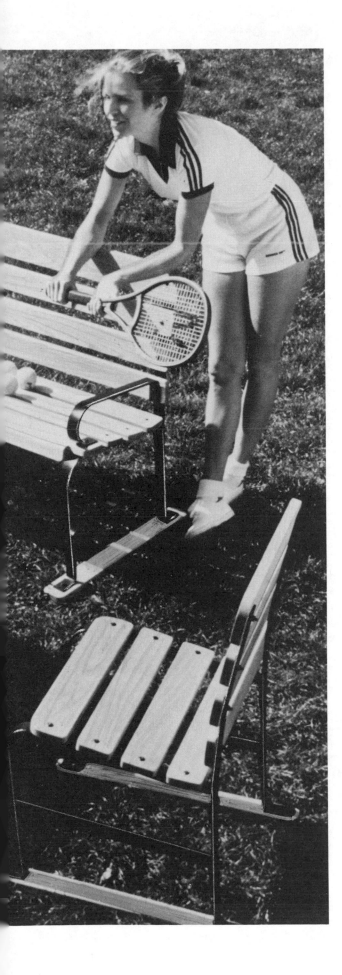

'Park-bench' furniture for your patio

We've designed a back-yard furniture suite based upon the familiar park bench of yesteryear. You bend the metal parts yourself

By ROSARIO CAPOTOSTO and HARRY WICKS

■ STARTING with the familiar-looking park bench, we've created an original patio furniture set that home craftsmen can duplicate. For a look of sheer elegance, we used oak for the wooden slats; the metal portions of the pieces are fashioned of ³⁄₁₆ by 1½-in. hot-rolled mild steel—a metal that you *can* work with.

The set consists of a bench, two chairs, a dining-sized table and a plant stand. The furniture is comfortable to use, easy to make and relatively inexpensive—in short, a nice project for a weekend workshopper to tackle.

If you have never worked with and bent metal before, you needn't be concerned. The fabrication procedures we have worked out have been especially tailored to meet the needs of a beginning metalworker. All the bending is done with simple, homemade jigs. Plans for making the jigs and information on using them are given on the following pages.

FURNITURE is built of oak and strips of mild steel. Countersunk nuts and bolts join parts.

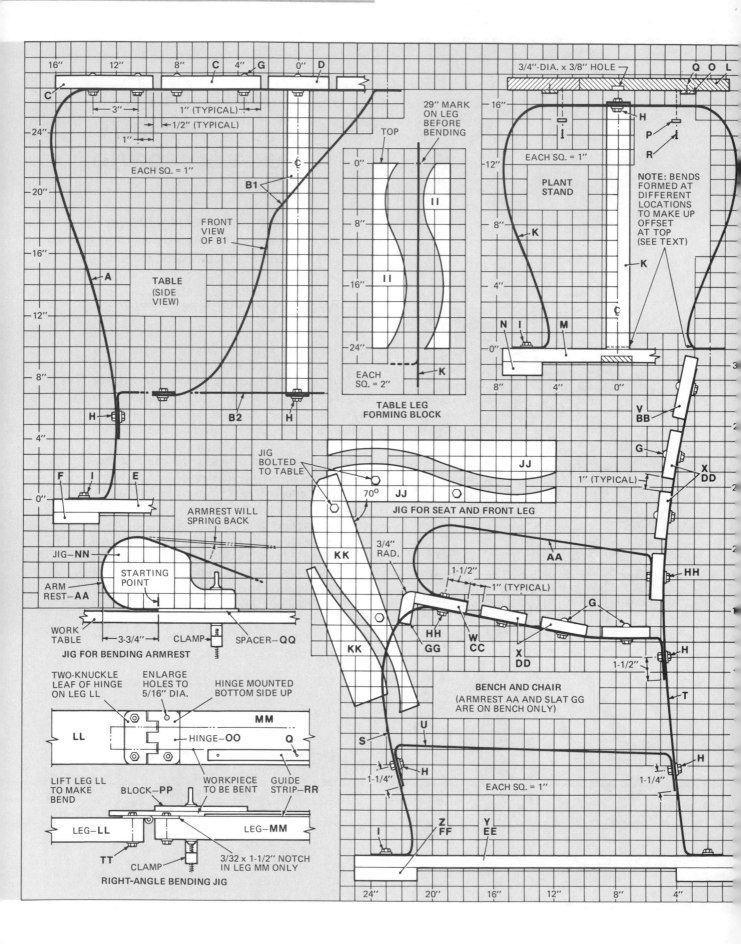

16"   12"   8"   C   4"   G   0"   D

3/4"-DIA. x 3/8" HOLE   Q O L

C

3"

1" (TYPICAL)

1/2" (TYPICAL)

1"

24"

EACH SQ. = 1"

B1

H

P

R

EACH SQ. = 1"

PLANT
STAND

NOTE: BENDS
FORMED AT
DIFFERENT
LOCATIONS
TO MAKE UP
OFFSET
AT TOP
(SEE TEXT)

20"

FRONT
VIEW
OF B1

16"

29" MARK
ON LEG
BEFORE
BENDING

TOP

0"

16"

12"

II

8"

K

A

TABLE
(SIDE
VIEW)

8"

8"

II

K

4"

12"

16"

II

V
BB

8"

H

B2

H

24"

0"

N I

M

0"

C

G

B2

K

1" (TYPICAL)

X
DD

TABLE LEG
FORMING BLOCK

EACH
SQ. = 2"

8"   4"   0"   3

JIG
BOLTED
TO TABLE

JJ

4"

F   I   E

70°   JJ

JIG FOR SEAT AND FRONT LEG

AA

G

0"

ARMREST WILL
SPRING BACK

JIG—NN

KK

3/4"
RAD.

HH

ARM
REST—AA

STARTING
POINT

1-1/2"

1" (TYPICAL)

G

WORK
TABLE

3-3/4"   CLAMP   SPACER—QQ

KK

HH
GG

W
CC

X
DD

H

JIG FOR BENDING ARMREST

1-1/2"

TWO-KNUCKLE
LEAF OF HINGE
ON LEG LL

ENLARGE
HOLES TO
5/16" DIA.

HINGE MOUNTED
BOTTOM SIDE UP

MM

BENCH AND CHAIR
(ARMREST AA AND SLAT GG
ARE ON BENCH ONLY)

T

LL

HINGE—OO   Q

S

U

H

LIFT LEG LL
TO MAKE
BEND

BLOCK—PP

WORKPIECE
TO BE BENT

GUIDE
STRIP—RR

1-1/4"   H

H

1-1/4"

LEG—LL

LEG—MM

EACH SQ. = 1"

TT   CLAMP

3/32 x 1-1/2" NOTCH
IN LEG MM ONLY

I   Z
FF

Y
EE

RIGHT-ANGLE BENDING JIG

24"   20"   16"   12"   8"   4"

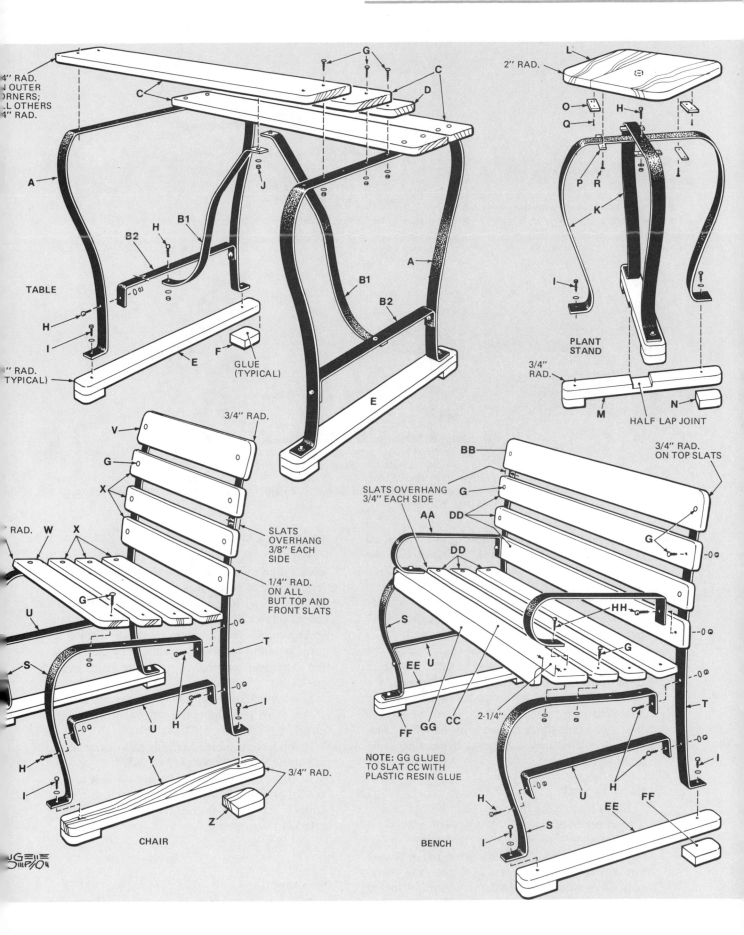

4" RAD.
N OUTER
ORNERS;
L OTHERS
4" RAD.

2" RAD.

L

O

H

Q

G

C

C

D

P   R

A

K

B1

B2   H

J

I

B1

H

A

B2

TABLE

PLANT
STAND

H

E

3/4"
RAD.

I

F

GLUE
(TYPICAL)

E

M

N

" RAD.
TYPICAL)

HALF LAP JOINT

V

3/4" RAD.

BB

3/4" RAD.
ON TOP SLATS

G

SLATS OVERHANG
3/4" EACH SIDE

G

X

AA   DD

G

RAD.   W   X

SLATS
OVERHANG
3/8" EACH
SIDE

DD

G

U

1/4" RAD.
ON ALL
BUT TOP AND
FRONT SLATS

S

HH

G

G

T

EE   U

S

U   H

GG   CC

2-1/4"

T

H

Y

FF

NOTE: GG GLUED
TO SLAT CC WITH
PLASTIC RESIN GLUE

H   U

H

I

Z

3/4" RAD.

I

EE

S

CHAIR

BENCH

FF

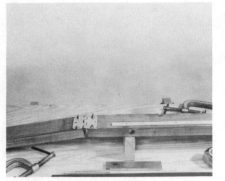

1 To make small-radius bender, attach hinge, upside down, between 2x4s. Two-knuckle leaf goes on short 2x4.

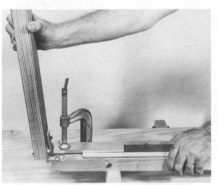

2 Clamp strip to be bent between the hinge and a steel hold-down block. Use a wood guide strip.

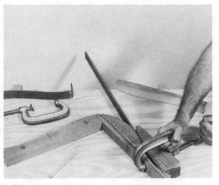

3 Squeeze mating curved blocks together to make leg's front contour. Small bend at end is formed before this.

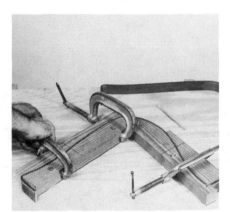

7 Return strip to contour jig, then apply pressure by squeezing clamps to complete forming strip.

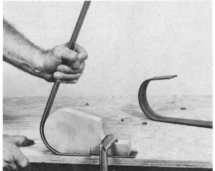

8 Clamp armrest-former jig vertically to worktable. Use a bar clamp over high spot to prevent block from lifting. Remove clamp after bend is started. Grasp the strip low.

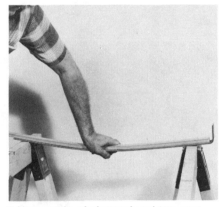

9 Use a strip of plywood and two sawhorses to fashion the large-radius, gentle curve for the rear legs.

The oak slats are ¹³/₁₆ in. thick—just as the wood comes from the lumberyard. You can buy the metal at a local iron-supply house, welding shop or from an ornamental iron worker. When you buy the metal strips, make certain you specify *mild steel* because anything that is tougher won't bend readily in the jigs we have designed.

To give an estimate of what the materials for the furniture should cost you (a difficult task in these times of almost daily price changes), the park bench and table shown cost approximately $35 each to produce. Each chair ran about $10 less. The plant stand can be built for under $15. All prices can vary somewhat depending upon area, of course.

where to start

Begin by making the three bending jigs shown. The curved sections can be cut with either jig, band or sabre saw. If, during the cutting, any irregular bumps are cut on the edge, make certain you smooth them out using a rasp and sandpaper—or you will transfer the bumps to the metal.

use a strong hinge

The long right-angle bender is made with a door hinge mounted back-side up between two lengths of 2x4 stock. It is *very important* that you select a strong hinge. While developing the prototype jig, we discovered that the quality of several unknown-brand hinges was poor: They fractured behind the knuckles when subjected to the force that was required to make the bends in the steel.

Stanley's 3½x3½-in. round corner hinge, No. 758, worked fine and is the hinge that we recommend.

If you have trouble obtaining this one, you can substitute Stanley's No. 742 or 741.

Rebore the two outer holes in each leaf to permit insertion of ⁵/₁₆-in. bolts. Attach the two-knuckle leaf to the shorter length of 2x4, as indicated in the drawing.

the bench

Cut a strip of steel 38 in. long to form the

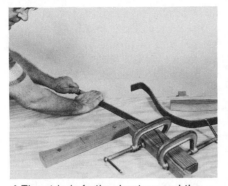

4 The strip is further bent around the corner by hand. Keep strip's edge flat against worktable.

5 Hold strip against former blocks, then mark block end. Temporarily remove strip and transfer to other jig.

6 Next, make the small radius bend. This view shows why seat contour must not be bent before this operation.

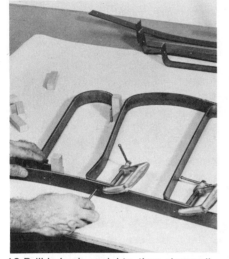

10 Drill holes in uprights, then clamp all pieces together to mark hole locations in abutting pieces.

Key	No.	Size and description (use)
		TABLE
A	2	3/16 x 1½ x 90″ steel (leg)
B	4	3/16 x 1½ x 28″ steel (brace)
C	4	13/16 x 6½ x 36″ oak (slat)
D	1	13/16 x 4 x 36″ oak (middle slat)
E	2	13/16 x 3 x 32″ oak (base)
F	4	13/16 x 3 x 3″ oak (base foot)
G	18	¼ x 1″ carriage bolt, nut and lockwasher
H	6	¼ x 1″ machine bolt, nut and lockwasher
I	4	¼ x 1½″ lagscrew and lockwasher
J	2	¼ x ⅞″ lagscrew and lockwasher
		PLANT STAND
K	2	3/16 x 1½ x 48″ steel (leg)
L	1	13/16 x 11½ x 11½″ oak (top)
M	2	13/16 x 2 x 15″ oak (base)
N	4	13/16 x 2 x 2½″ oak (base foot)
O	2	3/16 x 1 x 3″ wood shim
P	4	½ x 3″ mending plate
Q	4	½″ brads
R	8	1″ No. 8 fh screws
H	1	¼ x 1″ machine bolt, nut and lockwasher
I	4	¼ x 1½″ lagscrew and lockwasher
		CHAIR
S	2	3/16 x 1½ x 38″ steel (leg)
T	2	3/16 x 1½ x 34″ steel (back support and leg)
U	2	3/16 x 1½ x 23″ steel (brace)
V	1	13/16 x 4 x 18″ oak (top slat)
W	1	13/16 x 3½ x 18″ oak (front slat)
X	6	13/16 x 3 x 18″ oak (slat)
Y	2	13/16 x 2 x 24″ oak (base)
Z	4	13/16 x 2 x 3″ oak (base foot)
G	16	¼ x 1¼″ carriage bolt, nut and lockwasher

Key	No.	Size and description (use)
H	6	¼ x 1″ machine bolt, nut and lockwasher
I	4	¼ x 1½″ lagscrew and lockwasher
		BENCH
S	2	3/16 x 1½ x 38″ steel (leg)
T	2	3/16 x 1½ x 34″ steel (back support and leg)
AA	2	3/16 x 1½ x 25″ steel (arm rest)
U	2	3/16 x 1½ x 23″ steel (leg brace)
BB	1	13/16 x 4 x 43″ oak (top slat)
CC	1	13/16 x 3½ x 43″ oak (front slat)
DD	6	13/16 x 3 x 43″ oak (slats)
EE	2	13/16 x 3 x 25″ oak (base)
FF	4	13/16 x 3 x 4″ oak (base foot)
GG	1	13/16 x 2 x 38½″ oak (skirt)
G	12	¼ x 1¼″ carriage bolt, nut and lockwasher
HH	4	¼ x 1½″ machine bolt, nut and lockwasher
H	6	¼ x 1″ machine bolt, nut and lockwasher
I	4	¼ x 1½″ lagscrew and lockwasher
		JIGS
II	1	1½ x 5½ x 24″ fir (cut as shown)
JJ	1	1½ x 3½ x 15″ fir (cut as shown)
KK	1	1½ x 3½ x 16″ fir (cut as shown)
LL	1	1½ x 3½ x 24″ fir
MM	1	1½ x 3½ x 38″ fir
NN	1	13/16 x 5 x 9″ oak (cut as shown)
OO	1	3½ x 3½″ wrought steel hinge Stanley No. 758 (or Stanley No. 741)
PP	1	⅜ x 1½ x 6″ steel
QQ	1	3/16 x 1½ x 6″ steel
RR	1	⅛ x ¾ x 20″ fir
SS	4	1″ No. 8. fh screws
TT	4	5/16 x 2″ machine bolt, nut washer

front-leg/seat section. Make a grease-pencil mark 2¼ in. from one end. Place the mark over the center of the hinge. Clamp the strip to the long 2x4 together with a piece of ⅜x1½x5-in. steel (or use two pieces of scrap 3/16-in. working stock). Place this hold-down block ½ in. from the bend mark. Clamp firmly, close to the hinge, then lift the jig's short leg to form the bend.

Next, bolt the two sections of the leg/seat formers to a scrap board. Place the strip against the lower section, position the mating block, then squeeze with clamps. With the clamps in place, bend the strip around the corner by hand. Do *not* form the seat curve yet. Instead, make a mark for the small radius bend at the end of the former-block. Remove the strip from the jig and place it in the hinged bender. Locate the mark 1 in. from the center of the hinge (toward the long 2x4) and make the bend. Return the strip to the curved jig, and use clamps to form the seat curve. Center-lines marked on the jig pieces will aid alignment. Note that the fixed sections of the jig are positioned at an exaggerated angle to each other. This allows for spring-back.

To make the lower brace, use a strip 23 in. long. Mark bending lines 2½ in. from each end.

Center the mark over the hinge knuckles, clamp and make the bend.

The back upright is bent freehand because a jig of appropriate size would waste quite a bit of lumber. Use a 34-in. length of stock. Make the small-radius bend first, then place a strip of ½x2-in. plywood over the metal and put it over two sawhorses.

You should apply downward hand pressure at the center to obtain an even curve. Check the bend against the drawing.

The armrest is made with a 25-in. strip. Before forming the large curve, make a bend mark 3 in. from the other end.

Then clamp the armrest forming-block vertically to the work table over a piece of scrap strip. Slide the end of the work strip into the gap as shown in the drawing.

Use a bar clamp over the high point of the jig to hold it down during the initial phase of the bending. Bend the strip upward by hand, then remove the bar clamp and continue the bend. Transfer the piece to the right-angle jig and make the small-radius bend.

Mark the uprights for hole locations, then center punch and drill ¼-in.-dia. holes. Clamp the lower brace and armrest in place to accurately mark aligning hole centers. Scraps of wood the same thickness as the slats should be used as spacers when clamping the armrest in place.

Cut the wood stock to length, then rip to the necessary widths. Highly water-resistant plastic resin glue is used to join the 2-in. strip to the front slat and to make the base feet.

Apply metal primer and two coats of satin finish paint to the metal before final assembly. Krylon products will do the job; they are tough and quick drying. Also paint the bolts and screws for attaching the wood before final assembly.

To obtain a lasting clear finish to the wood, apply three coats of a quality weatherproof topcoat such as UGL Imperial ZAR.

planter

The legs for the planter are formed using the same jigs as for the bench, except the second part of the forming jig is not used. Since the legs cross over each other at the top, one set of legs is made slightly longer to make up the offset. This is accomplished by making the small-radius bends for the feet of differing dimensions.

Make a mark 1½ in. in from each end on one strip and 1¾ in. from the ends on the other. Place these marks over the knuckle of the hinge and make the bends.

Position and clamp the strip in the curve-forming jig so the corner of the small radius is 1 in. from the bottom end of the jig.

You should take up on the clamp to form the curve, then make the upper bend by hand while the strip is still clamped in place. Drill a hole for a ¼x1-in. bolt through the top center of both pieces. Also drill holes for ¼x1½-in. lagscrews in the feet.

Cut the top from a piece of 11½-in.-wide oak stock. Bore a blind ¾-in. hole ⅜ in. deep in the bottom center to allow clearance for the bolt head. The legs are secured to the top by bridging 3-in. mending plates over each leg section. Use two ³⁄₁₆-in.-thick wood strips, nailed in place, to shim the gaps resulting from the overlap. The base is made with two pieces of stock as shown.

table

A different forming jig is required for the table legs. Make it by cutting an "S" curve through a 24-in. piece of 2x6 lumber as shown.

Cut two pieces of strip 90 in. long, then make marks at 2¼ in. and at 29 in. in from each end.

You form the bends for the feet by setting the 2¼-in. mark over the hinge knuckle. Next, place the strip between the formers so the 29-in. mark lines up with the top edge of the blocks. Use two clamps to form the curve. With the clamps still engaged, make the upper bend by hand.

Four 28-in. lengths of steel are required for the table braces. To make the lower horizontals, make bending marks 2¼ in. in from each end; place the strip with the mark over the hinge knuckle and make the bend.

The curved braces are made using the chair-leg jig and a vise. Start by making the right angle bends 2¼ in. from the end. Then place the small bent end of the piece in a vise and make a slight return bend by hand. Form the sweeping curve in the chair-leg jig, using only the larger section. Clamp the flat end of the strip against the convex portion of the block and make the bend by hand.

Bore the holes for the bolts and screws as indicated in the drawing, then cut the wood to size.

The next step is to connect the braces; now lay out the tabletop slats on the work table, bottom side up and spaced ½ in. apart. Place the metal frame onto the slats and mark the center holes for the carriage bolts.

chair

The chairs are made in the same manner as the bench, but with the armrests excluded. Also, the stiffener strip under the front slat is not required.

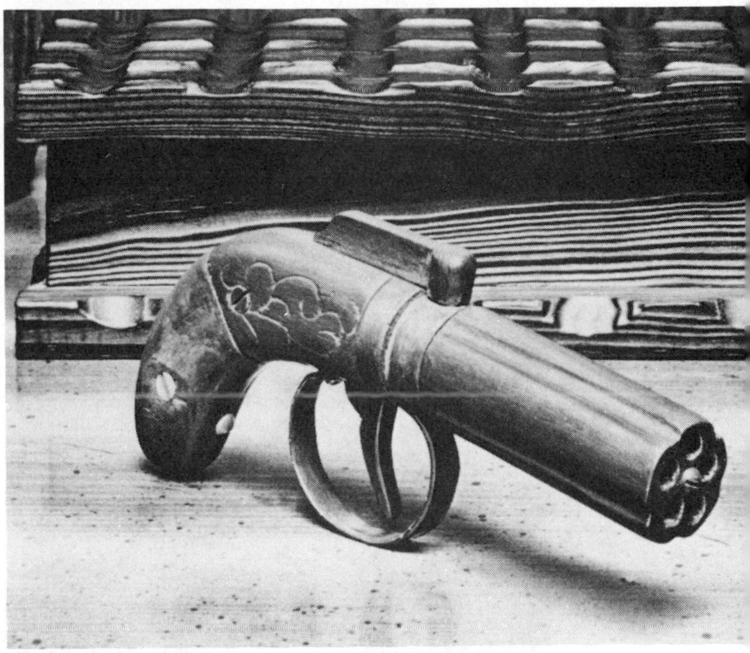

AN ATTRACTIVE decorating piece that hints of the California Gold Rush days, this pepperbox pistol is a reproduction of models made in Massachusetts by Ethan Allen circa 1845. You can duplicate it with wood and simple hardware.

Forty-niner's pistol

By RICHARD L. COULTON

■ CONTRARY TO POPULAR belief, the most popular handgun of the 1849 California gold rush was not the Colt revolver, but the pepperbox pistol. This was a firearm with three or more barrels encircling a central axis.

The reproduction shown is of a small .28-cal., five-shot, 3-in.-long barrel pepperbox made about 1845.

Cut out the grip. Draw a centerline around it to help you keep the model symmetrical. Round the grip to an oval cross section. Then cut the shallow grooves around the grips. Rough-sand with 80-grit sandpaper. Add simple engravings to each side of the frame if you wish. Final-sand with 100- or 120-grit sandpaper, dust, and tack off.

Add the flathead grip screws to each side and also add the round-head trigger tension screw to the front of the butt.

Cut the barrel cluster (A) of 1-in.-dia. round (dowel). Shape the end that attaches to the grip by diminishing its diameter. Using a 5/16-in.-dia. bit, make the five bores at the front about 1/2-in. deep. Then use a gouge to form the flutes between the barrels.

Next, carefully rough and final-sand the barrel with the grain, rounding off the edges of the flutes. Turn in the barrel screw. Glue the barrel cluster into position on the front of the grip; be sure that one of the bores is at the top.

Cut out the trigger (E) and the two parts of the hammer (C, D). Round the nose of the hammer to shape and reduce the thickness of the trigger and the blade of the hammer to 3/16-in.

Bore a hole in one end of the metal strip (F) and bend the strip into shape for the trigger guard so that the hole is in the rear.

To finish the gun, remove all screws except the one on the trigger guard. Treat the grips to two coats of a walnut stain, let dry, go over them lightly with 180-grit sandpaper and finish with tung oil. Paint all metal parts with gun-metal-blue paint (made by mixing equal parts of light blue and black enamel).

When the paint is completely dry, cut the gloss by rubbing with 4/0 steel wool; reassemble the pistol.

MATERIALS LIST—

FORTY-NINER'S PEPPERBOX PISTOL

Key	No.	Size and description (use)
A	1	1"-dia.×3 1/4" pine round (barrel cluster)
B	1	3/4×2 1/2×3" pine (grip)
C	1	3/4×2 1/2×3" pine (hammer blade)
D	1	3/4×2 1/2×3" pine (hammer nose)
E	1	3/4×2 1/2×3" pine (trigger)
F	1	1/4×4 1/4" metal strip; tin-can scrap
G	4	1/4"-dia.×3/8" fh wood screws
H	3	1/4"-dia.×3/8" rh wood screws

Misc.: Glue, walnut stain, tung oil, light blue and black enamel or metal paints.

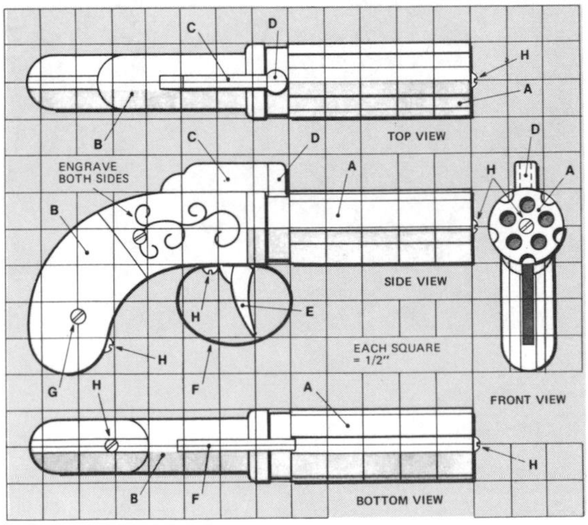

Kitchen door organizer

By ROSARIO CAPOTOSTO

UNIQUE STORAGE cabinet uses otherwise wasted space—the back side of the basement door. It corrals those kitchen items used every day—aluminum foil, paper products, cleaning supplies, etc.

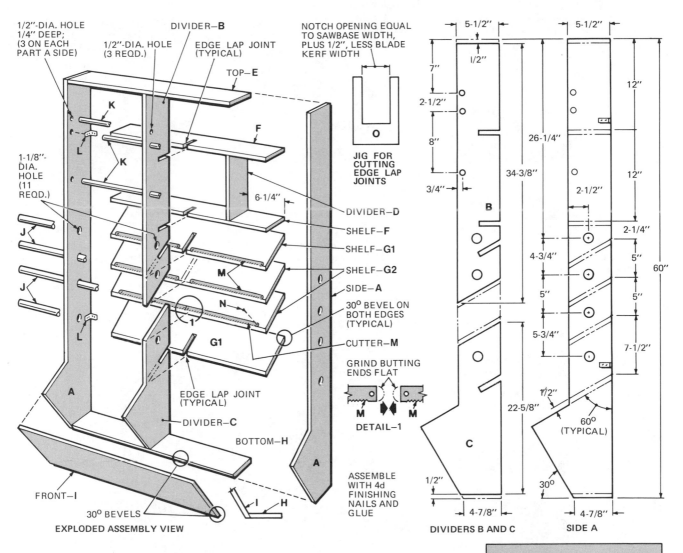

EXPLODED ASSEMBLY VIEW

1/2"-DIA. HOLE 1/4" DEEP; (3 ON EACH PART A SIDE)

1/2"-DIA. HOLE (3 REQD.)

DIVIDER—B

EDGE LAP JOINT (TYPICAL)

TOP—E

F

1-1/8"-DIA. HOLE (11 REQD.)

K

L

K

J

J

L

A

G1

EDGE LAP JOINT (TYPICAL)

DIVIDER—C

FRONT—I

30° BEVELS

6-1/4"

DIVIDER—D

SHELF—F

SHELF—G1

SHELF—G2

SIDE—A

30° BEVEL ON BOTH EDGES (TYPICAL)

CUTTER—M

GRIND BUTTING ENDS FLAT

M   M

DETAIL—1

ASSEMBLE WITH 4d FINISHING NAILS AND GLUE

BOTTOM—H

I   H

M

N

1

NOTCH OPENING EQUAL TO SAWBASE WIDTH, PLUS 1/2", LESS BLADE KERF WIDTH

O

JIG FOR CUTTING EDGE LAP JOINTS

5-1/2"   5-1/2"

1/2"

7"

2-1/2"

8"

3/4"

B

26-1/4"

34-3/8"

4-3/4"

5"

5-3/4"

22-5/8"

C

1/2"

4-7/8"

DIVIDERS B AND C

12"

12"

2-1/2"

2-1/4"

5"

5"

7-1/2"

1/2"

60°(TYPICAL)

60°

30°

4-7/8"

60"

SIDE A

■ MAKE THIS KITCHEN organizer and you'll find the whole family enjoying its conveniences. You can install it on the back of any door, such as the one leading to the basement, garage or pantry. It is so attractive, though, you may not want to hide it.

Designed by architect Lester Walker, the unit has received careful consideration for storing the most commonly used kitchen items. Toxic liquids are stored on the upper shelves out of reach of children; lower bins may contain paper cups, napkins and anything else children use regularly.

Perhaps the neatest features are the wrapping dispensers. Hacksaw blades serve as cutting edges for aluminum foil and the like and make the dispensing

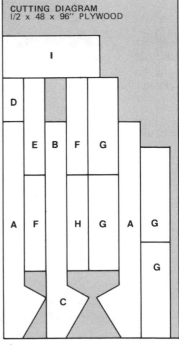

CUTTING DIAGRAM
1/2 x 48 x 96" PLYWOOD

MATERIALS LIST—KITCHEN ORGANIZER

Key	No.	Size and description (use)
A	2	½ x 10⅜ x 60" plywood (side)
B	1	½ x 3½ x 34⅜" (approx.) plywood (divider)
C	1	½ x 10⅜ x 22⅝" (approx.) plywood (divider)
D	1	½ x 5½ x 11½" plywood (divider)
E	1	½ x 5½ x 26½" plywood (top)
F	2	½ x 5½ x 26½" plywood (shelf)
G	4	½ x 6⅝ (approx.) x 26½" plywood (shelf)
H	1	½ x 5½ x 26½" plywood (bottom)
I	1	½ x 11 x 27½" plywood (front)
J	4	1"-dia. x 31" dowel
K	3	½"-dia. x 27" dowel
L	4	1½" corner brace with eight ½" No. 6 fh screws
M	6	12" hacksaw blade
N	1	½" No. 6 rh screw (as reqd.)
O	1	¼" x 8 x 12" hardboard or plywood (jig)

Misc.: Carpenter's glue, paint, sandpaper.

MAKE LOWER, angled cuts of sides with circular saw and guide strip.

RESET GUIDE, even for short cuts, each time you make a cut.

ALWAYS EXTEND guide strip beyond edge of workpiece. Cutting diagram allows removal of waste.

SECURE CUTTING jig to workpiece, using hand-screw or C-clamp. Make opening in jig long enough to cut both 60° and 90° slots.

SHOWN HERE READY for assembly are parts of the kitchen organizer cut from one 4x8 plywood panel. Use MDO (medium density overlaid) plywood for best results.

of these materials a fast, one-hand operation. You can also see when you're getting low on wraps, as the rolls are not concealed in awkward boxes.

The unit shown is painted with PPG Industries' semigloss latex enamel: Bohemian Blue for the sides, Candle Glow on all inside surfaces and New Rust on the dowels.

materials used

The unit is constructed of ½-in. MDO (medium density overlaid) plywood. Having a very

smooth surface, this is more costly than ordinary fir plywood, but it is well worth the difference for several other advantages. It is made with good-quality inner plies and thus there are no large voids or splintery areas. An MDO panel does not warp easily and doesn't splinter at the edge when sawed. Its smooth, flat surface is especially well suited for painting.

cutting plan

All required pieces can be cut from one 4x8 panel if you follow the cutting plan shown. The

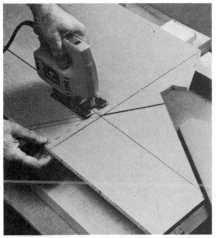

COMPLETE CIRCULAR saw cuts with sabre saw. Cut slowly with steady hand or use a straightedge positioned to give clean line.

SANDWICH-CLAMP three vertical members together (before centerpiece is cut). Sand exposed edges with 120-grit, then 150-grit paper.

USE DRILL press or portable guide to assure boring holes straight. Place workpiece on scrap for a clean hole. Pilot holes make job easier.

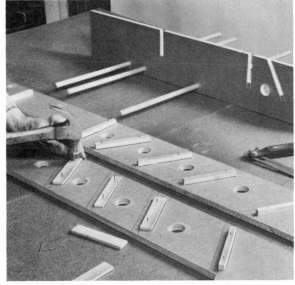

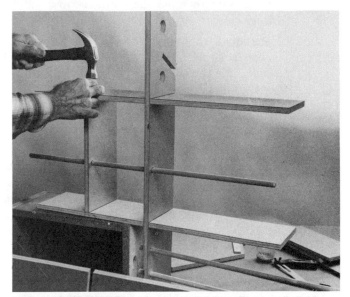

TEMPORARY CLEATS are tack-nailed below each shelf location to simplify assembly.

EVEN DULL hacksaw blades will work well as cutting edges for the various wrappings.

BEGIN ASSEMBLING shelves and dividers. The small divider must be placed in position with dowel before attaching end.

AFTER ALL PARTS are attached to center divider, including dowels, sides are easily added using nails and carpenter's glue, with cabinet turned on its side as shown.

initial cuts can be made with a sabre saw or circular saw. Whatever saw you use, be sure to use a smooth-cutting plywood blade and set up your guides carefully so that you will have finished cuts in one step. Remember to allow for the saw kerf when you lay out the cutting pattern.

A 4x8 panel can be cumbersome to work with, so always have it properly supported for its entire length. Readjust your supports after each cut and avoid a situation in which it will be awkward to make the full length of the cut in one run.

Make the first cut across the panel to yield the piece from which the front (I) is cut. This procedure will allow you to make several lengthwise cuts to get smaller sections that are easier to handle. Next, use clamps and a straight strip of wood as a guide to make the angled cuts for the sides. Cut to within 1 in. of the inside corners with the circular saw, then use the sabre saw to finish the corner cuts.

Although the center divider consists of two pieces (B and C) initially, cut it as a single unit exactly like the two sides. Then clamp all three together and finish-sand the edges that will be exposed.

boring the dowel holes

Mark center points for the 1⅛-in.-diameter dowel holes on one side of the sandwiched pieces. Use a 1⅛-in. spade bit and be sure to back up the work with a wood block to prevent tearing as the bit breaks through. Since good alignment of the holes is important, use a guide with your portable drill or use a drill press.

Before separating the three pieces, mark off the measurements for the shelves on both sides. Join these respective marks across the edges, front and back, with a straight pencil line.

Now, separate the sides and centerpiece and mark the center points for the ½-in.-diameter dowel holes in the centerpiece. Note that the holes for the small dowels are bored through the centerpiece, but are bored only ¼ in. deep in the inside surface of each sidepiece. This requires the use of a twist drill with a bit stop.

After the holes have been bored in the centerpiece, connect the marks on the front and back edges to produce the 60° and 90° angle lines. Cut piece B-C into the two dividers, B and C.

The angled shelves are cut to size with a 30° bevel on the front and back edges. A table saw is ideal for these cuts, but they can be made as well with a guide and a portable circular saw.

a jig for edge-lap joints

Edge-lap joints are used to attach the shelves to the center dividers. These are cut with a sabre saw and a simple jig.

To make the jig, cut a piece of ¼-in. plywood or hardboard to 8x12 in. To determine the width of the slot in the jig, measure the width of the saw base and add ½ in. (thickness of the stock). Then subtract the kerf (thickness of the saw blade).

The length of the slot should be more than 3⁵⁄₁₆ in. (half of the angled shelf width before bevels), plus the distance from the front edge of the sabre-saw shoe. Cut the slots before you make the bevels. Note that the slots in shelves F should be exactly half the width of the shelf and the divider (B) or 2¾ in., as these joints are both positioned at right angles.

Before using the jig on a workpiece, make test cuts in scrap to check the fit of the joint produced. The parts should fit together easily without gaps.

assembling the organizer

Attach the two upper shelves to the center divider and nail in the short vertical divider (D). Insert the ½-in. dowels.

The shelves will automatically be positioned on the center dividers, but you should use temporary cleats tacked to the sides in order to obtain an easy, accurate assembly of the sides to the shelves. Tack cleats to the sides with finishing nails. Leave the heads protruding so the cleats can be removed easily after assembly.

Use carpenter's glue and 1½-in. (4d) finishing nails on all butt joints. If you bore small pilot holes for the nails in the sides in advance, you'll have an easier time getting them in line and centered. Attach the front panel last.

Now, set all nailheads and cover them with a wood filler. Finish-sand with 120-grit paper and round over all edges slightly.

positioning the blades

Buy inexpensive hacksaw blades or use old ones. Use ½-in. No. 6 roundhead screws to attach them to the shelves. Position the blades so that the serrated edges overhang the shelf by about ⅛-in. If you grind the rounded ends square, the cutting edges of abutting blades will be continuous for a nice finishing touch.

Attach four 1½-in. corner irons flush with the back to permit hanging.

OUTDOOR RECEPTACLES

IN-GROUND GARBAGE CAN

BASEMENT ENTRY

HOSE BIB

Five conveniences for your yard

We've rounded up the five most wanted back-yard conveniences and created the how-to you need so you can install them, too. Any of these will add to your summer enjoyment

■ WARM WEATHER means more time for the great outdoors—your own comfortable back yard. Here are a few ideas that can make yard life more enjoyable.

The convenience of outdoor electrical receptacles is obvious to anyone who spends much time in the yard. Whatever electrical appliance you wish to use outside may be plugged in on the site. Then it is no longer necessary to run a long—and possibly dangerous—extension cord into the

house through an open window or through a screen door forced to stand ajar by the cord.

Remember that all electrical work must be done in accordance with the National Electrical code, or your local code, whichever is more stringent. In fact, it's very possible that your local building code may require the work to be done by a licensed electrician.

All approved electrical systems are protected with circuit breakers or fuses, but the National

Electrical Code requires that outdoor receptacles be further protected with a special device called a Ground Fault Interrupter, shown above and on the following pages. Fuses and circuit breakers protect against overloads and short circuits, but GFIs protect you from a fatal shock, so don't forget to use them.

An in-ground garbage can serves two purposes. First, you can keep the can convenient, yet virtually out of sight. The second advantage is that animals can't get to it; thus, tipped-over cans are eliminated.

Another idea is to add a yard entrance to the basement of the house. As both basement and yard are used for recreational activity, easy passage makes everything more fun. Installing a basement entrance is a major construction job, but you will find the basics for installing an entryway on the following pages.

The maker of the door shown in the photographs also includes complete "how to" installation instructions.

There's no doubt that a hose bib in the yard makes life there more convenient. With the use of plastic vinyl tubing, you no longer need a plumber to install an outdoor faucet.

TWO ELECTRIC RECEPTACLES

■ DECIDE WHERE you want exterior receptacles in the wall of the house and then adjust the position slightly if necessary to locate it between studs. Be careful not to cut the opening oversize, as the electrical box has ears with screw holes for attachment to the wall.

Trace the box outline onto the wall, then bore two ⅜-in. holes centered at the top and bottom. These holes allow clearance for receptacle-to-box connecting screws and permit blade entry to complete the cutout.

Inside, run the cable to the box, making certain it is securely fixed to the framing with staples spaced no more than 24 in. apart. Cut the cable and install it in the box, using the appropriate connector. Do not connect the circuit to the house service panel until the box installation is completed.

The remaining work is done from the outside. Bare the ends of the black and white leads and join them with solderless connectors to the black and white leads that extend from the receptacle.

JOIN WHITE to white, black to black and the ground wire to the green lead. Cap unused red and gray leads.

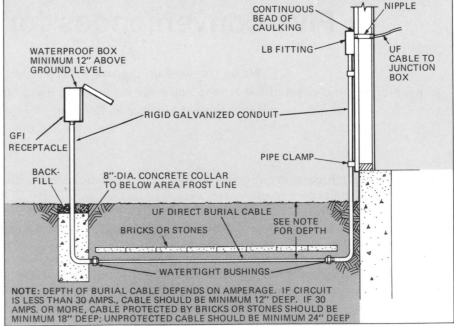

CONTINUOUS BEAD OF CAULKING

NIPPLE

LB FITTING

UF CABLE TO JUNCTION BOX

WATERPROOF BOX MINIMUM 12" ABOVE GROUND LEVEL

RIGID GALVANIZED CONDUIT

GFI RECEPTACLE

PIPE CLAMP

BACK-FILL

8"-DIA. CONCRETE COLLAR TO BELOW AREA FROST LINE

UF DIRECT BURIAL CABLE

BRICKS OR STONES

SEE NOTE FOR DEPTH

WATERTIGHT BUSHINGS

NOTE: DEPTH OF BURIAL CABLE DEPENDS ON AMPERAGE. IF CIRCUIT IS LESS THAN 30 AMPS., CABLE SHOULD BE MINIMUM 12" DEEP. IF 30 AMPS. OR MORE, CABLE PROTECTED BY BRICKS OR STONES SHOULD BE MINIMUM 18" DEEP; UNPROTECTED CABLE SHOULD BE MINIMUM 24" DEEP

USE AN AWL to mark holes for the screws. Bore pilot holes with a drill. Use gasket to cover the mounting plate. Add an extra piece of gasket underneath if plate holds gasket away from the wall.

RECEPTACLE has a reset button which pops out when a fault or slight leak occurs in the circuit. To test interrupter, press test button. If it doesn't pop out, interrupter isn't working.

Connect the bare ground wire to the receptacle's green lead. One red and one gray lead marked LOAD on the box (not visible in photo) are capped with solderless connectors.

If the receptacle that you are installing were not a terminal receptacle (end of run), those installed downstream from this one would also be GFI-protected.

Fold all wires neatly inside and then attach the receptacle to the box. Next, mark and make pilot holes for the screws to secure the flange to the wall. Use four flathead screws.

The cover plate comes with a waterproof gasket, but the flange may hold this gasket away from the wall of the house. If you anticipate this situation, buy a second gasket and cut ¼-in.-wide strips from it to insert around the perimeter of the flange.

After attaching the spring-loaded cover plate, connect the cable to the panel box. Test the unit as indicated in the detailed instructions provided by the receptacle maker.

The GFI shown on this page is called an SIR (Slater Interrupter Receptacle, made by Slater Electric Inc., Glen Cove, NY 11542). It retails for approximately $28.

in-ground receptacles

Codes may permit the use of UF cable that can be buried directly in the ground, requiring only that conduit be used for those portions where the cable is not in the ground (from house to ground and from ground to fixture). Some codes require conduit throughout.

A trench for direct-burial UF cable should be 12 in. deep (at least 24 in. deep for a 30-amp cir-

cuit). Plastic or thin-wall conduit must be buried at least 18-in. deep.

The installation shown in the drawing is for a UF direct-burial installation. Galvanized rigid conduit is used to protect the cable from the point where it leaves the wall to a depth of 18 in. in the ground. A 30-in. length of conduit is used at the in-ground receptacle secured in a concrete collar. The NEC requires in-ground receptacles 12 in. to 18 in. above ground and the box secured to the conduit with a threaded bushing.

An LB fitting is used on conduit to carry the cable from the house down to the ground. A nipple joins the LB to a junction box inside the house. This fitting, threaded both sides, has a removable plate which permits fishing the cable around the bend. A rubber gasket keeps water out. A weatherproof box houses the junction.

Begin by locating the site for the in-ground receptacle. Lay out and dig the trench from the power location at the house to the receptacle site.

If your lawn is in good shape, make neat slices so that the sod can be lifted out and saved for reuse.

With the trench dug to desired depth, install a plywood form across the trench end, braced by stakes, so you can pour the concrete collar around the conduit. Bend the conduit to shape and position it in the form. Secure it in the vertical position, using three diagonal stakes and wire.

The lower end of the conduit, of course, must exit through the form at the desired elevation. Wrap both ends of the pipe to prevent any chance of concrete entering.

Pass the cable through the plastic bushings and then fish the cable up into the receptacle and junction box. Tighten the bushings.

Bricks or stones provide natural protection from a stake or some other object driven into the ground. They also act as a warning reminder that the cable is present at the time of a later excavation. Before placing the bricks, bury the cable with three or four inches of soil. Tamp the soil firmly around the cable, then lay in the bricks tightly together.

Screw the LB fitting to the conduit. Connect the LB fitting to a junction box on the interior wall using a nipple of the required size. Remove the knockout from the back of the junction box, pass the nipple through, then secure it with a star nut. Screw on a plastic bushing. Strap the conduit to the wall.

Fish the cable through. Connect the in-ground receptacle box with a threaded bushing, then pass the cable through. Connect the GFI receptacle.

Inside the house, join the outdoor cable to a cable running to the panel box. Caulk around the LB fitting on the exterior wall.

BASEMENT ENTRYWAY

■ FIRST, decide how you will use your basement, and lay out a plan showing where various activities will take place. Locate the new entrance where it does not interfere with partitions, utilities, piping or with any outside construction.

When considering the outside access area, a low grade will save steps and simplify construction. The grade should also slope away from the areaway to provide good drainage.

Our photographs show installation of a door made by the Bilco Co., New Haven, CT 06505. The maker claims the materials cost less than $300. Bilco provides a complete installation booklet, including the steps outlined here.

Draw vertical lines on the foundation to indicate the location and width of the opening. Stake off the area to be excavated, allowing at least an extra foot all around for the footing and for application of waterproofing materials.

To lay out the areaway square with the wall, use the 3-4-5 triangle method: Measure along the wall three units from one corner of the areaway to start. Then measure four units out at approximately a 90° angle. The hypotenuse between the marks must be five units to make the lines square with the wall. Lay out the areaway, leaving adequate room for the footings.

Do all excavating first. Dig to a depth of 4 in. below the level of the basement floor. Then dig a footing trench around the areaway to the depth of the house footing and about 12 to 16 in. wide. After the footing has been poured and has set for two or three days, masonry work begins.

Hollow blocks used to construct the areaway are called stretcher blocks and have both ends hollowed. There are also corner blocks which have one end flat. Each course takes two corner blocks.

The first course is most important; it's a good idea to lay it out without mortar. Check for alignment and square with house and footing.

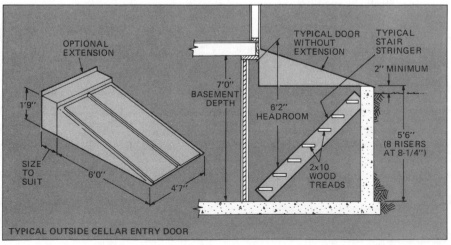

AFTER THREE OR FOUR blocks have been laid (top left), the corner block is used for correct alignment. Below left, adjustments are made before the door is attached. Here, the header slips under the siding.

OPTIONAL EXTENSION

1'9"

SIZE TO SUIT

6'0"

4'7"

TYPICAL DOOR WITHOUT EXTENSION

TYPICAL STAIR STRINGER

2" MINIMUM

7'0" BASEMENT DEPTH

6'2" HEADROOM

2x10 WOOD TREADS

5'6" (8 RISERS AT 8-1/4")

TYPICAL OUTSIDE CELLAR ENTRY DOOR

Use the triangle method again. When satisfied with position of the first course, remove the blocks, spread and lay on mortar to create a ½-in. joint.

Cement blocks are laid with their thick surface up (the side with the smaller holes); this provides a larger surface by the mortar bed. For vertical joints, only the ends of the face shells are "buttered" with mortar. Each block is brought downward into the mortar bed and against the previously laid block, thus producing well-filled mortar joints.

Vertical joints between blocks on successive courses should be staggered. The top course should come slightly above ground level and about 3 in. from the required areaway height as given in the instructions. Should the standard block not permit this, half blocks may be used.

The deepest areaway will require about nine courses while most require only four or five. After mortar has set for two or three days, apply a masonry waterproofing material to the exterior wall following the instructions on the can.

The next step is to assemble the frame of the areaway door. Position it over the wall and against the house. Use stone or block shims if necessary to get the door into the desired position. Be certain to locate the frame exactly as you want it. Mark the frame's outline against the house.

Remove the door and, following its outline, cut out the shingles or clapboard.

Start pouring the cap and, when it is an inch or so below the desired height, set the door back in position with the header flange between the siding and the sheathing underneath. Make sure the frame is square. Insert the mounting screws with the spring steel nuts in the side pieces and sill, and embed in the wet concrete.

Continue pouring the cap, bringing the concrete flush with the bottom of the sill and side-piece flanges. Don't bring the capping above the bottom of the door; the door should rest *on top of* the foundation. With a little extra work, the cap outside the door can be chamfered to ensure good positive water runoff.

If you have not done so already, you may want to break through the foundation wall into the basement. The opening should be the full inside width of the areaway to take full advantage of the new entry. In block foundations, it can be cut with a cold chisel and hammer, but a masonry bit in a power drill is faster.

If the basement wall is reinforced concrete, a heavy-duty electric hammer with chisel attachment will be required. Either way, call in an engineer to determine the best method for breaking out the wall, and whether you will have to install additional support above.

Drill and chisel from the outside and knock the wall out from the inside to minimize the rubble in your basement. You can now clean up the areaway and pour the floor to the same level as the basement floor.

If you plan to use a vertical door in combination with the areaway door, have it on hand when you break through. Give this matter consideration—you don't want to leave your home unprotected.

Keep an eye on the weather when planning this project. You don't want to chop a large hole in your foundation at the onset of a rainy period, for example. When the job is completed, the doors are watertight and designed to ensure water runoff.

The areaway doors are easily installed once the concrete cap has set around the screws which are threaded through the frame.

If the frame does not wiggle, doors may be attached as soon as the frame is in place.

IN-GROUND GARBAGE CAN

■ HERE'S A SMART way to keep a garbage can by the back door—yet virtually invisible. In-ground units have retainers and inserts. Available in 10-, 15-, and 20-gal. sizes, the units have all parts made of galvanized steel. The retainers are made with single- or double-action covers. They are intended as temporary receptacles for the garbage. It would be transferred to larger cans for final disposal. The single-action unit on the next page is a 20-gal. size retailing for about $50 and made by the Dover Stamping Co., 427 Plymouth Ave., Fall River, MA 02722.

Dig a neat hole 1 in. wider than the retainer. Then dig a ring as shown in the drawing and set up a form for the collar. Using any packaged premixed concrete, mix it with water and fill the ring halfway. Lay in a few rings of heavy wire for reinforcement and then fill up the ring. After surface water has disappeared, level with a wooden float. When the concrete has set but is still wet, you can round over the edges as indicated by the arrows in the drawing. You may also need to carve out a small indentation in the collar to accommodate the lever hinge on the lid.

continued on the next page

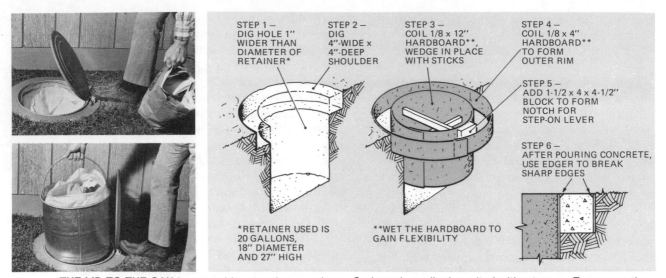

STEP 1 —
DIG HOLE 1"
WIDER THAN
DIAMETER OF
RETAINER*

STEP 2 —
DIG
4"-WIDE x
4"-DEEP
SHOULDER

STEP 3 —
COIL 1/8 x 12"
HARDBOARD**,
WEDGE IN PLACE
WITH STICKS

STEP 4 —
COIL 1/8 x 4"
HARDBOARD**
TO FORM
OUTER RIM

STEP 5 —
ADD 1-1/2 x 4 x 4-1/2"
BLOCK TO FORM
NOTCH FOR
STEP-ON LEVER

STEP 6 —
AFTER POURING CONCRETE,
USE EDGER TO BREAK
SHARP EDGES

*RETAINER USED IS
20 GALLONS,
18" DIAMETER
AND 27" HIGH

**WET THE HARDBOARD TO
GAIN FLEXIBILITY

THE LID TO THE CAN is opened by stepping on a lever. Garbage is easily deposited without mess. To remove the garbage, the insert is lifted out. Can stays clean with a plastic bag liner.

EXTRA HOSE BIB

■ TO INSTALL a hose bib, you'll need to tap into the cold-water supply line in the house. This is done by inserting a tee fitting in the line.

We chose the Qest polybutylene system that features "Magic Seal" fittings which will let you make positive, sound joints without solder, solvents or the need for threading.

The tools required are few: tubing cutter, knife and wrench. The cutter is needed to cut into an existing copper system.

After shutting off the water, use the tubing cutter to remove a section of the cold-water line equal to the length of the tee fitting with connecting nuts removed. Slip the nuts over the ends of the pipe; then slide a ring and cone over each end.

Make up the branch assembly to include a shutoff valve inside the house. This indoor valve allows you to cut water off to the exterior during the winter when water near the bib could freeze and cause it to crack.

Use a sharp knife to cut the plastic tubing to length. Bore a hole through the outside wall. Make the hole just large enough to pass the fitting through, thus allowing enough wall material around the hole to receive two screws to hold the faucet.

Engage the cone and fitting and turn the nut onto the fitting hand-tight. Next, wrench-tighten it one to two full turns until you hear a squeak.

Now you can attach a coupling adapter to the hose-bib faucet for the transition from threads to threadless tubing. Here you must use Teflon tape to seal the joint.

Seal the opening around the faucet with caulk, after you have marked and bored pilot holes for the screws. Pass the faucet through the wall and secure it with the screws. Then make the final connection to the elbow.

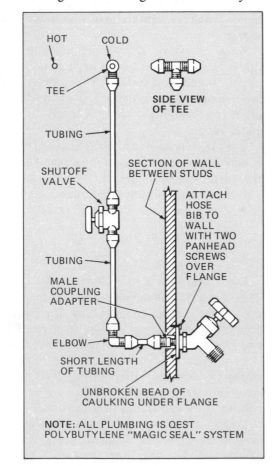

HOT

COLD

TEE

SIDE VIEW
OF TEE

TUBING

SHUTOFF
VALVE

SECTION OF WALL
BETWEEN STUDS

ATTACH
HOSE
BIB TO
WALL
WITH TWO
PANHEAD
SCREWS
OVER
FLANGE

TUBING

MALE
COUPLING
ADAPTER

ELBOW

SHORT LENGTH
OF TUBING

UNBROKEN BEAD OF
CAULKING UNDER FLANGE

NOTE: ALL PLUMBING IS QEST
POLYBUTYLENE "MAGIC SEAL" SYSTEM

COUNTERTOP GRILL brings the flavor of outside cooking inside without the smoke. Enjoy charcoal taste year 'round.

Install your own counter grill

■ ADDING THE FUN and flavor of a countertop grill to your kitchen is a surprisingly easy do-it-yourself operation. Using a drill and a sabre saw, you should be able to make all the cuts in the countertop, cabinet, floor and through the house wall to install the unit.

The Jenn-Air grill shown is Model G100, which operates on electricity. It comes with in-structions and a template for positioning both the grill and venting duct. The ductwork is not in-cluded, but it is available at many hardware, plumbing and heating-supply stores.

First, lay out and cut the hole in the countertop using a sabre saw. To avoid marring the lami-nate, put masking tape on the saw's shoe.

USING manufacturer-supplied template, mark the countertop for the grill location. Because the unit eliminates the need for an exhaust hood, it can be placed just about anywhere you want it.

AFTER you have cut the countertop, use the same template to mark the location of the smoke-vent ductwork. By lining up the duct carefully now, attaching the two will be much easier later.

install the duct

Next, position the duct and make all necessary cuts accurately. The grill attaches to the duct, so there is no margin for error. After the ductwork is through the floor, make the necessary turns using elbows to run it outdoors. The duct run should be as short and straight as possible. The manufacturer supplies a table for figuring the ideal duct length for your particular model. Follow these instructions.

Use the vent itself to precisely locate the hole to be cut in the outside wall. For the neatest job, locate and bore through at center, then finish making the hole from the outside. If you have a brick-veneered house, bore with carbide-tipped masonry bits and secure the wall cap, using anchors intended for masonry.

a one-day project

Allow at least one day to make the installation, not including the wiring, which should be done by a licensed electrician (unless you have the electrical knowledge to do it yourself).

For complete information write: Jenn-Air Corp., 3035 Shadeland, Indianapolis, IN 46226.

WHEN DUCTWORK is positioned (left), the grill can be lowered into it and attached. Secure joints with at least four sheet-metal screws, staggered on both sides of the joint. A hole is cut to the outside just below the floor level (photo below) and the wall cap is installed. The cap contains a damper to prevent backdrafts when the grill is not in use. The grease trap (below right) is a glass jar that removes for cleaning.

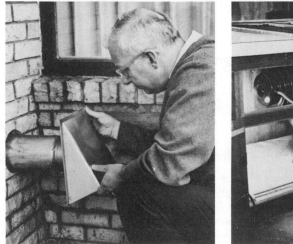

TO OPEN the garage door, turn four knobs to the proper positions and press the button.

Electric lock for your garage door

Fool intruders with this combination electric lock. You set the combination and then open the door without keys or magnets. Here's how to install it yourself

By THOMAS A. GAULDIN

■ THIS COMBINATION lock for a garage-door opener lets you activate the opener at the touch of a button without using easy-to-lose keys or magnets. I made it for under $10 in less than 30 minutes.

You can purchase the components at an electrical supply house or from a Radio Shack store (see parts list, below). You'll need a drill, screwdriver and soldering iron.

To make the opener work, you must complete an electrical circuit through four 12-position rotary switches and a momentary-contact pushbutton switch; then press the pushbutton switch that is normally open. You must know the correct position of all four rotary switches.

You can attach the device to the front of your garage or in another convenient spot. For additional safety, you might add a tamper switch that sounds an alarm if the box is removed.

To begin assembly, lay out the positions of the four holes for the rotary switches and the hole for the pushbutton on the cabinet. Allow a minimum 1¼-in. space between centers. Bore ⅛-in.-dia. pilot holes; bore ⅜-in.-dia. holes for the rotary switches and a ½-in.-dia. hole for the pushbutton. Feed the drill slowly to prevent grabbing or denting the aluminum face.

Install the rotary switches and pushbutton

switch. Tighten the nut provided with each switch.

As a first step in wiring, solder a 2-in. piece of insulated wire to the center lug of the first rotary switch. Then solder this wire to any of the outside lugs of an adjacent rotary switch. Repeat this process for the second, third and fourth rotary switches. The fourth switch should be located next to the momentary-contact switch. With a 2-in. piece of wire, connect one of the outside lugs of the fourth rotary switch to a lug of the momentary-contact switch.

Strip two 2-in. pieces of insulated wire and solder the end of one piece to the remaining lug of the momentary-contact switch. Solder the remaining piece of insulated wire to one of the outside lugs of the first rotary contact. These short pieces of wire connect to the low-voltage wiring from your door operator.

Using bolt cutters, snip off the excess shaft supplied with the rotary switches. Install the knobs by sliding them over the shafts and tighten the mounting screws. Rotate all knobs so they point to the 12 o'clock position. Scratch or etch a mark on the faceplate above each knob. Then rotate each knob one click and repeat the process until the 12 positions have been marked.

KNOBS rotate to a predetermined position.

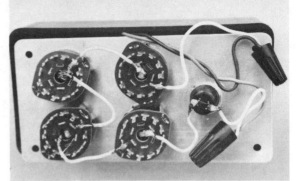

WIRE the rotary and pushbutton switches. Use solderless connectors to connect to the door opener.

figuring the combination

To figure your combination, while facing the back of the panel, rotate each knob until the center wiper contact inside each switch is aligned with the terminal of the rotary switch that has been soldered to the wire. With all four switches aligned, note the position of each knob on the face of the panel. This is the combination of your lock.

By using any of the 12 positions on each rotary switch, any combination is possible. Prior to installing the combination lock, check continuity with an ohmmeter, if you can.

Carefully plan the installation position of the lock on the outside of your home or garage. Select a spot that provides some weather protection, or shelter it in a wooden box.

Mount the box securely to the garage by boring its back in three locations and securing it to the wall with sheet-metal screws. Next, bore a ⅜- or ½-in.-dia. hole through one side of the box and garage wall to permit the bell wire from the garage-door opener to be pulled into the box.

remove electrical hazard

Note: To prevent accidental operation or electrical hazard while wiring, disconnect the power at the circuit breaker or unplug the garage-door opener from the connection to the house power supply.

Install the bell wire between the combination lock and the low-voltage contacts of the garage-door opener. Most have a two-screw terminal, so a doorbell button can be used from indoors to operate the door. Connect each wire to a screw on this terminal, tightening screws *securely*. Pull the other end of the bell wire into the combination-lock box, leaving 6 in. exposed. Connect the two short pigtails from the switches to the two ends of the wire, using solderless connectors. Test and install the faceplate.

Be sure to rotate all knobs after each use. This will prevent someone from gaining entrance by pushing the switch, or copying the combination for later use.

```
PARTS LIST—ELECTRIC LOCK
Amt.  Description
 4    Mallory No. 382 templates numbered 1-12 (optional)
 1    Archer No. 270-233 mini-utility box
 4    Archer No. 275-1385 12-position rotary switches
 1    Archer No. 275-609 pushbutton switch
 4    Archer No. 274-416 1″ molded knobs for ¼″ shaft
      18-ga. insulated bell wire (length to suit)
 1    door operator
 2    solderless connectors
 3    No. 8 × 1½″ sheet-metal screws
```

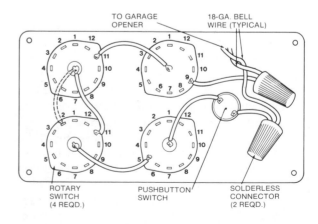

COMBINATION is now 5-11-11-9. Proposed change (dotted wire) would be 5-2-11-9.

QUAINT BUILDING features sliding barn doors plus a greenhouse to give you a jump on the season.

Build this solar garden shed

DICK RAYMOND'S harvest crop started as seedlings in the greenhouse section of building.

Famous New England gardener Dick Raymond shares the plans for his dual-purpose gardener's building

By HARRY WICKS

■ GARDENING CONSULTANT Dick Raymond built the super-useful multipurpose shed above almost as an aside on an assignment recently. Gardens for All (the nonprofit National Assn. for Gardening) asked Raymond to design, plant and evaluate the much-publicized 25x30 ft. "Independence Garden."

Dick's Independence Garden, which was designed for an average back yard, produced $497 worth of vegetables. The garden plan and Raymond's techniques are featured in a basic vegetable gardening guide called *Your Independence Garden for the '80s.* To get a free copy, send $1 to cover postage and handling to Gardens for All, Dept. PM, 180 Flynn Ave., Burlington, VT 05401.

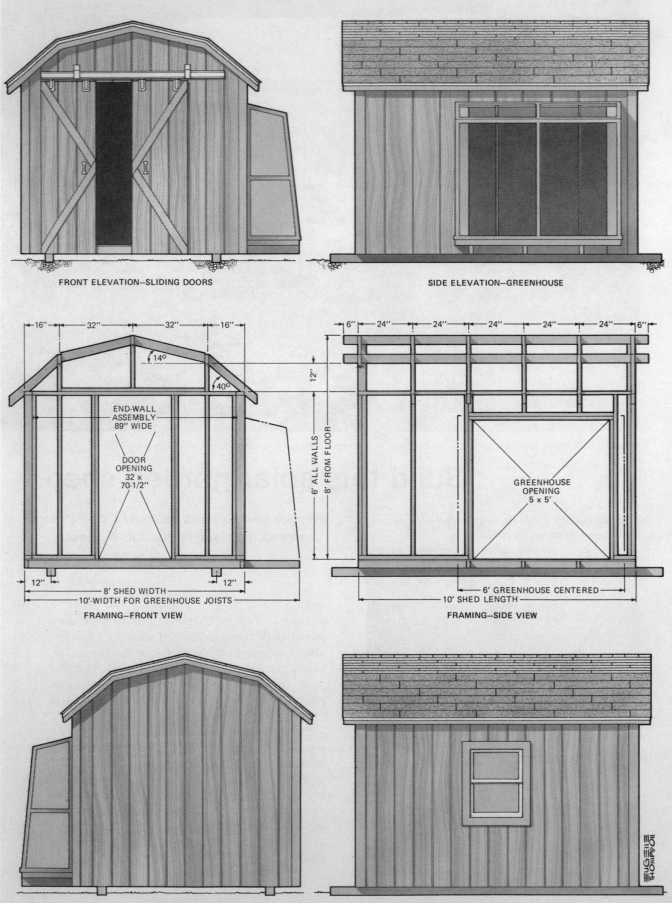

FRONT ELEVATION—SLIDING DOORS

SIDE ELEVATION—GREENHOUSE

16"   32"   32"   16"

14°

40°

END-WALL
ASSEMBLY
89" WIDE

DOOR
OPENING
32 x
70-1/2"

12"   12"

8' SHED WIDTH
10'-WIDTH FOR GREENHOUSE JOISTS

FRAMING—FRONT VIEW

6"   24"   24"   24"   24"   24"   6"

12"

6' ALL WALLS
8' FROM FLOOR

GREENHOUSE
OPENING
5 x 5'

6' GREENHOUSE CENTERED
10' SHED LENGTH

FRAMING—SIDE VIEW

BACK ELEVATION

SIDE ELEVATION—OPTIONAL WINDOW

PAIR OF SLIDING doors provides an opening big enough to drive a yard tractor through.

BECAUSE STRUCTURE lacks any collar beams, the roof is beefed up with gussets over all joints.

What we spotted—and liked—in Dick's garden was the attractive shed shown in detail on these pages. It's built using conventional building techniques and a minimum of material. What's different about this back-yard shed is that it serves two purposes:

■ Its generous size lets it hold all the gardening tools you are likely to own, plus a small tractor.
■ The easy-build greenhouse lets you get started early in the season—so you are sure of an early harvest for many of the crops. You will find complete plans on these pages.

it's built on skids

For several reasons, Raymond built his shed on skids, rather than on a permanent foundation. First, the building can be moved with tractor and cable if desired, so that ground usage can be rotated. Second, in many areas of the country a back-yard building, erected over permanent footing and block walls requires a permit. A shed on skids usually doesn't. Check your building department.

Because the building rests on the ground, Dick used pressure-treated lumber for the skids and all flooring.

Conventional framing is used throughout. The easiest way to assemble such a shed of this type is to build the floor first and use it as a work platform for the walls.

Construct the walls one at a time, tipping each up into position as it's assembled. You'll need a helper to lift the wall and hold it steady while you check both vertical planes with a spirit level. When wall is plumb, use two diagonal braces to hold it until other walls are placed.

GREENHOUSE IS a simple structure of 1x2 stock that is covered with hefty plastic sheeting.

FRAMING ASSEMBLY

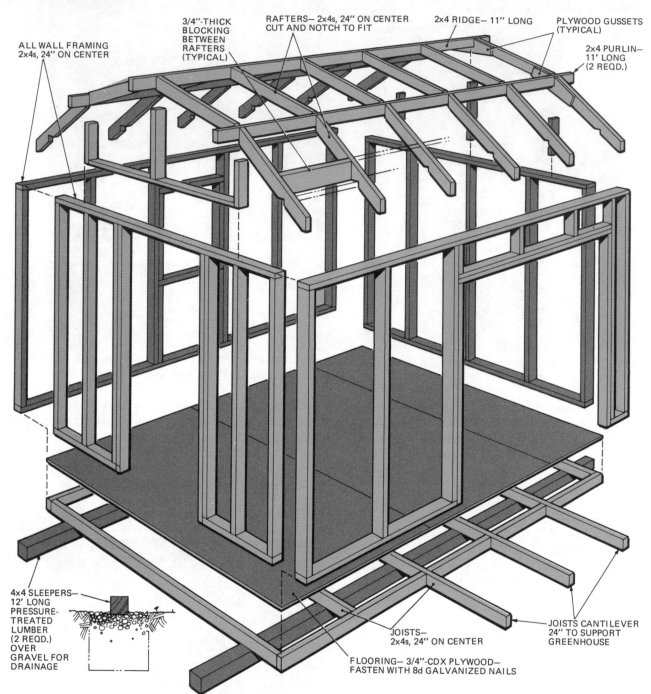

ALL WALL FRAMING
2x4s, 24" ON CENTER

3/4"-THICK
BLOCKING
BETWEEN
RAFTERS
(TYPICAL)

RAFTERS— 2x4s, 24" ON CENTER
CUT AND NOTCH TO FIT

2x4 RIDGE— 11" LONG

PLYWOOD GUSSETS
(TYPICAL)

2x4 PURLIN—
11' LONG
(2 REQD.)

4x4 SLEEPERS—
12' LONG
PRESSURE-
TREATED
LUMBER
(2 REQD.)
OVER
GRAVEL FOR
DRAINAGE

JOISTS—
2x4s, 24" ON CENTER

FLOORING— 3/4"-CDX PLYWOOD—
FASTEN WITH 8d GALVANIZED NAILS

JOISTS CANTILEVER
24" TO SUPPORT
GREENHOUSE

The braces can be 1x4 material; tack-fasten them to a pair of studs (up near the wall's top plate) at one end and to a floor-mounted cleat at the other. When all walls are up, plumb and braced, join the corners using 16d common nails.

Next, frame the gambrel roof. Raymond used a ridgeboard, purlins and plywood gussets to en-sure good weight-bearing capabilities. Install the two end rafter sections first to hold ridgeboard and purlins secure, then the other rafter sections.

Skin the walls with Texture 1-11 exterior ply-wood and the roof with ⅜-in., sheathing-grade plywood. Once the walls are covered with ply-wood, remove the diagonal braces.

SIDING, ROOFING AND GREENHOUSE DETAILS

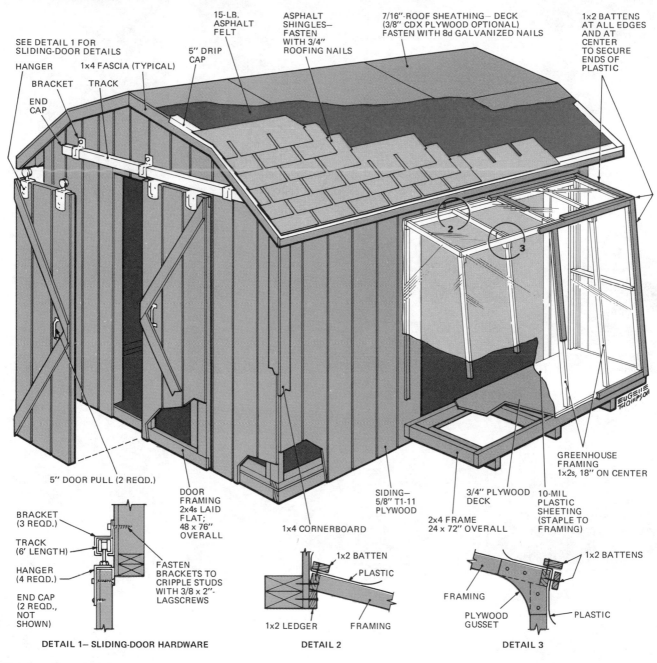

SEE DETAIL 1 FOR SLIDING-DOOR DETAILS

HANGER

BRACKET

END CAP

1x4 FASCIA (TYPICAL)

TRACK

15-LB. ASPHALT FELT

5" DRIP CAP

ASPHALT SHINGLES— FASTEN WITH 3/4" ROOFING NAILS

7/16"-ROOF SHEATHING— DECK (3/8" CDX PLYWOOD OPTIONAL) FASTEN WITH 8d GALVANIZED NAILS

1x2 BATTENS AT ALL EDGES AND AT CENTER TO SECURE ENDS OF PLASTIC

5" DOOR PULL (2 REQD.)

DOOR FRAMING 2x4s LAID FLAT; 48 x 76" OVERALL

1x4 CORNERBOARD

SIDING— 5/8" T1-11 PLYWOOD

2x4 FRAME 24 x 72" OVERALL

3/4" PLYWOOD DECK

10-MIL PLASTIC SHEETING (STAPLE TO FRAMING)

GREENHOUSE FRAMING 1x2s, 18" ON CENTER

2

3

BRACKET (3 REQD.)

TRACK (6' LENGTH)

HANGER (4 REQD.)

END CAP (2 REQD., NOT SHOWN)

FASTEN BRACKETS TO CRIPPLE STUDS WITH 3/8 x 2"- LAGSCREWS

DETAIL 1— SLIDING-DOOR HARDWARE

1x2 BATTEN

PLASTIC

1x2 LEDGER

FRAMING

DETAIL 2

FRAMING

PLYWOOD GUSSET

1x2 BATTENS

PLASTIC

DETAIL 3

Door hardware is available at local hardware stores and from retailers such as Sears, Roebuck and J.C. Penney.

Cover the roof with overlapped layers of 15-lb. felt followed by 235-lb. asphalt shingles with self-sealing edges. Apply a coat of exterior stain to the outside of the Texture 1-11.

The greenhouse cover is of 10-mil polyethylene sheet plastic, available at lumberyards and home centers. One brand name is Flex-O-Pane.

If you'd like to move the shed in your yard, install a hefty eyebolt through the end joist so you can pull it easily with cable and tractor.

Four handsome planters you can build

■ ONE OF THE quickest and least expensive ways to upgrade the looks of your home—indoors and out—is by adding a handsome planter or two. Three of the four designs shown can be used in either place. One, because it features a built-in bench, is intended solely for patio use.

Idea No. 4 is a clever, caster-mounted stand that is ideal for use beneath heavy house plants. Using it makes it a snap to move small trees and the like to sunlight, or for cleaning purposes.

which wood to use?

California redwood is an excellent choice for planters. It boasts the unbeatable combination of natural beauty and good durability. Redwood is resistant to decay and to attack by insects.

When building a planter, choose one of the all-heartwood grades, such as Clear All Heart, Select Heart or Construction Heart. There are also grades available containing some sapwood, which run slightly lower in cost. These are available on special order from your lumberyard. To get longevity from the material you buy, it should be used following certain recommendations from the California Redwood Assn.

Use only noncorrosive nails to build any planter which will be parked outdoors. Conventional steel nails (common and finishing), when wet, will react with redwood's chemicals and cause unsightly stain streaks. To prevent such staining, choose aluminum-alloy, stainless-steel or high-quality hot-dipped galvanized nails. (*Note:* If you use the latter, remove any nail whose galvanized surface is cracked by an angled hammer blow. When the nail's galvanized surface is broken, it rusts like any ordinary nail.)

After completing construction, the redwood can be left as is. But you might consider doing some finish work on the planters.

finishes

The Redwood Assn. recommends using a water repellent on all exterior redwood. This is especially true for sapwood-containing grades. The application task is easier, and you will have a better job, if you apply the repellent before constructing the planter. Coat all edges, sides and ends of lumber. Be aware that using water repellent slows down natural weathering, but since it reduces the effects of moisture, it also protects the wood from dirt and grime. A water repellent can serve as the finish, or it can serve as the undercoat for additional finishes such as bleaching or staining.

If you do not plan to follow with another finish, you should apply a second coat of the repellent.

You can use a commercially prepared bleach to speed up the driftwood gray effect (that appears as a result of natural weathering). If you decide to bleach, read all of the manufacturer's use instructions on the label.

If you prefer a darker color, you will have to stain the planter. A pigmented oil-base stain can be used or you can choose a latex exterior stain. Either way, make certain the stain you buy is intended for outdoor use.

Do not use varnish or any other clear, film-forming finish on your redwood planter. Such finishes deteriorate rapidly when exposed to sun and weather.

Plants can be planted directly in a soil-filled planter or you can place potted plants inside. If you want the former, make certain that bushes and the like are planted using accepted garden practice. Plants, of course, must have adequate drainage: Too much moisture will drown a plant.

roll-around plant stand

Dimension the stand to suit the size of your pot. You can make it by gluing up circular segments, or a block as shown. The latter permits sawing the skirt in one piece.

1 Plant container/bench combination is an eye-pleasing, functional setup that will improve the looks of most decks. Unit surrounds a post.

2 Clean lines of planter let the plants inside steal all the applause. For appearance, clear kiln-dried redwood was used throughout.

3 Redwood planter can be used on outdoor deck or entryway, but is handsome enough to serve as a container for large tree inside.

4 This good-looking and practical roll-around container, intended for large indoor planters, was designed by PM reader Harold S. Hodge.

PLANT CONTAINER/BENCH COMBINATION

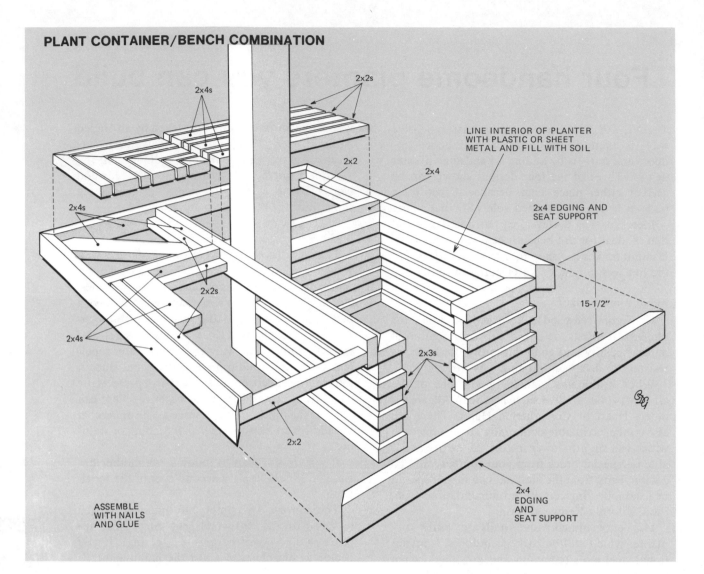

2x4s

2x2s

2x2

2x4

LINE INTERIOR OF PLANTER
WITH PLASTIC OR SHEET
METAL AND FILL WITH SOIL

2x4 EDGING AND
SEAT SUPPORT

2x4s

2x2s

15-1/2"

2x4s

2x3s

2x2

ASSEMBLE
WITH NAILS
AND GLUE

2x4
EDGING
AND
SEAT SUPPORT

Make the block by sandwich-gluing 12 pieces of wood with joints alternately overlapped. For swivel plate casters (with typical 1⅛-in.-dia. wheels and overall height of 1⅞ in.), the sandwich should have two layers of ¾-in. stock with a ¼-in. layer in between. Drive nails in the waste areas to keep the glued pieces from sliding about when the clamps are applied.

Tack-nail two pieces of ¼-in. plywood to the block, locate block center and drive a nail through and into a board clamped to the band saw (or jigsaw) table. This serves as a pivot to make a perfect circular cut. Locate the pivot the desired radius distance from the saw blade and make the cut.

Next, remove one plywood piece to use as is for the platform. On the remaining two, make a freehand tangent cut through the edge of the disc to get the blade to the inside. Reinstate the pivot and complete the internal cut to obtain a ⅜-in.-thick wall.

Glue the platform to the skirt, then add the ring. The spaces made by the blade are filled by gluing in thin filler strips.

Install the three casters with flathead machine screws and nuts.

The stand shown was sanded smooth, dusted off and sealed with a coat of shellac thinned 50 percent with denatured alcohol. Next, the surface was sanded with 180-grit paper, dusted and wiped with a tack cloth. To finish, two coats of latex semigloss enamel were applied; light sanding with 220-grit paper was done between coats.

BOX PLANTER

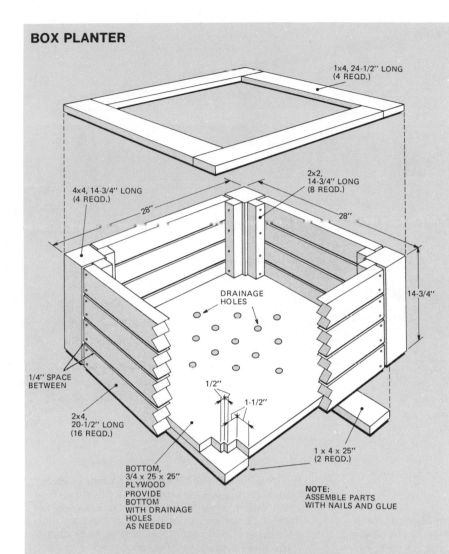

1x4, 24-1/2" LONG
(4 REQD.)

4x4, 14-3/4" LONG
(4 REQD.)

2x2,
14-3/4" LONG
(8 REQD.)

28"

28"

14-3/4"

DRAINAGE
HOLES

1/4" SPACE
BETWEEN

1/2"

1-1/2"

2x4,
20-1/2" LONG
(16 REQD.)

1 x 4 x 25"
(2 REQD.)

BOTTOM,
3/4 x 25 x 25"
PLYWOOD
PROVIDE
BOTTOM
WITH DRAINAGE
HOLES
AS NEEDED

NOTE:
ASSEMBLE PARTS
WITH NAILS AND GLUE

REDWOOD PLANTER

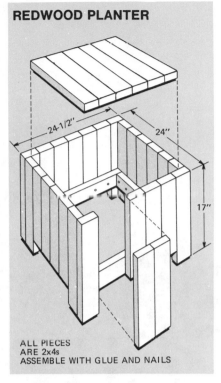

24-1/2"

24"

17"

ALL PIECES
ARE 2x4s
ASSEMBLE WITH GLUE AND NAILS

ROLL-AROUND CONTAINER

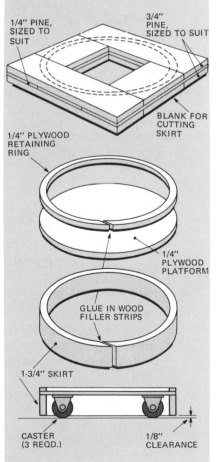

1/4" PINE,
SIZED TO
SUIT

3/4"
PINE,
SIZED TO SUIT

BLANK FOR
CUTTING
SKIRT

1/4" PLYWOOD
RETAINING
RING

1/4"
PLYWOOD
PLATFORM

GLUE IN WOOD
FILLER STRIPS

1-3/4" SKIRT

CASTER
(3 REQD.)

1/8"
CLEARANCE

TO CUT circles from block, shift pivot point after tangent cut is made.

GLUE AND NAIL platform first, then add fillers and the retaining ring.

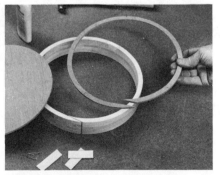

THREE PIECES are ready for gluing. Thin strips are used to fill kerf gap.

VIEW FROM BOTTOM: Three plate-type casters make planter easy to move.

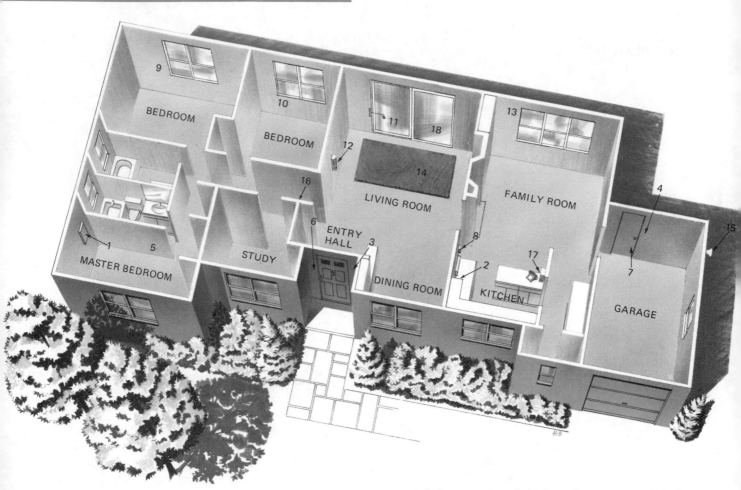

HOW TO PUT an electronic "fence" around your home: Studies show that alarms triggered by a network of detectors throughout a house will scare away 98 percent of all burglars. While most homes will not have all the security devices indicated on the house plan above, they show the wide variety of aids available. They are: 1. master control; 2. remote master; 3. indoor remote switch; 4. outdoor remote switch; 5. manual emergency (panic) button; 6. reset button; 7. shunt switch; 8. light-flasher relay; 9. surface-mount magnetic detector; 10. recessed magnetic detector; 11. glass-break sensor; 12. ultrasonic detector; 13. alarm-wired screen; 14. pressure-sensitive floormat; 15. outdoor alarm horn; 16. indoor horn; 17. automatic telephone dialer; 18. photocell detector. System parts by NuTone Div., Scovill, Madison and Red Bank Rds., Cincinnati, OH 45227.

Burglar-alarm systems for your home

Here's how a central alarm system can save your valuables—and peace of mind

By JOHN INGERSOLL

■ "WE DON'T NEED a burglar alarm when we're home," said a Philadelphia contractor. Not true. While he and his family were eating dinner last summer, a "cat burglar" hoisted himself up to a small second-story balcony outside the master bedroom, entered quietly through French doors, swept valuable jewelry into a pillowcase and left as he came.

"The house is completely locked. We aren't worried about thefts," said a Minneapolis couple.

Wrong again. Returning from a two-week vacation, they found their house stripped. The thief had broken a window, reached in to release the sash lock and entered easily.

"I always leave the door unlocked. Nothing ever happens here," said a bachelor in Laramie, Wyo. Back from an evening movie, he found his house ransacked.

In all three cases, the owners slammed the barn door after the horse was stolen. They now have

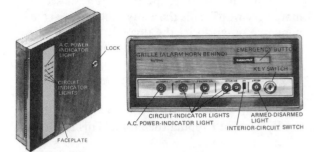

CIRCUIT-INDICATOR LIGHTS   ARMED-DISARMED
A.C. POWER-INDICATOR LIGHT   LIGHT
    INTERIOR-CIRCUIT SWITCH

MASTER CONTROL PANEL (above left) connects all components in system. LEDs indicate if system is operating properly and, if not, where trouble lies. It has standby battery and connections for extra circuits. Remote master (above right) is similar, but styled for use in bedroom, kitchen, or other living areas. It has its own alarm horn behind decorative grille, panic button and indicator lights.

burglar-alarm systems.

Alarm systems—all of which consist of a network of detectors connected to a central control—range in price from $120, uninstalled, to $5,000, installed and monitored by a private security agency for a monthly fee of $15 to $25.

A full alarm system runs one or more perimeter circuits from a central control, arming all windows and outside doors. It may also include one or more interior circuits, laying traps for an intruder who manages to elude the perimeter loops. A full system generally ties in fire protection as well.

A number of systems are sold in kit form, with instructions for do-it-yourself installation. Inexpensive systems are the easiest to install, mainly because they consist of fewer and simpler parts. As the price goes up, so does the sophistication and the time it will take to hook everything up. The actual wiring, however, is fairly simple, since alarm systems almost universally operate on 12 volts, permitting the use of easy-to-run, low-voltage cable. A transformer is connected between house current and the central control, and there's usually a standby battery to provide backup power in a blackout.

Here are the parts common to most systems:

central control panel

The central control panel is the heart of any full alarm system. It contains a relay that transmits signals from the detectors to an audible alarm in the house or to the security station monitoring your system. Most controls also display signal lights, indicating power on/off and whether or not the circuits are armed.

Control panels are used for both wired and radio-transmitted alarms. Choose a wireless network if it's too much of a hassle to conceal the wires and surface wiring will appear too unsightly.

In a radio system, the central control plugs into a 115-volt outlet and has a 12-volt backup battery. Battery-operated radio transmitters, wired to perimeter detectors, send a signal to the control panel when a break-in occurs, and the panel sounds the alarm. This system goes in more easily than the wired type, but does have a drawback: Not everyone remembers to replace batteries regularly, and a dead one could knock out your protection.

In a wired system, the central control panel is

REMOTE KEY switch fits standard electrical wall box, allows you to arm or disarm system at points distant from master control. Similar switch is made in weatherproof style for outdoor use so you can control the system from a porch deck or patio.

PANIC BUTTON lets you sound alarm manually if you suspect intruder is trying to break in. You can have one by your bed, others elsewhere. Similar control boxes house reset buttons for rearming system after it's been triggered and shunt switches to temporarily disarm door or window.

connected through a transformer to your house wiring and contains a rechargeable battery for emergency backup power. Wires connect it to your door and window detectors, forming a continuous loop of protection. A break in the circuit at any point in the loop causes the alarm to sound.

remote controls

A master remote panel is similar to the central control panel, but can be installed in any remote location where you want to keep tabs on the system. Often it's attractively styled so it can be openly displayed in living areas, such as the kitchen or master bedroom. Its signals tell you the same information as the main control panel—sometimes more. It can also house an

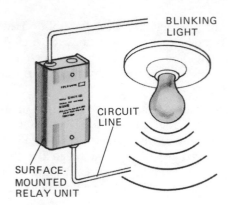

LIGHT-FLASHER relay turns on house lights (up to 1000 watts) if a detector is tripped. It can also blink lights on and off to scare away a thief.

alarm of its own, usually behind a decorative grille. What the panel gives you is a second opportunity to oversee the system.

exit/entry devices

Obviously, you and the members of your family must have a way to enter and leave the house without triggering the alarm yourselves. Several options are open to you: digital signals code-set to allow you time to enter or leave, key locks that let you disarm the system momentarily, or a simple button switch to deactivate the system for a

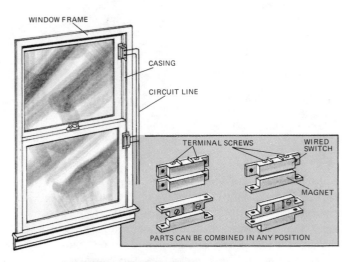

MAGNETIC DETECTORS install on windows and doors to form continuous loop of protection to encircle the house. Magnets and their magnetically controlled switches are arranged in closely spaced pairs. The surface mount type shown here is the easiest to install.

preset interval, usually just long enough to let you get in or out the door.

Whatever its form, the exit/entry device is both a necessity—and a nuisance. It's been labeled by many alarm-system owners as the "false-alarm trigger." The device—or actually

the failure to use it properly—seems to set off more "cry wolf" calls than any other single component. You go to let the dog out, forget to disarm the system and suddenly—wham!—off goes the alarm with a deafening blast, disturbing neighbors and sometimes bringing the police on the run.

A shunt switch allows you to open a door briefly without tripping the alarm. This is a form

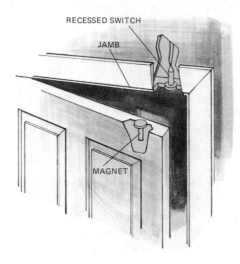

MAGNETIC DETECTORS can also be installed in door and window jambs as shown here. They look neater and are harder for a burglar to spot than surface types, but are more difficult to install.

of disarming control, but it deactivates only one detector, not the whole system. The switch releases the door detector from the perimeter circuit loop until the switch is flipped on again. The same switch lets you open a bedroom window at night for fresh air without setting off the alarm or having to deactivate the entire system. You must remember to reset a shunt switch, however. Unlike a timed exit/entry control, it will not reset itself automatically.

emergency switches

Emergency switches—more familiarly known as panic buttons—do just what their name implies. They allow you to trigger the alarm manually any time you think an intruder is attempting to break in or in other emergencies where a loud alarm might be useful in calling for help. Install the buttons at key locations, such as next to your bed and in an upstairs hallway.

Another type of remote control is a reset button that puts the system back into operation after the alarm has been set off by an intruder—or a forgetful child. In some systems, this is a key-operated switch instead of a button, but it does the same thing. Install a reset next to the central control panel if it doesn't contain its own reset (some do). Another possibility: alongside entry doors, where many false alarms are triggered.

magnetic detectors

Magnetic detectors are used to protect entry doors, sliding glass doors, garage doors and any form of window that opens. These consist of two parts: an unwired magnet and a wired switch that is controlled by the magnet. The two are arranged with a slight gap between them so as to maintain a constant magnetic field.

The clever part about this system is that it's constantly energized so that a break anywhere in the circuit—not just at a detector—will automatically trigger the alarm. Thus, if a thief attempts to deactivate the alarm by cutting the wires, he instantly sets it off.

GLASS-BREAK DETECTOR

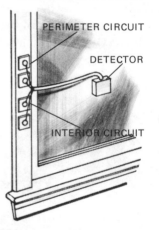

GLASS-BREAK detector is tiny device that sticks to large picture window or sliding glass door. Sensitive to vibration, it sounds alarm if glass is broken, but won't trip if jarred only by wind gusts.

hidden detectors

If you prefer a concealed system, recessed types of magnetic detectors are also available. These fit flush into the edges of doors and windows and are almost invisible. They take a lot more work to install, but they improve the looks and, more important, disguise your protection from an intruder peering inside. If a thief can see the magnets, he might attempt to defeat the system. (Some alarm systems *can* be fooled, but we think it best not to discuss the methods here.)

Another type of door and window detector is mechanical and less reliable. Called a plunger detector, it signals for an alarm when its plunger is depressed as little as 1/8 inch. Its problem is that

moisture in the air can corrode the plunger, eventually jamming it.

There's more. You've seen how commercial establishments are protected with strips of metallic foil around the edges of windows. This system is also available for home installation and is not a bad idea for a large expanse of fixed glass. Smashing the glass breaks the foil tape, instantly sounding the alarm. The tape can be wired into the same system as magnetic detectors so you can have magnets on windows that move and the foil on those that don't.

sophisticated sensors

Area protection inside the house is provided by some of the more dramatic devices. Newest among these is the infrared heat sensor. It sends out finger-slim beams of invisible infrared light, ready in an instant to detect any change in temperature. It won't trip when morning sun streams in a window, but will sound the minute a human body at 98° F. passes through the beams.

Another type, the ultrasonic detector, sends out sound waves inaudible to human ears. The device is both a transmitter and receiver. When the pattern of sound waves received is different

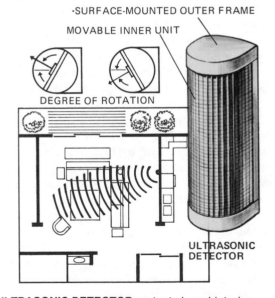

ULTRASONIC DETECTOR protects broad interior spaces. It sends inaudible sound waves through a room. If waves are disturbed by someone crossing their path, it sounds an alarm. Transmitter swivels to aim it for desired area of coverage. Other area-type detectors use microwaves or heat-sensing infrared.

from that of the waves sent out, it indicates that the waves have been disturbed by someone crossing their path, and the alarm sounds.

A third device, the microwave detector, is also a transceiver. It floods the area with high-frequency radio waves (not injurious to health). The

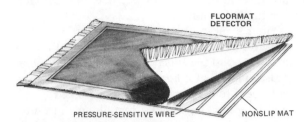

PRESSURE-SENSITIVE floormat hidden under a rug or stair runner flashes the alarm if stepped on. They're good for doorways, halls and other high-traffic areas.

detector, monitoring the reflected energy, notes when the waves have been distorted by someone moving through them and sounds the alarm. A problem: Pets or small children can trigger the alarm.

Sliding glass doors and other doorways can also be protected by photoelectric cells using beams of invisible infrared light. A transmitter and reflector are installed on opposite sides of the door. If someone breaks the reflected beam, the alarm sounds.

pressure-sensitive mats

Pressure-sensitive floormats, laid under rugs or stair carpet, will signal the central control when a person (even a dog) walks on them. These are good for doorways, halls and sliding glass doors, but can be a problem when someone sleepily goes downstairs for a late-night snack and forgets to disarm them.

An audio detector should be mentioned, too. Stationed centrally in the house, it detects the sound frequency made by breaking glass. It's a good idea if your house has a lot of vulnerable glass area, but shouldn't be needed if the perimeter is well protected by other devices.

Alarm-wired door and window screens offer added protection. You might want to consider them if your house is hidden from street view or in a remote location where a burglar would have more time to work unnoticed. An alarm sounds if the screen is cut or removed.

indoor and outdoor alarms

The alarm itself is either a loud bell or blaring horn. You can choose an indoor type, an outdoor type—or both. An indoor alarm is loud enough to wake you when you're home and is usually frightening enough to scare off an intruder even when you're away. However, it probably won't be heard by neighbors.

An outdoor alarm will rouse the entire neighborhood and perhaps even get the attention of a

nearby patrol car. On the other hand, you can't always count on neighbors to call the police for you—they may not be home or, more likely, may tire of the game after about the third false alarm. For this reason, most installations include both an inside and outside alarm. An added bonus: If a thief cuts the wires to an outside alarm, the inside one will still sound.

What happens if a thief cuts your 115-volt house wiring? Will the alarm be deactivated? No. It will immediately switch over to power from the 12-volt backup battery and remain armed. If the intruder then interrupts the perimeter wiring at any point, the alarm will go off. This gives you protection if the power goes out for any reason, but at the same time, prevents the alarm from sounding during a storm-related blackout.

telephone alerts

Three less noisy options are also open to you. One is a simple light-circuit relay. When signaled, it switches on all house lights connected to its circuit. It can also be set to flash the lights on and off. Often, this is enough to frighten off an intruder.

OUTDOOR ALARM horn sounds electronic wail at 102 decibels, loud enough to rouse entire neighborhood. Indoor horn at 85 db. wakes sleepers. Most installations include both. If outdoor alarm is cut, indoor one will sound.

The second is an automatic telephone dialer combined with a tape recorder. You prerecord a message on tape, saying your house is being burglarized. When an actual break-in occurs, the dialer silently rings a preselected number—a friend, neighbor or the police. Unfortunately, the police in some areas may not permit automatic dialers to be set to their number (because of the nuisance of false alarms).

Better is a silent, digital telephone dialer that sends a coded signal to a central security station. This is the most expensive route to take, but also the closest to being foolproof. False alarms are intercepted before neighbors or the police are unnecessarily alerted.

All about water filters

While a filter can't guarantee health benefits, it can improve taste and remove odors and sediment

By JOHN H. INGERSOLL

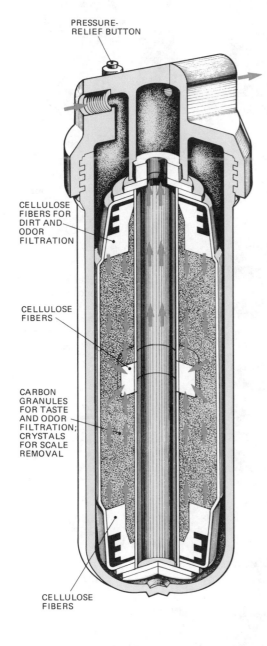

PRESSURE-RELIEF BUTTON

CELLULOSE FIBERS FOR DIRT AND ODOR FILTRATION

CELLULOSE FIBERS

CARBON GRANULES FOR TASTE AND ODOR FILTRATION; CRYSTALS FOR SCALE REMOVAL

CELLULOSE FIBERS

COMBINATION water filter works this way: Carbon granules improve taste and odor, spun cellulose fibers remove sediment, and salt crystals cut back lime scale. Tap water flows between the outer cylinder and inner filter cartridge. Line pressure forces the water through the filter agents to the inner core and to the faucet.

■ IF TAP WATER from a community supply were filtered by one family, and another family consumed it straight from the faucet, which family would expose itself to a health risk?

That's the question I asked Dr. Joseph Cotruvo, director, Drinking Water Standards, En-

vironmental Protection Agency (EPA). He said, "There would be no way you could prove any differences in their health were traceable to the water."

Neither Dr. Cotruvo, water-supply engineers, nor environmentalists would fault U.S. water companies. The opinion was unanimous: We still have the safest processed water in the world.

That doesn't mean officials are closing their eyes to potential dangers. It's true that toxic chemicals have seeped into some surface water that's been processed for home consumption. Several chemicals react with chlorine, the purifying agent that's used almost universally to produce trihalomethanes (THMs). Lab tests show that, in some cases, high concentrations of THMs are carcinogenic in small animals. While that doesn't translate into an immediate threat for humans, the EPA has already set standards for the presence of THMs in treated water (100 parts per billion).

well water

"What about well water?" I asked.

"Quantitatively, 99 percent of U.S. ground water is pure," according to Dr. Jay Lehr, executive director, National Well Water Assn. "It's true, however, that in isolated areas, toxic industrial wastes have leached into aquifers serving a number of private wells. But the nationwide risk has been overblown and has needlessly alarmed people who draw pure water from wells."

Then why, one would ask logically, are home water filters among the fastest selling appliances on the market today? According to makers, most people buy them for the advertised advantages: ". . . removes disagreeable taste and odor, sediment, rust and dirt. . . ."

Yet a growing number of families are opting for filters because they've become anxious over what they can't see in their tap water—micro-

SIX WAYS TO CLEANER WATER

WHEN YOU WANT filtered water for cooking or drinking, push the side button on this faucet-attached carbon filter made by West Bend. Otherwise, the filter is bypassed.

A TYPICAL under-sink filter kit includes (left to right, rear): hanging bracket, tubing, replaceable filter cartridge, tubing adapter, outer cylinder. Front: mounting screws, filtered water spout and self-tapping needle valve.

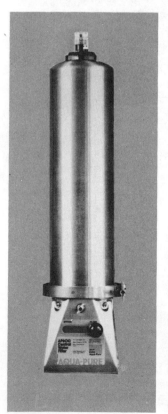

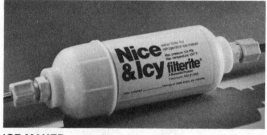

ICE-MAKER water filter from Filterite attaches to the copper or plastic tubing at the rear of the refrigerator. The filter eliminates annoying odors and tastes in ice cubes.

THE AP600 model filters out bad tastes, odors, rust and grime, and inhibits scale. An indicator pops up when the cartridge is dirty and needs changing.

THIS PORTABLE electric water filter forces water up into activated charcoal and out the spout at the top into a special container. It's made by Dynek and costs under $50.

WATER MASTER by American Purification delivers one cup of water at a time. The hourglass filter fits over the cup. Water takes under a minute to seep through.

scopic fragments of asbestos, petroleum derivatives and other chemicals.

If you buy a filtering device for advertised reasons, you won't be disappointed—as long as you install and maintain it as recommended. If your purchase is intended to protect the health of your family, you'll cover some of the bases partially and miss others entirely.

Filters containing activated charcoal *do* block many frightening compounds, such as THMs. But even the best filters don't remove *all* of these substances. Those packed with a large volume of charcoal generally weed out more organic material at the start of cartridge life; performance falls off less rapidly in time than does that of containers with only a small amount of charcoal.

With few exceptions, performance specifications of each filter are printed on the shipping carton, the canister or both. You'll learn what the filter sifts from the water and, generally, the estimated life of the cartridge under normal conditions. The flow rate in gallons per minute is also noted.

fiber filters block sediment

Not all filters contain charcoal. Another group, aimed at taking out turbidity (suspended sediment), contains fibers of spun cellulose or rayon. The tightly wrapped fibers form a cylinder around a tubular opening. Tap water surrounds the cylinder and line pressure forces the water through the wrappings. These fibers trap the silt and pass along clean water to the inner opening that leads to the faucet.

Fiber filters are marked according to the size of particles that they trap. A tightly wrapped fiber could sift out everything over about 5 microns. (The diameter of a human hair is about 100 microns. The smallest particle visible to the human eye is 40 microns.) More loosely wound and less expensive filters catch everything over about 60 microns.

All the wrapped cylinders fill up with particles eventually and then it is necessary to replace them.

ceramic filters

A ceramic filter, intended for the same duty, is permanent. Designed to weed out larger particles—in the 250- to 350-micron range, or about the size of the tiniest visible grain of sand—it is cleaned by backwashing for a recommended period. Then you remove, soak and wash it thoroughly, and it's ready for use again.

Cold-water dirt filters are plentiful and operate at temperatures between 40 and 100°F. But if you want to catch rust before it stains clothes in the washer, buy a hot-water sediment filter. Some withstand temperatures as high as 275° F., but those withstanding 200° are more than sufficient.

Activated charcoal (carbon) filters remove bad taste, odor and many of the chemical compounds with the tongue-twisting names. For most people, the primary taste that they are trying to remove is that of chlorine; where it prevails, hydrogen sulfide (the "rotten egg" compound) runs a close second. Carbon doesn't remove fluorine or any natural minerals.

Recently, some makers have infused their activated carbon with a silver compound aimed at squelching minute bacteria growth on the surface of the carbon. However, according to extensive EPA tests, there is no significant difference in bacteria count between filters with silver and those without.

While the bacteria is virtually benign in such small quantities, it is still a source of concern for some. To cleanse the carbon surface of the filter, simply run water through the filter for five or six seconds.

preventing lime buildup

Finally, there are filters packed with salts to impede lime buildup or scale on the piping and inner walls of hot-water heaters. These small filters are not intended to supplant water softeners. They are designed only to remove the worst of the calcium in hard water.

A number of companies offer cartridges containing filter combinations. One, in fact, is said to block taste and odor (carbon), sediment (spun cellulose) and lime (salts). Such filters, however, don't perform as well in each category as canisters of the same size that are packed with a single filtering material.

The best cure for hard, rusty, chlorine water is to install three separate filters—one each to solve a specific problem.

Of course, the catch is cost. One combo unit might run around $50. Three single-purpose devices could exceed $140, not considering your time required to install the system (or the cost of paying someone to do it).

six types of water filters

Costs for filtering devices run the gamut, from as low as $12 to nearly $400. Here are the highlights of six types of filters and what they'll do for you:

1. Faucet-attached filters are at the base of the

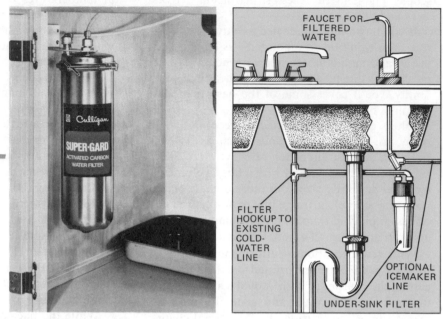

INSTALLATION UNDER A KITCHEN SINK

THE UNDER-SINK taste-and-odor filter by Culligan mounts on a bracket and delivers fresh water to its own water spout. The handy unit is packed heavily with carbon. The filter installs on an L-shaped bracket on the cold-water line. The line maintains pressure through the filter to its spout and to the optional ice-maker line.

price ladder—from about $12 to $40. You just remove the faucet aerator and attach the filter fitting. Older faucets may not take the fitting directly. But you can buy adapter rings from a plumbing supply or hardware store. Choose a filter that provides a bypass for unfiltered water. Otherwise, you'll needlessly shorten the life of the cartridge by filtering water to wash, say, the kitchen floor.

2. Under-sink models fasten to supply piping. Generally, these in-line models fall into two categories: (1) units that hook up to cold-water supply piping and feed an existing faucet, and (2) systems that divert water from the cold-water line to the filter and send clean water to a separate spout.

Spout models deliver filtered water when you need it, allowing water for general purposes to flow through the faucet. Some in-line devices have a bypass feature, a valve built into the canister head.

If you buy in-line cylinders without a bypass, install the valve on the supply side. This way, you won't have to trudge to the cellar to turn off the house water before changing filters. A valve on the delivery side prevents water in the line from draining back during a change.

wide range of prices

Prices for under-sink models span the widest range—from around $35 to nearly $400. Replacement cartridges run from about $6 to $75. Variations that account for the wide range of prices include: different amounts of carbon; plastic versus stainless-steel cylinders; canister alone versus canister plus spout and piping accessories; activated carbon inside the cylinder versus activated carbon plus additional mechanical filters.

Before mounting an in-line canister, make sure the supply pipe is strong enough to support the added weight. If you decide it isn't, support the unit with a wall bracket.

3. In-line sediment filters are identical in appearance to under-sink models (and can be installed there). Generally, families want sediment removed from all their water. For that purpose, the filter is installed in-line at the service entry, just beyond the shutoff valve.

Prices for these start at about $35 and run to $150. Replacement cartridges cost from $5 to $22. Essentially, price differences relate to size. Bigger models take out sediment over a longer period of time.

4. Ice-maker filters attach to the flexible copper or plastic tubing that delivers water to a cold-water/icemaker refrigerator or a standard ice maker. You attach it to the line just before it enters the appliance. It costs from $12 to $40 for the original and $12 to $16 for replacements.

5. Portable filters freshen water on a recreational vehicle, boat or at a campsite, assuming you start with potable water. Most of these units are simple pour-through systems. They cost between $5 and $25.

Electric models by Dynek are intended for both in-house or out-of-house use. One model,

INSTALLATION ON HOUSE SUPPLY LINE

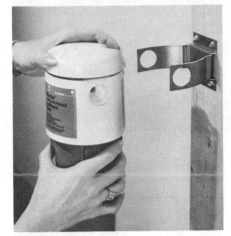

THIS SEDIMENT filter is installed on the main cold-water line. The pipe openings line up with bracket holes.

A MALE-THREADED pipe fitting holds the filter securely in its bracket. The adapter allows you to hook up the filter to the existing piping.

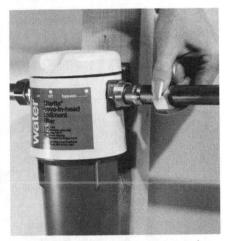

SLIP A NUT over the pipe and put pipe in the joint opening. This system eliminates the need to thread the pipe.

TIGHTEN NUT firmly, but not excessively. This in-line filter has a water by-pass valve to ease cartridge changes.

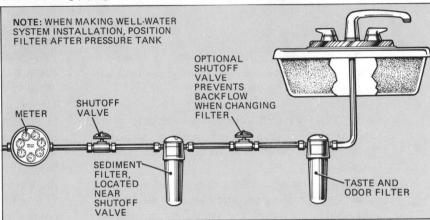

SUGGESTED LOCATIONS for the sediment and taste-odor filters are shown in the diagram. The shutoff valve prevents backflow when changing filter.

under $50, operates on 115-v. house current. Another, under $55, works off a 12-v. line. You pour water into the container, and a small electric pump forces water up through a bed of activated carbon, then out a spout at the top. A standard filter replacement for $8 removes taste and odor; a special filter ($10) also removes fluorine and some minerals.

6. Scale filters connect to the hot-water heater supply line. A smaller model prevents scale buildup in humidifiers. Prices range from about $35 to $90.

maintaining the filters

Maintenance is vital for all of these filtering devices; you can't install and forget them. As time passes, the filtering agent becomes less efficient. Eventually, it needs to be replaced.

How long the filter lasts depends on the filter size, the condition of your water and how often you use the filter.

The easiest way to determine when the filter needs a change is to check the water flow. When water from the filter slows to a dribble, a change is overdue: The filtering agent is clogged.

You can also tell that your filter is due for replacement when the water begins to taste bad again, or when it shows a slight turbidity. Manufacturers usually give you a ballpark figure for filter life, as well.

More than anything else, water filters improve your meal-time enjoyment. As one Florida homeowner said, "I'd forgotten that a simple cup of coffee could taste so good."

A thermostat controls this fan

By RUSSELL JAMES

LINE-VOLTAGE thermostat (under ridge, far right) activates the fan as the temperature rises.

IDEAL FAN HEIGHT from the floor is 10 to 12 ft. The switches are to the right of the window.

■ IF YOU THINK ceiling fans are only good for summer use or nostalgia, you'll be surprised to learn their practical value during the heating season, too.

During summer, ceiling fans create a cooling effect by increasing the circulation of air around our bodies. In winter, the same fan can increase our comfort and the efficiency of our heating systems by recirculating the warm air that has a natural tendency to rise and nestle against the ceiling. The higher the ceiling, the greater the air-temperature difference. The upper layer of air in a cathedral-ceiling room may be over 90° F., while air by the room thermostat, 5 ft. from the floor, is only 70° F.

However, it is neither desirable nor fuel efficient to leave the fan spinning continuously, especially when your heating system is off.

The solution for homeowners is to use a line-voltage thermostat to control the fan. When installed on the ceiling in a series circuit with the fan, a heat-control system is established that keeps the room more comfortable and saves fuel.

When the house temperature drops to the lower limit of the thermostat's setting, the heating system is activated, and warm air is generated. As the warm air rises and begins to concentrate heat near the ceiling, the contacts in the high-voltage thermostat begin to close. This thermostat is set

at a temperature 7° to 10° warmer than the house thermostat. At the ceiling, this temperature is reached soon after the heat begins to concentrate. When the contacts close, the fan turns on and sets the warmer air in circulation.

An evenly heated room is more comfortable, of course, but that's not the only advantage. The temperature equalization allows the house thermostat to reach its shutoff setting sooner, saving fuel.

We installed a Hunter fan with a 52-in. blade spread (about $200) in a 17x20-ft. room with a 14-ft.-high cathedral ceiling. We also installed a thermostat-override switch, in a handy location. Next to it, we installed a variable-speed-control switch (about $12).

For more information about Hunter fans, send $1 for a catalog from Robbins and Myers Inc., Box 14775, Memphis, TN 38114, or call toll-free, 1 (800) 238-5358.

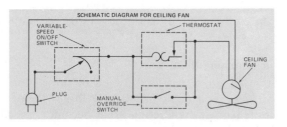

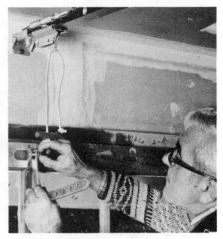

AN OBSTRUCTION in the path of the invisible light beam between two sensors will cause a closing door to reopen—the door doesn't have to be touched. The sensor is the dark object near the bottom of the door frame.

FOUR-SECTION tee rail is assembled with carriage bolts and secured to the opener chassis. A heavy-duty chain wraps around the drive sprocket and trolley and is secured with two master links.

TEE RAIL is held on header-wall bracket with a clevis pin (top). Door is attached to trolley with V-shape hardware plate and door-mounted bracket.

ATTRACTIVE chassis has built-in lights that turn on when the opener is activated. All adjustments and wiring connections are made on outside of chassis.

SPECIFICATIONS—DOOR OPENER

Motor: ⅓ hp, 1500 rpm, 120 v.a.c., 4.8 amps.
Drive mechanism: length, 1.16 in.; headroom, 1 in.; weight: 52 lbs. 6 oz.; price: about $200.
Safety features: automatic reversal in either direction, independent up and down adjustment screws, motor overload protector, low-voltage pushbutton wiring, circuit actuated by limit nut, limited adjustment, low-voltage pushbutton, keyswitch or radio control.
Manufacturer: Chamberlain Manufacturing Corp., 845 Larch Ave., Elmhurst, Ill. 60126.

CODE in radio control can be set or changed by altering digital switch positions. Code used must be the same in the transmitter and receiver.

Sensor monitors garage door opener

■ AN INVISIBLE light-beam obstruction sensor is a feature of Chamberlain's newest heavy-duty opener for use with all types of overhead garage doors. Any break in the light beam, which is installed about 6 in. above the floor, causes a closing door to reopen or prevents an open door from closing. The door doesn't have to "bump" someone to reverse.

A solid-state trinary radio receiver, Model 444 has an on/off switch to prevent operation through a transmitter signal during vacation periods or whenever garage security is desired. The digital radio controls are easy to change to one of 3,375 code possibilities. There is automatic on/off built-in lighting with a 4½-minute duration, independent up and down force adjustment and pull-cord emergency disconnect for manual door operation in the event of a power failure.

The package comes with all necessary hardware and an easy-to-follow installation instruction manual. You can install the unit in several hours using a few ordinary household tools.

Model No. 444, now available at home centers, is about $200 and is made by the Chamberlain Manufacturing Corp., 845 Larch Ave., Elmhurst, IL 60126.

LANGHORNE CUT steel end plates (above), then fitted curved blades to complete the turbine (top).

FOUR voltage-sensitive relays kick on in sequence to add load when power supply exceeds demand.

MOUNTAIN STREAM is diverted to enter supply pipe, lined with polyethylene. Screen keeps out debris.

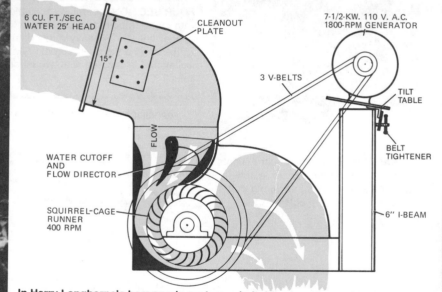

6 CU. FT./SEC. WATER 25' HEAD

CLEANOUT PLATE

7-1/2-KW. 110 V. A.C. 1800-RPM GENERATOR

15"

3 V-BELTS

TILT TABLE

FLOW

BELT TIGHTENER

WATER CUTOFF AND FLOW DIRECTOR

SQUIRREL-CAGE RUNNER 400 RPM

6" I-BEAM

In Harry Langhorne's homemade system, a belt drive transfers turbine energy to a 7.5-kilowatt generator mounted on a tilting table. Water flows to the turbine through 100 feet of pipe running from a concrete box that collects diverted water.

Back-yard power plants: Energy by the bucket

Now you can fish watts from flowing water by using miniature hydroelectric equipment. It's possible to do it in your own backyard if you have a small stream, spring or river. You may even be able to sell energy to the utility company

By JOHN INGERSOLL

LANGHORNE attached 450-watt heating element to stone coffee table which helps heat his house.

ANOTHER HEATING element warms chair seat. Hydro supplies 80 percent of electricity used in house.

■ HARRY LANGHORNE of Lowesville, Va., gets his hot water from a cold mountain stream.

Langhorne enjoys a hot, leisurely shower every morning without worrying about his energy bills. He also runs lights and a few appliances and even heats up millstone tables to help heat his house—all with a 6.5-kilowatt hydroelectric plant he built himself. The little homemade turbine, which can spin out more than 130 kilowatt-hours per day when the stream is high, meets about 80 percent of his electrical needs.

Langhorne is not alone. Backyard hydropower is gaining enough popularity to worry a few private and public utility officials. They view it as an erosion of their monopoly, rather than as a solution to foreign oil dependence.

Tiny generating plants are springing up, and they're being encouraged by the Department of Energy (DOE) and protection from the Federal Energy Regulatory Commission (FERC). DOE

HOW TO MEASURE FLOW RATE

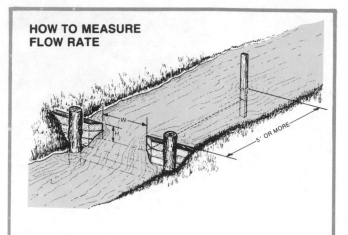

Is back-yard hydro practical for you? It depends in part on flow rate (see accompanying article).

In small streams, you can measure flow by diverting the stream into a drum of known volume and timing how long it takes to fill up. In larger streams, however, that can be difficult. And that's where the *weir method* of measuring flow comes in.

Begin by building a temporary dam with an opening large enough to let through all water in the stream without the water spilling over the top of the dam. The width of the dam opening (W) should be at least three times the opening height (H). Sink a stake into the stream at least five feet up from the dam. Run a piece of cord from the lip of the dam to the stake. Use a mason's line level on this line (water won't hurt it) to make sure the bottom of the dam lip is level with the point where the cord attaches to the stick.

Now carefully measure the distance in inches along the stake from the cord attachment to the water surface. Move to the weir table (which we have abbreviated below) and determine what rating equals the measurement. Multiply the rating by the width of the dam opening in inches. The result will be the cubic-feet-per-minute (c.f.m.) flow for the stream. It's important during measurements that leakage does not occur in the dam; caulk any leaky seams with clay-filled mud.

Depth on stake (in inches)	C.F.M. per inch of notch width	Depth on stake (in inches)	C.F.M. per inch of notch width
1	0.40	13	18.87
2	1.14	14	21.09
3	2.09	15	23.38
4	3.22	16	25.76
5	4.50	17	28.20
6	5.90	18	30.70
7	7.44	19	33.29
8	9.10	20	35.94
9	10.86	21	38.65
10	12.71	22	41.43
11	14.67	23	44.28
12	16.73	24	47.18
C.F.M. = Cubic feet per minute.			

estimates that there are hundreds of such installations supplying millions of kilowatts.

The fundamentals are simple. Moving water contains energy, converted to electricity through a water-spun turbine (basically a sophisticated water wheel), which turns a generator. "Water power is the most efficient, most dependable source of energy known to man," says Ron Corso of FERC. Moreover, it is environmentally clean.

big savings in oil

A DOE/Army Corps of Engineers report predicted that redevelopment of existing dam sites, development of new sites and backyard power-plants could raise the contribution of hydro to 160,000 megawatts, saving 727,000 barrels of oil daily. At that level, hydro power—from tiny 500-watt generators to mammoth 500-megawatt plants—would deliver five percent of the country's power, or about 24 percent of total electric-power needs. Hydro now meets 15 percent of national electrical demand.

With so much in hydro's favor, why isn't it sweeping the nation? One pragmatic reason is its cost. The National Center for Appropriate Technology in Butte, MT, estimates that labor and materials for a system to generate house power would cost between $800 and $1500 per kilowatt of generating capacity. Estimates of peak demands for a household vary between 1 kilowatt (for a cabin with just a few lights) to more than 12 kilowatts. The DOE estimates *average* demand at any given time—including nights—at 1 to 1.5 kilowatts. Still, buying hydro equipment to meet peak demands could easily cost $10,000 installed, and some people have spent up to $40,-000 for 12-kilowatt equipment. By comparison, Langhorne paid less than $2100 for materials in 1975 to build his plant, which is capable of producing about 6.5 kilowatts when water is gushing.

small users bypassed

Why are there such extremes? For decades, companies here and in Europe have made huge turbines and generators to supply the big utilities. Small power users were bypassed or given scaled-down versions of the monster systems. These units were expensive and rated for high performance.

hardware shrinks, prices drop

But today, new companies are introducing product lines specifically designed for small plants. These entries are cheaper than older systems, and competition could drive the prices even lower.

That's the good news. The bad news is that no accepted standards for microhydro equipment (from .5 to 5000 kilowatts) exist at present.

Drastically reducing or eliminating electric bills is one spur for the enthusiastic new wave of microhydro developers. The second spur is *making* money.

sell your power

John and Susan Craft own and direct the Liliwaup Falls Research Station in Washington. Flowing water on their property generates 160 kilowatts with existing equipment. But the potential power in their stream, they estimate, is 1200 kilowatts.

When this is tapped, the Crafts intend to draw what they need for the research center and sell the remainder to local residents. This income will be plowed back into research—essentially of a biological nature.

In 1980, the Crafts were visited by a local utility representative who had gotten wind of their plans. At first, he was pleasant and patient in trying to dissuade them. When that proved futile, he implied that the power company could stop them legally.

official protection

Whether a utility could take such action was debatable then. Now it isn't. On Oct. 29, 1980, the Commissioner of FERC offered official protection to anyone producing hydroelectric power up to 5000 kilowatts.

Ron Corso of FERC says, "Once the individual's application is submitted and approved (which takes about 120 days), the property is exempted from licensing, which means no one—private or public utility, state or city—can condemn or take away their site or prevent them from developing hydropower.

"Second, this individual may sell power at whatever rate he wishes.

"Third, privately developed power can be sold to a utility, and the utility must buy it, but at rates established by the state commission."

This new rule frees the Crafts to develop their stream. It also gives people with much smaller operations a chance to make money.

running the meter backward

For example, a house with a 10-kilowatt demand may be served by a plant generating 15 kilowatts. Five kilowatts is available immediately

7.5-KILOWATT hydro powerplant is from Energy Independence Research Corp., Bellingham, WA. It maintains continuous output under changing loads.

for sale back to the grid. As demand in the house drops, the homeowner can sell more of his power. A standard meter, running backward, keeps track of electricity sent to the grid in kilowatt-hours. At the end of each month, the owner may receive a check, instead of mailing one.

Sound enticing? It is. Sound easy? It isn't. While the technology for large hydro systems was perfected decades ago, the engineering of microhydro is an emerging art. The most fundamental and critical problem associated with sending power back to a utility grid is generating 60-cycle current with a wave form that precisely matches that of the grid with consistency and no transient voltage.

Another potential problem: Private power can zap linemen working to restore a public-power outage.

FERC and DOE have laid the groundwork for small private-power sales. But the details that are going to protect owners *and* utilities have yet to be hammered out.

Here are some common questions and answers to serve as a guideline for your further research.
■ *How much water is required?* More than a trickling spring, but probably a lot less than you expect. Alan Van Hook of Nooksack, WA, draws 6 kilowatts from a small, but steady spring. His powerplant works because the spring is 350 feet above his turbine. In hydro terminology, the system operates on a 350-foot "head."

Head, or the vertical drop from water source to turbine, and *flow,* the quantity of water moving past a given point in gallons or cubic feet per minute, are the two conditions of moving water that determine power potential.

To generate house power, a high head and low flow will serve as well as a low head and high flow.

A rough rule of thumb equates high head with smaller, less costly equipment; low head with larger, more expensive turbines.

simple way to measure

Because the slope from water source to turbine is almost always gradual, you can use simple surveyor's measurements to calculate head. You don't need to rent a transit, though you can. You can manage with a tripod, spirit level, tape rule and a tall pole or stick marked, at least, in one-foot increments.

Stand the tripod close to the water at the top of the slope. Place the spirit level on the tripod platform. Measure the height of the level above the water.

You'll need a partner to hold the pole. Move him down the slope to a point at which the upright pole is just within sight across the top of the spirit level. Aim the level as you would sight a rifle.

Make certain the level bubble is centered; have your partner record the span between the ground and the level on the pole intersected by your line of sight.

Move down below the pole position and set up the tripod so its top is even with the bottom of the pole. Have your partner move down the slope and repeat the process. Continue until your partner reaches the turbine site, then sight the last measurement.

To compute the head, add up all the sighted elevations and subtract the height of your tripod.

measure your flow

You can measure flow in a small stream or spring by diverting the entire flow into a container of a known size. For example, suppose the water fills a 55-gallon drum in 32 seconds. That translates to 1.72 gallons/second or 103.13 gallons/minute, or 13.79 cubic feet/minute.

Flow in a larger body of moving water is measured by the method shown in the drawing on page 80.

To determine the potential power in a moving stream, insert head and flow into this formula: $P = (Q \times h)/709$, where P = theoretical power in kilowatts; Q = flow in cubic feet per minute; h = head in feet.

For example, suppose the head turned out to be 20 feet, and the flow was 8 cubic feet/minute. Theoretical power would be 8 times 20 divided by 709—0.23 kilowatts or 230 watts. At that figure, your stream wouldn't represent enough potential to justify investing in costly equipment.

Measurement should always be taken in the dry season, when the water is running at its lowest. If the potential meets requirements at that time, it will always suffice.

■ *There's no water on your property. How do you gain access to water?* If possible, buy land nearby on which there is running water. Or apply to tap a public source.

■ *What kind of turbine is best?* Harry Langhorne built a cross-flow or Banki turbine, and it has served him well. Most small power developers choose some form of a Pelton wheel, which looks like a collection of tiny cups on the edge of a metal wheel.

obtaining the best turbine

Choosing the best turbine for your site is a decision you ought to make with the manufacturer, given your particular set of head, flow and demand facts.

■ *How do you direct water from source to turbine?* By pipe, or open sluice or penstock. Most home power developers choose polyvinyl-chloride pipe, which is noncorrosive, relatively inexpensive and easy to install. However, some users report cold-weather cracking and breaks in the joints, according to Bill Kitching, manager of Small Hydroelectric Systems. Longer lasting, but more expensive materials include clay culvert pipe banded with concrete at the joints, and wood pipe.

■ *Is it easy to switch from home hydro to public power?* Yes. A transfer switch at your service entrance allows you to use hydro power up to maximum, and public-utility power for the balance.

■ *Are there regulations that govern a home hydro system?* For a system under 5 kilowatts, perhaps not. But check before you invest in equipment. In many states, especially in the West, laws on water rights are strict. You may need to obtain a water-use permit.

And in some areas, tapping water for energy, even on your own property, is checked by an environmental agency (such as a fish and game commission).

If you intend to build a plant that will generate more than 5000 kilowatts, you must secure a license from FERC, and almost surely from state agencies, as well.

Two sources for additional information are: Volunteers in Technical Assistance (VITA), 3706 Rhode Island Ave., Mount Rainier, MD 20822 and U.S. Department of Energy, Idaho Operations Office, Hydropower Program, 550 Second St., Idaho Falls, ID 83401.

THIS SOLAR water heater can supply at least 46 gallons of hot water on sunny days.

COLD-WATER PIPE with valve (right) bypasses electric heater and leads to solar system. Pipe entering from left is hot-water return from solar tank.

■ THIS SOLAR water heater is an auxiliary to an existing water heater—electric or gas. It has cut our electric bill in Florida an average of 200 kw. hours per month.

Aluminum solar fins on the copper tubes conduct absorbed solar heat to water in the tubes. Water circulating by thermosiphon action keeps warm water rising to a 42-gal. insulated storage tank above the panel. This water feeds to the existing water heater.

Build a solar water heater

By KARL F. FRANK

The solar water panel must face directly south. Its angle (degree of pitch) depends on its geographic location and latitude. Note: In freezing climates, the solar heater must have a cold-water bypass that runs to the existing heater, because the solar-heating system must drain.

Begin by boring holes for the tubes in the headers and reaming them to exact size. Clean the ends of the tube with steel wool in order to assure good solder contact; solder all tubes to one header first. Solder the brass plugs in place.

The simple cover has a groove for wedges glued to secure the vinyl sheet. Fishing line passed over the vinyl, then passed through holes bored in the cover frame, with the ends wound around nails, helps hold the vinyl.

To insert the headers in the frame, elongate the frame holes and slide the headers in at an angle. Later, you can fill the holes.

A simple die of a 2-in. oak cube helps shape the solar fins. Bore a $^{13}\!/_{32}$-in.-dia. hole in the wood and cut through the hole lengthwise so that $^{5}\!/_{16}$ in. of the diameter remains. Shape the fin to the block's contour with a $^{3}\!/_{8}$-in.-dia. steel rod. Press-fit the fins on the underside of the tubes and spray-paint the metal black. Fasten the cover and install the panel securely.

MATERIALS LIST—SOLAR HEATER

Key	No.	Size and description (use)
A	2*	1$^{1}\!/_{8}$" o.d. × 53" type "L" copper tubing (headers)
B	15*	$^{3}\!/_{8}$" o.d. × 57$^{7}\!/_{8}$" type "L" copper tubing
C	2*	$^{3}\!/_{4}$ × 3$^{1}\!/_{2}$ × 49" redwood (frame)
D	2	$^{3}\!/_{4}$ × 3$^{1}\!/_{2}$ × 63" redwood (frame)
E	2*	$^{3}\!/_{4}$ × 1$^{1}\!/_{4}$ × 50$^{1}\!/_{2}$" redwood (cover)
F	2	$^{3}\!/_{4}$ × 1$^{1}\!/_{4}$ × 64$^{1}\!/_{2}$" redwood (cover)
G	1*	$^{1}\!/_{8}$ × 48 × 62" hardboard (frame bottom)
H	1*	$^{3}\!/_{4}$" × 6 sq. ft. Styrofoam insulation sheeting
I	1	8-mil vinyl sheet, Sears catalog, No. 32KY42292C
J	2*	$^{1}\!/_{8}$ × $^{3}\!/_{8}$" × 20"* redwood (wedges)
K	120*	2 × 4$^{3}\!/_{32}$" × 22-ga. aluminum sheet, 10 sq. ft. (fins)
L	2	$^{1}\!/_{16}$ × 1.025"-dia. brass discs (end plugs)
M	1	42-gal. storage tank with insulation
N	4	3 × 4 × 4" sheet-metal angles (corner reinforcements)
O	4	1 × 4 × 4" sheet-metal angles (corner reinforcements)
P	48	$^{3}\!/_{4}$" No. 10 sheet-metal screws
Q	†	Braided steel fishing line (secure vinyl)
R	†	Nail to secure fishing line ends

Misc.: 1$^{1}\!/_{2}$" No. 8 fh woodscrews, flat, black heat-resistant paint, solder, Elmer's professional cabinetmaker's contact cement.
*Increase by the number of increments that the unit will be enlarged. †As required.

FRAME DETAIL

F J I
L (NOT SHOWN)
2-1/4" 3-1/8" A
3/8"-DIA. HOLE FOR B (TYPICAL)
1-3/4"
2-1/4"
D
H G

1-1/8"-DIA. HOLE FOR A

63"
58-1/2"

D

2-1/4"
3-1/2"

K A B C N

I
F
E O R P Q

TO COLD-WATER INLET OF EXISTING WATER HEATER

M
FROM COLD-WATER LINE

3-1/2"

K

D
3/8" 5/16"
SOLAR FIN—K (SIDE VIEW)

STORAGE TANK— 1' MINIMUM HEIGHT ABOVE SOLAR HEATER

Surprise! Softwood causes no more creosote

By JOHN E. GAYNOR

■ FOR YEARS, conscientious homeowners have fretted about firewoods. Because they believed hard, dry woods would reduce the creosote hazard in the flue, wood-stove and fireplace users avoided the less expensive, more plentiful, soft and green woods. But recent tests conducted by Auburn University's mechanical engineering department, with aid from the Department of Energy, have produced some surprising discoveries.

Under certain conditions, hardwood can produce more creosote than softwood. Other tests indicate that seasoned wood may produce more creosote than green or wet wood. Although these tests were conducted on "airtight," free-standing stoves with metal flues, the results apply to any duct in which wood smoke is conducted away from a fire.

Creosote is a substance created by incomplete combustion. Some unburned matter (tars, or hydrocarbons as the scientists call them) always escape the fire. These hydrocarbons are absorbed by water vapor that is also given off by the fire, and the mixture goes up the chimney as smoke.

How creosote forms is shown in the drawing at right. In the cool, upper surfaces of the flue or chimney, the vapor mixture condenses. This condensed water vapor, mixed with hydrocarbons, is the highly flammable, black, sticky stuff called creosote.

As it builds up, creosote runs down the flue or chimney and collects on ledges, elbows and junctions. If not cleaned out regularly, it can eventually ignite, causing a serious and inaccessible fire.

Until recently, hardwood was thought to produce less creosote than soft (resinous), wet woods. But the tests show otherwise.

The scientists at Auburn collected smoke from a probe stuck into a flue. They kept the smoke hot and filtered it to remove the particles with no function in forming creosote. Then they bubbled the smoke through cold water. This caused the creosote hydrocarbons to be absorbed and remain in the water. The scientists measured the quantity of hydrocarbons produced by identical amounts of hardwood and softwood in the same

length of time. The tests showed clearly that hardwood produces more creosote.

Scientists theorize that the quicker burn rate of hardwoods causes more unburned hydrocarbons to escape up the flue. This, in turn, produces more creosote.

In other tests, scientists collected creosote as it condensed and ran down the inner wall of a double-walled flue in which cold water was circulating. This setup approximated the cooler conditions of a chimney or flue where it's near the exterior of the house. In the laboratory, the creosote collected in beakers. Scientists then measured the liquid collected under controlled circumstances.

The researchers used a special device to pass light through the creosote solutions and measure the creosote concentration. Again, there was less creosote in solutions produced from wet wood than from dry wood.

Scientists think a secondary combustion process occurs in softwoods, which they attribute to the "water-gas" reaction. As wood burns, water vapor, hydrocarbons and gases are forced from the core, through the charring surface areas of the wood. Here, additional gases are produced which help burn the heavier constituents of creosote in the fire.

The other explanation is called the "water-dilution effect." Wet wood sends more water vapor up the flue, which lowers the vapor dew point and causes more condensation to occur. But more vapor also goes out of the chimney and into the air, carrying hydrocarbons with it. Although you may get more condensation, your chimney will collect less creosote.

The question remains: What does one do about creosote? The only answer is to check your flue or chimney regularly. Check horizontal parts and couplings. Remove creosote by scraping it off.

To reduce creosote buildup in airtight stoves, allow a small, but fairly hot fire, to burn freely for 15 to 20 minutes. The hot, fast-moving exhaust tends to have a cleansing effect. This practice also works well in brick fireplaces, but only after flues and fireplaces have been cleaned thoroughly.

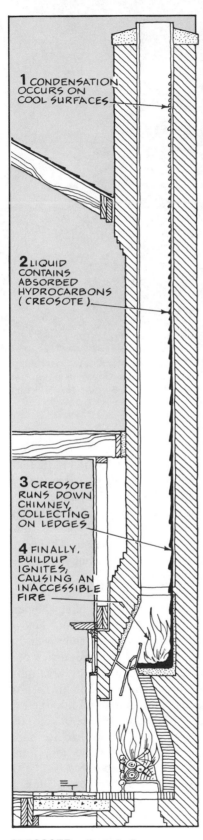

1 CONDENSATION OCCURS ON COOL SURFACES

2 LIQUID CONTAINS ABSORBED HYDROCARBONS (CREOSOTE)

3 CREOSOTE RUNS DOWN CHIMNEY, COLLECTING ON LEDGES

4 FINALLY, BUILDUP IGNITES, CAUSING AN INACCESSIBLE FIRE

CREOSOTE collects in flue or chimney conducting smoke away from a solid-fuel fire. Check for creosote buildup regularly.

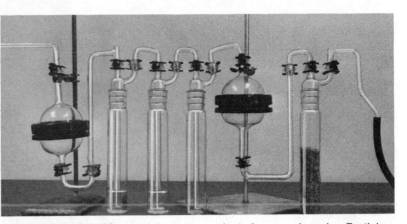

SETUP REPRESENTS one of the tests conducted on wood smoke. Particles are filtered out in container at left from hot smoke from flue. Creosote condenses in cold water in the three middle bottles. Residual matter collects in the containers at the right.

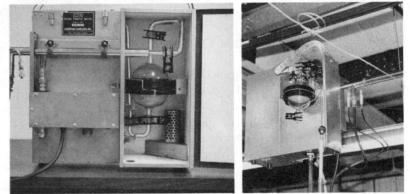

ACTUAL LABORATORY equipment looks like this. The particle-filter beaker is shown in its heated chamber (left). Smoke tube passes to the other side, where creosote is collected in bottles (not visible). Scientists call this equipment a Methods 5 Emissions Train.

AUBURN UNIVERSITY may have the only wood stove known with hot and cold running water. The cold water circulates through a double-walled flue, causing creosote to condense and collect in the beakers (right). Hot water and steam circulate to clean the flue.

Coal makes a comeback

Modern burners are designed to get best results from abundant coal. Here's what you should know to keep the home fires burning

By CONRAD M. STOWERS

EMPTYING ASH PAN assures efficiency. Coal requires more attention than gas or liquid fuels, but less than wood. The model shown is Surdiac No. 508 from Classic Stove Works.

■ MORE THAN 300,000 coal stoves were sold in one recent year, according to the Department of Energy. Coal distributors were swamped with orders from eager homeowners.

Assisting the central heating system with a space heater can save lots of money. Highly efficient coal is a natural choice of fuels for this purpose.

Bituminous and anthracite are the two major kinds of coal. Anthracite, in the size of "pea" or "nut," is the coal used in most space heaters and new home furnaces. It is celebrated for its high efficiency, low sulfur content and production of little ash and practically no smoke. Because anthracite is harder than bituminous coal, it is also relatively clean to handle. It was the soft, crumbly, bituminous coal used in home furnaces in the '40s (now largely used in industry) that gave coal its "dirty" reputation.

availability of coal

One of coal's most attractive features is the amount buried under our feet, rather than in the sands of some Arabian desert. Industrial engineers estimate that the nation's coal reserves are so abundant they will last for centuries.

It is comforting to know that the fuel is domestically abundant, but the question of cost and economy is nevertheless complicated.

Coal is both mined and transported by labor-intensive industries. This means that supply and price can be affected by strikes and the state of the nation's economy.

Also, 90 percent of all anthracite coal is located in a small area of northeastern Pennsylvania. Therefore, transportation costs are an important factor for this kind of coal.

One expert we contacted suggested this rule of thumb: Given the present price and wage structure in the industry, if you are located more than 700 miles from the mine, one of the other fuels is probably a better deal for your fuel dollar.

Called "coking," burning coal actually becomes liquefied as it gives up its volatile compounds in the combustion process. The combustion area may be very small, but the heat is intense, reaching temperatures in excess of 2,200° F.

Coal requires its primary source of air (80 percent) to come up through the bed from below, while the other 20 percent must come in over the top of the fire. As it burns, it produces a very fine ash which remains in the combustion area until the bed is shaken very gently to allow this ash to sift through the coals, the grate, and into the ash pan below. This is a delicate feature of coal, for improper shaking can disturb the bed so much that the flame is extinguished. In addition, if disturbed too much, ash may become mixed with the liquefying coal and form "clinkers." Clinkers look like volcanic rock and are a nuisance. They stick to grates and other stove parts and waste fuel.

Our knowledge of coking allows us to set some requirements for the well-designed stove. One essential feature is some form of baffle to help ab-

BASIC STOVE

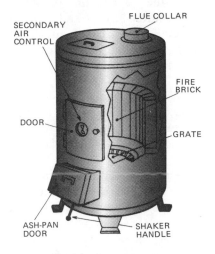

SECONDARY AIR CONTROL

FLUE COLLAR

FIRE BRICK

DOOR

GRATE

ASH-PAN DOOR

SHAKER HANDLE

BECAUSE FUEL is hand-fed into fire chamber in simple stoves, these designs require most attention.

INTERNAL HOPPER

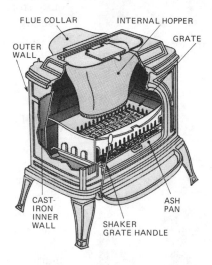

FLUE COLLAR

INTERNAL HOPPER

OUTER WALL

GRATE

CAST-IRON INNER WALL

ASH PAN

SHAKER GRATE HANDLE

CONVENIENT internal hoppers are popular for space heaters. A double-walled stove can hold day's fuel supply.

AUTOMATIC STOKER

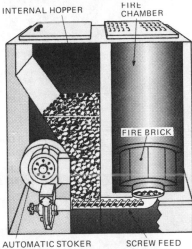

INTERNAL HOPPER

FIRE CHAMBER

FIRE BRICK

AUTOMATIC STOKER MOTOR

SCREW FEED

IN THE MOST convenient space heaters (not typical), and furnaces, an automatic screw feeds coal.

sorb and disperse the intense heat evenly in the immediate area of combustion. Most stove manufacturers insist this requirement is best met by a fire-chamber lining of firebrick—very much like that used in industrial ceramic kilns. The immediate and apparent drawback is that any such stove is going to be very heavy. Some manufacturers claim that a lighter, double-wall stove with a cast-iron interior helps to do the same thing—air passing between the walls draws heat from the hot spot. In either case, the heat must be drawn out efficiently or it will begin to melt the interior of the stove.

Because of the primary and secondary air re-

THIS FIREBRICK-LINED stove from Shenandoah Manufacturing includes all features of basic design: Primary air control is usually built into ash-pan door. Ceramic-glass doors allow a view of the glowing coals. Prices of basic stoves range from $200 to $1000.

INTERNAL HOPPER model by Ceramic Radiant Heat has ceramic face panels to distribute heat. Hoppers range in cost from $350 to $1200.

IN APPEARANCE, Tekton's furnace boiler is typical of larger coal burners, whether fed by hand (as this) or fed automatically. Versatility of coal furnaces produces a wide price range from $350 to $3000.

SHENANDOAH, like many stove makers, also offers a fireplace insert stove. Some inserts burn cannel coal brightly. Prices: $400 to $1200.

quirements of coal, the grate design is also important. Usually composed of one stationary part and one movable part, it must allow for gentle shaking of the entire bed at once and be designed to support the coal, yet allow the unimpeded passage of primary air up through the bed.

Airtight construction is a must for burning coal efficiently. A well-designed stove will have controls for primary and secondary air supplies.

Basic stoves come in a multitude of sizes and shapes. Depending on decorative features, prices can vary widely. The main drawback of the simple stove is that it must be stoked regularly.

For convenience, the most popular coal stove has an internal hopper which can allow up to 1½ days' supply of coal to be fed to the stove at a time. Most internal hoppers work on a gravity-feed principle. As the coal burns, the bed settles; this allows more coal to descend from the hopper into the fire chamber. Most internal hopper stoves have double-walled construction instead of a firebrick lining.

A few space heaters have not only an internal hopper, but also a thermostatically controlled stoker system which feeds the coal to the burning chamber by means of a screw mechanism (drawing on right, page 87). Because of the machinery and storage size of the hopper, this design is usually used for hot-water heaters and central-heating furnaces. One drawback of automatic stokers is that they produce an intermittent disturbing, crunching noise when the screw-feed is working.

One of the great myths about wood stoves is now apparent: You cannot burn coal in a wood stove without probable damage from intense heat, unless the firebox and grates are designed to handle both fuels.

Stove makers are under great pressure to provide versatile stoves that can burn a variety of fuels. But the challenge of producing an efficient coal and wood stove is considerable, because of the marked differences in the ways these fuels burn. The fact is, a stove that will burn both will burn neither efficiently.

While efficiency is the key word in coal stoves, be wary of any maker claiming an efficiency greater than 70 percent. All fuels have their limits, regardless of burner design.

tips on burning coal

■ The kindling temperature of coal is around 800° F. This means a kindling fire of wood is necessary to get the coals started.

■ If smoking occurs during the fire, there is probably something amiss in the flue. This is the most common problem with coal stoves.

■ Make sure that the size coal specified by your stove is available. Don't burn other sizes or kinds of coal or your grate won't work properly.

■ Because it is a small industry, there is less flexibility in delivery and supply systems of anthracite coal. Order early.

■ Develop patterns of checking your coal stove regularly. Even the automatic stokers require ash removal by hand on a regular basis.

■ Never disturb the bed of burning coals with a poker, as used to be the practice with old potbellies burning bituminous. This disturbance will produce clinkers and defeat the purpose of the well-designed grate.

■ Finally, remember to follow the maker's instructions carefully to get maximum stove performance from this highly efficient fuel. Burning coal, however, does require a certain modification of your lifestyle. Unlike gas or liquid fuel, which you may never even see, coal is handled and the stove must be tended. Rather than thinking this inconvenient, some homeowners seem to feel that they want to be closer to the basic household necessities.

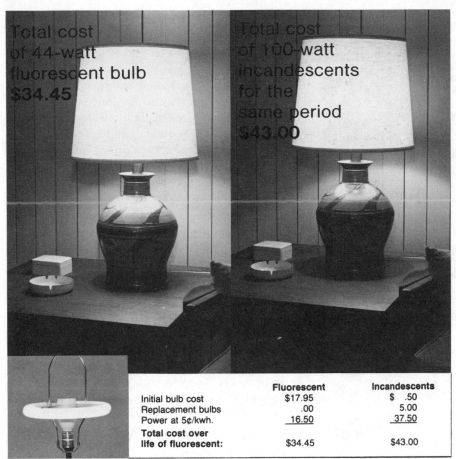

Total cost
of 44-watt
fluorescent bulb
$34.45

Total cost
of 100-watt
incandescents
for the
same period
$43.00

	Fluorescent	Incandescents
Initial bulb cost	$17.95	$ .50
Replacement bulbs	.00	5.00
Power at 5¢/kwh.	16.50	37.50
Total cost over life of fluorescent:	$34.45	$43.00

COMPARISON OF GE's Circlite (above left and inset) with a standard 100-watt incandescent (above right): Fluorescent sheds as much light for less money.

Save money with low-energy lighting

New lights deliver the same brightness as—or more than — equivalent incandescent bulbs, at lower cost

By JOHN H. INGERSOLL

■ WHERE CAN YOU BUY more for less these days? One bright answer rests with new lighting products, where you can find a better deal than putting your money into standard incandescent bulbs.

Here's a quick rundown on the advantages of these new products (though not all deliver all the advantages).

■ You gain more light for less money.

■ These sources deliver illumination over a longer period of time—sometimes over 25 times as long, and are therefore more convenient to use.

■ With new sources in place, the electric meter spins more slowly.

If all this is true, why isn't everyone rushing out to buy? For three reasons: 1. The initial cost is higher than what you pay now for standard incandescent bulbs; 2. for pin-contact fluorescent tubes, you may have to buy a fixture as well; 3.

it's likely you'll have to search beyond the supermarket to locate the right "color" fluorescent tubes or one of the newer, energy-saving offerings described here.

table-lamp fluorescents

Now you can simply toss out a spent incandescent bulb from that end-table lamp and screw in a fluorescent. As the photos above show, illumination is every bit as good using a fluorescent—if not better. You're also due cash savings in two ways: There's less draw on your electricity with a fluorescent; its long life will cut your bulb bill.

Fluorescence demands only a small amount of electric power before it's aglow. For example, in a year-long comparison, assuming lights are on in the house for about five hours a day (roughly normal), Duro-Lite matches one 40-watt Vita-Lite fluorescent against two 75-watt incandescents. Over the 365 days, the two incandescents

NEW ENTRIES IN THE LIGHTING MARKET

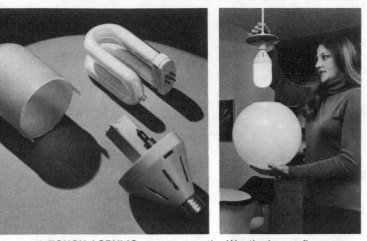

A TOUGH ACRYLIC cover wraps the Westinghouse fluorescent and its compact, instant ballast. The cover fits as handily as an incandescent bulb into a globe fixture.

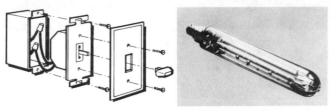

NORELCO'S sodium outdoor light spreads bright yellow light for one-quarter acre. It features low energy use.

LUTRON'S easily installed dimmer is made to work on incandescents.

burn up $16.43 worth of energy, while the fluorescent consumes a mere $4.38—both figures based on a moderate rate of 6 cents per kwh.

In this example, there's a bonus. The two bulbs, burning at a 150-watt rate, produce 1,980 lumens (standard measure of light output). The 40-watt fluorescent tube delivers 2,180 lumens.

(Note: A 40-watt fluorescent in use actually draws 54 watts, the difference made up by electricity demand for the ballast—a device that controls voltage, wave pattern and current delivered to the vapor within the near-vacuum tube. The $4.38 figure above is based on 54 watts.)

During the same year's period, a number of incandescents (note plural) will cost more than a fluorescent (note singular). How much more? Lithonia Lighting did a study based on 1980 retail prices. Two 60-watt incandescent bulbs were

tagged at $1.62, while a lumen-equivalent circular fluorescent of 32 watts (35-watt total with ballast) was $8.85.

During the year those incandescents kept burning out. Replacements ran up a bill of $17.82. The fluorescent continued to work. As with the Duro-Lite test, figures were based on average home use of light. The final score: incandescents—$19.44; fluorescent—$8.85, a saving of $10.59.

At the heart of the new table-lamp fluorescents is a redesigned ballast, small enough to screw into the existing socket. Over the ballast shaft slides the fluorescent unit. Once in place and reshaded, the lamp operates the same. The difference: The light just lasts and lasts.

Three major producers, General Electric, Sylvania and Westinghouse, have introduced table-lamp fluorescents. GE and Sylvania offer an adaptation of the circular fluorescent introduced in the 1940s (and still available), a dinner-plate-diameter tube that often found its way to the kitchen ceiling. Westinghouse developed a U-shaped, mini-fluorescent packed into a tube not vastly different from an incandescent bulb.

For three-way fixtures, GE offers a two-way fluorescent delivering the brightness level of a 50-watt and 100-watt incandescent, but doing it on 16 and 44 watts. The company also produces similar units at one-level brightnesses of 60 watts (actual 22 watts), and 100 watts (actual 44 watts). At 22 watts, Sylvania's entry puts out 75-watt brightness and Westinghouse's small tube throws out light of 60 to 75 watts on a demand of 27 watts.

One of these five new fluorescents ought to fit just about any standard-size socket in your home, including wall sconces and ceiling fixtures. Replacing every bulb in an average three-bedroom house could bring year-end savings of $200 to $400.

Read the fine print, though. For example, GE warns you not to close in its two-way tube with a frosted glass-covered ceiling fixture or globe-shaped swag light. Heat buildup within the confined space could knock out the tube.

A subtler reason than inconvenience has kept fluorescents out of living areas for years. "Colors look crazy under that light," say many who have tried them. This is partly true. Under the harsh light of cool white fluorescents, a bright fire-engine-red pillow could look almost gray. People tend to look wan and unhealthy.

soft white fluorescents

Unfortunately, not many know there are more "colors" than cool white. Recognizing the problem, all three makers produce table-lamp fluorescents in a "soft white" rendering, which makes clothes, food and you look more the way you expect.

Yet the cool-white conventional unit remains for anyone wishing to buy fluorescent tubes in 20-, 30-, or 40-watt sizes. Savings easily equal, and sometimes exceed, those you reap with the new table-lamp units. Fixture makers have also designed attractive new covers for ceiling-mounted fluorescents.

Manufacturers of incandescents are also redesigning for efficiency. From GE and Westinghouse come three-way bulbs at 15/135/150 watts, replacing the conventional 50/100/150 watts. The concept: Who needs 50 watts for conversation, watching TV, or as a security light when 15 watts will do? Because of a redesigned tungsten coil, the 135-watt setting produces 8 percent more light than the 150-watt level on the older bulb.

Need a close-up light for shop, study or as an accent on a piece of art? GE recently introduced a watt-saving reflector bulb. This 50-watter is housed in its own swivel fixture for around $11. Because the light is concentrated, the subject is illuminated as much as it would be by a standard 100-watt bulb.

Sylvania has joined the energy-saving clan with four bulbs at slightly less wattages than standard. For example, it offers a 69-watter to do the work of an ordinary 75-watt bulb.

Floodlamps for outdoor safety and security are effective, but they eat up energy dollars.

sodium lights

However, Norelco offers a low-pressure sodium light that will economically illuminate up to one-quarter acre, or 10,000 sq. ft. There is a yellow cast to the light, but if safety and security are concerns, this fixture is a good investment.

Light dimmers help you chip away at your electric bill and lengthen bulb life. Incandescent light dimmers are simple to install. One type replaces a wall switch; another cuts into a fixture cord and a third kind wires to an existing table lamp. Prices are $5 to about $25.

Fluorescent dimmers work only on standard 30 to 40-watt, rapid-start fluorescent tubes. In addition, each tube must have a special ballast to replace the original one. Price of the ballast: about $30. The dimmer, which costs $40 to $50,

LIGHTING STRATEGIES THAT SAVE ENERGY

LOW-WATT fluorescents from GE placed under kitchen cabinets serve as security lights as shown above.

BUILT-IN DOWNLIGHTS from Duro-Lite reflect off glass and a mirror back into the room.

works on one or up to 30 fluorescents.

Savings do accrue using any dimmer. Suppose you consistently burn a 100-watt incandescent at 70-percent capacity. That results in a 17.5-percent saving in electricity, which translates to $3.06 at 6 cents per kwh, for the average year, not including added life of the bulb.

Common sense suggests other ways to trim your bills; for example, dining by candlelight and chatting by firelight. What could be nicer?

IN THIS CAREFULLY planned workshop, all of the available space is used for handy storage of tools and hardware. Good lighting is a must to do quality work.

Nine ways to keep your shop organized

By JORMA HYYPIA

■ FEW WORKSHOP problems are more frustrating than being unable to find that certain tool or jig when you know it's around somewhere. Projects may even be discouraged through lack of organization. That was the situation in my garage workshop before organization fever struck. Catch this bug and you, too, will be surprised how inventive organizing a workshop can be. I suggest that you start by clearing everything out and cleaning up the space. You might even repaint.

After all the junk has been tossed out, lay out tools and useful materials in function-oriented groups. This will give you an idea of how much space is needed for storage of each group. Consider ways in which valuable floor space can be saved and made flexible.

1 GROUP TOOLS BY USE

ALL SIMILAR TOOLS (saws, clamps and wrenches) are stored in the same area. To gain work space, table saw rolls partially under radial saw.

2 KEEP TOOLS NEARBY

EASY ACCESS is important. Bits and accessory tools for drill press are to immediate left of machine.

3 INCREASE STORAGE AREAS

■ By reinforcing the legs of this old table with ½-in. plywood, it is stable enough to support my wood lathe and it provides more storage space in the process. I left mine open underneath, but if more shelving is needed, this would be ideal.

PLYWOOD SKIRT on old dining table provides storage for lathe tools. Large items are stored underneath.

4 DESIGN A FLOOR PLAN

FLOOR PLAN—WORKSHOP

Key	Description
A	Main workbench
B	Cupboard (portable power tools)
C	Nail, screw and bolt storage shelves
D	Grinder bench (handsaws below)
E	Table saw
F	Radial-arm saw
G	Belt and disc sander
H	Sabre saw and router table
I	Roll-out shop vacuum
J	Storage cabinet (old dishwasher)
K	Drill press
L	Lathe table
M	General storage shelves
N	Lally column
O	Tool storage wall
P	4-ft., single-tube fluorescent light
Q	4-ft., double-tube fluorescent light
R	3-ft., single-tube fluorescent light

Note: Overall garage dimensions are about 19½ × 22 ft.

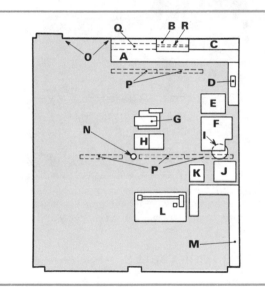

5 MAKE LIFT-OUT DOORS

■ Conventional doors under a workbench have drawbacks. Sliding doors leave the storage space half-closed. Conventional doors require swinging space at cabinet front. The door shown solves both problems. The 28x60-in. door is hinged at the bottom to swing open bin-fashion. When you need repeated access to the storage space, the entire door can be pulled out.

First, bore the dowel holes in a length of 2x4 to size. Bore the holes 3 in. deep and about 8 in. from the ends. Rip the 2x4 down the middle to make two pieces about 1½ in. wide by 1¾ in. thick. Keep the cut-edge sides face-to-face so dowel holes remain aligned; then attach one

piece to bench or to legs to form stationary rail. Mark and set butt hinges as shown on the other rail and doorframe rail. A ⅛x½ in.-deep groove was cut in door frame to suit panel.

MATERIALS LIST—REMOVABLE DOOR

Key	No.	Size and description (use)
A	2	1½ × approx. 1¹¹/₁₆ × 60″ upper and lower rails (ripped from same 2 × 4)
B	2	¾ × 2 × 60″ mitered rails
C	2	¾ × 2 × 28″ mitered stiles
D	1	⅛ × 25 × 57″ finished panel
E	1	¼ × 1 × 26″ stiffener
F	4	2½″ corner irons (Stanley No. SP999)
G	2	2″ butt hinges (Stanley No. 808BP)
H	2	⅝ × 3″ wooden dowels
I	2	5¾″ door pulls (Stanley No. CD482)

Misc: Carpenter's glue, fh wood screws

keeping shop organized, continued

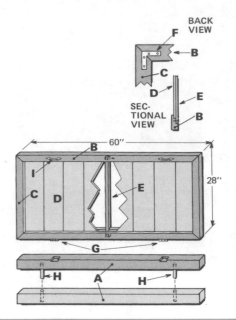

PULL TOP of door out slightly and lift evenly on door handles to disengage dowels. Door can be set aside for full access to storage.

6 STORE ITEMS IN JARS

■ As numerous shop owners discovered long ago, baby-food bottles are ideal keepers for storing all kinds of small items. In my shop, I changed several large shelves above my workbench to accommodate over 100 of these jars. By adding a smaller shelf between, I could fit three rows and still have space left on the wider shelves for tools I want to keep nearby.

If you want to hang the larger bottles from underneath as shown, allow adequate finger clearance when attaching the caps; otherwise the jars will be difficult to loosen. Stick-on labels should be used to identify those jars with similar contents. I also recommend a small utility light—like the gooseneck lamp shown—for sorting and selection.

BABY-FOOD JARS can store nails, screws, nuts, plus assorted items. Larger bottles aligned on lower shelf hang by caps. Attach caps with centered screw and off-center brad.

7 COMBINE TOOL TABLES

■ This combination table serves two useful purposes: It keeps the router and sabre saw (used as substitute shaper and jigsaw) handy at all times and saves floor space by combining the two tools into one fold-up unit. The framework shown was originally used to hold industrial electronic equipment; it was salvaged from the local dump. Admittedly, you won't find a duplicate, but it would be easy to build a similar table from angle iron welded or bolted together, or even from wood.

The easiest way to mount the sabre saw on the top level is to use a commercial sabre-saw table that comes with saw-mounting and accessory hardware to make the tool a jigsaw. I added a wood frame around the metal saw table to cus-

tom-fit it to the slightly larger framework.

You can also add a hold-down, spring-loaded arm as shown in the photo. By fastening a plastic pill-bottle cap over the slotted working end of the arm, you protect the sabre saw blade.

MATERIALS LIST—HOLD-DOWN ARM

Key	No.	Size and description (use)
A	1	8", 2 × 4 vertical support
B	1	¾ × 1½ × 14½" arm
C	1	compression spring
D	1	3½" long, 1½" angle iron
E	1	¼" machine screw
F	2	nuts
G	1	washer
H	1	dowel (spring retainer)
I	1	¼ × 4" threaded rod
J	2	nuts
K	2	washers
L	1	pill bottle and cap

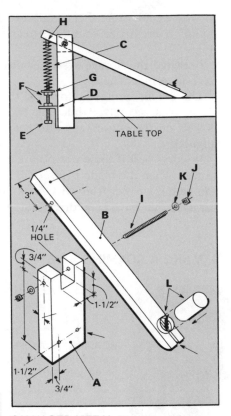

SALVAGED METAL frame provides a handy place for sabre saw table on top level, and makes the router a shaper on the lower slide-in table. Commercial saw table was adapted to the stand dimensions by adding a frame. An optional hold-down arm includes a ''pill bottle'' safety feature to protect the blade and your fingers.

8 HANG SAWS TEETH IN

HANDSAW STORES under a narrow shelf. Clips hold larger saws; a coat-hanger wire is bent to grab the smaller saws. A closed loop in a piece of wire is attached to the shelf bottom with a screw eye. Saws sorted this way need less space while the blade teeth remain well protected.

keeping shop organized, continued

■ Most people store their handsaws flat, and by doing so use space that is better left to other things.

I created the storage system shown under my 8x48-in. grinder shelf.

The 2¾-in. spring clamps hold the top of my large saws securely, while the two ½-in.-thick dowels on the bottom serve to keep each blade aligned.

It works best if these dowels are loose enough to turn when the blade is inserted. Smaller saws can be hung either from wire hooks, or from finish nails that have been driven into the wall.

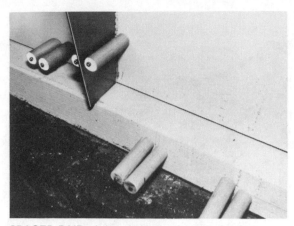

SPACED PAIR of dowels keeps the saw tips from swinging. Install them by using 8d nails.

9 MAKE A ROAMING VISE

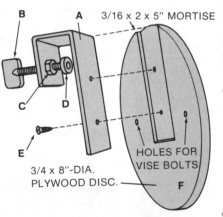

ROAMING VISE uses a clamp that came from an old dough mixer. It's an easy-to-make clamp.

3/16 x 2 x 5" MORTISE

3/4 x 8"-DIA. PLYWOOD DISC.

HOLES FOR VISE BOLTS

■ An extra vise can be converted into a roaming vise by mounting it on a piece of ¾-in. plywood and then clamping this unit wherever it's needed. You can make your own clamp by bending flat-iron bar stock into a U-shape and welding a large nut on the lower arm to accept a wing bolt. If the vise vibrates when doing heavy work, just slip a thin wood shim between the base and the bench. When the wedge is properly fitted, the play will disappear and you can glue it to the base to make the adjustment permanent.

MATERIALS LIST—VISE

Key	No.	Size and description
A	1	³⁄₁₆ × 2 × 9½" flat iron bar
B	1	4" thumbscrew
C	1	nut, welded to flat iron
D	1	collar to suit nut
E	2	¾", No. 7 fh screws
F	1	¾ × 8"-dia. plywood disc

MORE TIPS FOR GETTING MORE ENJOYMENT FROM YOUR SHOP

Try to avoid the temptation to hang a lot of tools, such as spring clamps or wrenches, from one nail. Although it may save space, the tool you want always seems nearest the wall. The space saved may cause some aggravation and usually isn't worth it.

Once your shop is organized and everything is in place, make a special effort to keep it that way. Allow time for cleanup after each work session. I find myself more eager to get back to my projects when I know everything is in order. On the other hand, if I leave the shop or project in a mess, I am less anxious to get back to the job.

If you have youngsters, or particularly a teen-age son with an interest in your shop, keeping it orderly will encourage a tool's return to its proper place. It doesn't work like magic, but it helps.

Lumber, pipe, panels and rarely used cutting jigs are best stored high up and out of the way. Ceiling joists or collar beams are usually exposed in a garage workshop and these make instant racks for this purpose. Remember to store large items in a way that allows easy retrieval. Trying to move heavy objects about while working over your head is an easy way to injure your back.

An organized shop is a safe shop, but remember that your shop is only as safe as you are. Power tools make work more enjoyable, but they require extra attention when in use. Always keep safety glasses near your power tools as a reminder to use them.

After my initial organization of the shop, I wanted to change my original plan. Don't hesitate to refine your plan through shop use.—J.H.

Tool holders from hardware cloth

By WALTER E. BURTON

■ INEXPENSIVE SCRAPS of hardware cloth are ideal for making tool holders in a variety of shapes. The ready-made openings in the wire mesh save the work of boring holes in wood racks, and they accommodate a wide assortment of tools.

Two easily made racks are shown here: one for use on a bench and one for wall mounting. Three mesh, galvanized hardware cloth has three openings to the inch and accepts tools with shanks up to about 5/16 in. in diameter. Two-mesh cloth has two openings per inch and takes somewhat larger tools.

To keep tools neatly upright, you need two levels of mesh—one at the top and one underneath to catch the tips. In the wall rack, this is accomplished by rolling an 8x9-in. piece of mesh into a 2¼-in.-diameter cylinder. This looks attractive and allows you to insert tools at various angles. The cylinder is held at the ends by wood discs glued into a U-shaped bracket. The back of the bracket extends 3 in. below the cylinder to keep the tips of slanted tools from scratching the wall.

The bench rack is just a U-shaped wood stand fitted with two levels of mesh about 1½ in. apart. Bend the edges of the mesh down at 90° all around to add stiffness. Shape the pieces first before determining final dimensions for the stand. The mesh is held in place by small bolts.

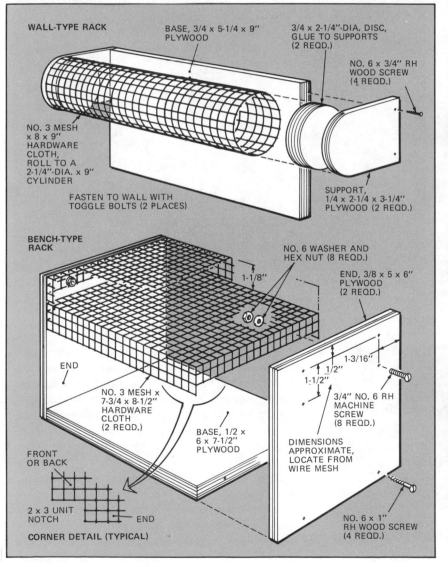

WALL-TYPE RACK

BASE, 3/4 x 5-1/4 x 9" PLYWOOD

3/4 x 2-1/4"-DIA. DISC, GLUE TO SUPPORTS (2 REQD.)

NO. 6 x 3/4" RH WOOD SCREW (4 REQD.)

NO. 3 MESH x 8 x 9" HARDWARE CLOTH, ROLL TO A 2-1/4"-DIA. x 9" CYLINDER

FASTEN TO WALL WITH TOGGLE BOLTS (2 PLACES)

SUPPORT, 1/4 x 2-1/4 x 3-1/4" PLYWOOD (2 REQD.)

BENCH-TYPE RACK

NO. 6 WASHER AND HEX NUT (8 REQD.)

END, 3/8 x 5 x 6" PLYWOOD (2 REQD.)

1-1/8"

END

NO. 3 MESH x 7-3/4 x 8-1/2" HARDWARE CLOTH (2 REQD.)

BASE, 1/2 x 6 x 7-1/2" PLYWOOD

1-3/16"
1/2"
1-1/2"

3/4" NO. 6 RH MACHINE SCREW (8 REQD.)

DIMENSIONS APPROXIMATE, LOCATE FROM WIRE MESH

FRONT OR BACK

2 x 3 UNIT NOTCH

END

CORNER DETAIL (TYPICAL)

NO. 6 x 1" RH WOOD SCREW (4 REQD.)

PORTABLE BENCH rack puts small tools within easy reach.

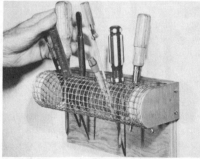

WALL RACK uses hardware cloth formed into a cylinder.

EASY WAY to shape the cylinder is to roll mesh around a caulking cartridge.

Two classic toolboxes you can build

By HARRY WICKS

BOTH ORIGINAL toolboxes were found in Wheeling, WV, antique shops. They are good examples of carpenter design—built by their owners.

OUR LIDDED REPRODUCTION is crafted of ½- and ¾-in. cherry; we added a tray for chisels and such. With lid down, box can be used as coffee table.

OPEN CARPENTER'S toolbox is handy for conventional carpentry tools or to display magazines.

■ A trip to an antique fair or shop is almost certain to turn up one or more old toolboxes. At least, that has been my experience during the past year. They are still around in a variety of shapes and forms—from the rare master craftsman's box made of hardwood that seems to accommodate every tool imaginable to a simple carpenter's pine box like the one shown at the left.

The majority of old toolboxes we were fortunate enough to find were obviously crafted by their owner-users. Typically, the design details were kept simple and the boxes were extremely functional. The craftsman knew what he wanted to store or take to the job and designed the box to

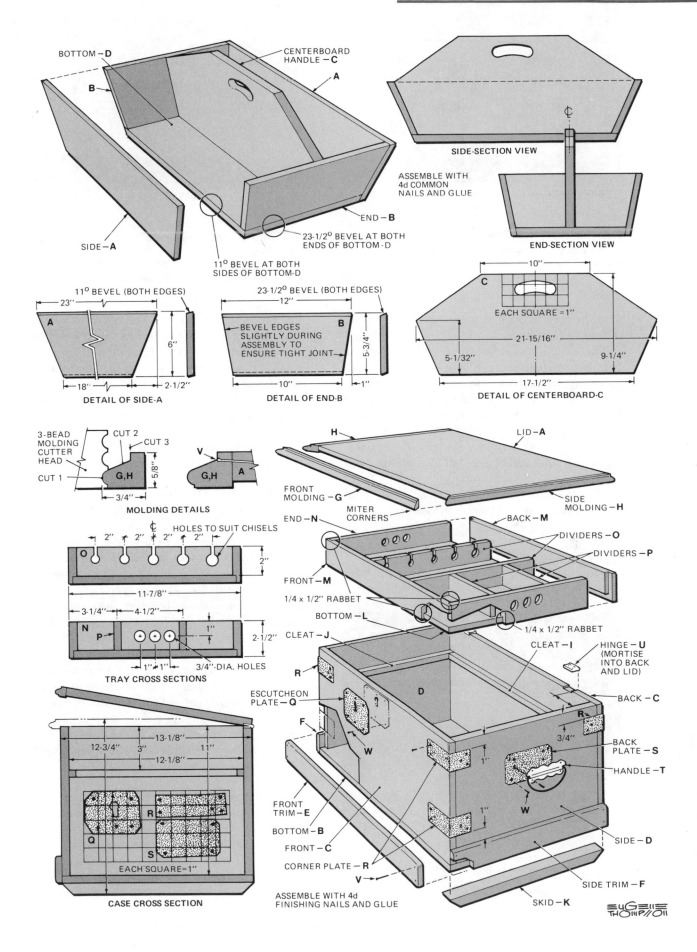

BOTTOM – **D**

B

SIDE – **A**

CENTERBOARD HANDLE – **C**

A

END – **B**

23-1/2° BEVEL AT BOTH ENDS OF BOTTOM - D

11° BEVEL AT BOTH SIDES OF BOTTOM-D

SIDE-SECTION VIEW

ASSEMBLE WITH 4d COMMON NAILS AND GLUE

END-SECTION VIEW

11° BEVEL (BOTH EDGES)

23"

A

6"

18"

2-1/2"

DETAIL OF SIDE-A

23-1/2° BEVEL (BOTH EDGES)

12"

B

BEVEL EDGES SLIGHTLY DURING ASSEMBLY TO ENSURE TIGHT JOINT

5-3/4"

10"

1"

DETAIL OF END-B

10"

C

EACH SQUARE = 1"

21-15/16"

5-1/32"

9-1/4"

17-1/2"

DETAIL OF CENTERBOARD-C

3-BEAD MOLDING CUTTER HEAD

CUT 2

CUT 3

CUT 1

G, H

5/8"

3/4"

V

G, H

A

MOLDING DETAILS

HOLES TO SUIT CHISELS

2" 2" 2" 2"

O

2"

11-7/8"

3-1/4" 4-1/2"

N

P

1"

2-1/2"

1" 1"

3/4"-DIA. HOLES

TRAY CROSS SECTIONS

13-1/8"

12-3/4" 3" 11"

12-1/8"

R

Q

S

EACH SQUARE=1"

CASE CROSS SECTION

H

LID – **A**

FRONT MOLDING – **G**

MITER CORNERS

SIDE MOLDING – **H**

END – **N**

BACK – **M**

DIVIDERS – **O**

DIVIDERS – **P**

FRONT – **M**

1/4 x 1/2" RABBET

BOTTOM – **L**

CLEAT – **J**

CLEAT – **I**

1/4 x 1/2" RABBET

HINGE – **U** (MORTISE INTO BACK AND LID)

ESCUTCHEON PLATE – **Q**

R

F

W

D

BACK – **C**

3/4"

BACK PLATE – **S**

HANDLE – **T**

R

1"

1"

W

FRONT TRIM – **E**

BOTTOM – **B**

FRONT – **C**

CORNER PLATE – **R**

V

SIDE – **D**

SIDE TRIM – **F**

SKID – **K**

ASSEMBLE WITH 4d FINISHING NAILS AND GLUE

EUGENE THOMPSON

THE ORIGINAL HANDLES were probably handcrafted by the box's journeyman builder. A search of old hardware catalogs failed to turn up any that had the same look so we created our own.

WE CREATED our version using available hardware-store handles and a backup plate fashioned from 28-gauge sheet metal. Metal parts are painted with flat-black latex and coated with varnish.

meet his needs. So it is with the boxes that we picked to reproduce.

The closed box is the more elaborate of the two; the original is made of ½- and ¾-in. stock (pine and maple). It was severely distressed when we found it with many nicks and gouges in the pine. We created the copy in the same thicknesses and, for sheer good looks, opted to use cherry for the case and mahogany for the tray. These hardwoods not only add beauty but also strength and durability.

The inside tray was missing from the original so we crafted our own version to accommodate

THIS END VIEW of the box shows the severe distressing that exists on the original. It's important that you resist the urge to overdo it when putting ''antique'' marks on your reproduction.

our needs. The result is a tray sized to suit my collection of fine chisels. You can, of course, alter the members' shapes and locations to suit the tools that you plan to store in the tray. Careful design and planning before you begin will result in having the tools where you want them when you are working on a project. Or, if you choose to use the toolbox as a coffee table with storage, eliminate the small partitions completely so that the tray can be used as a server.

making the box with the lid

The cherry for the box is available from The Woodworker's Store, Industrial Blvd., Rogers, MN 55374, or any other mail order distributor or lumberyard that stocks hardwood. Use our materials list to prepare your order. The hardware is hand-fashioned, using 28-gauge sheet metal as described later in the building instructions. All metal parts can be purchased at your local hardware store.

Start by laying out all parts according to the dimensions in the drawing. Use a square to ensure accurate cuts and cut all the parts to size. The wide boards for the top and bottom can be created by edge-joining narrow boards. For the original, the boards were joined using ¼-in. dowels in the joint, and ½-in. corrugated fasteners into both ends across the joint.

moldings made with handtools

Notice the decorative edging on the lid. This apparently was the journeyman's way of "showing off" his skills. The original moldings, in all likelihood, were fashioned using handtools. Though we did some of the shaping with power tools, we, too, had to resort to hand work to closely match the original molding shape.

Start by cutting the three molding pieces to width, depth and length. Then, set up your table saw with the molding cutterhead shown. You *must* use an auxiliary wooden fence to make the cut as shown in the drawing (see page 106, *You Can Master Fine Wood Joinery,* for information on auxiliary wooden fences).

You should also use both a hold-down and a hold-in to avoid any chance of accident to yourself when making the moldings. This will also result in greater accuracy. Make the initial pass over the cutterheads to achieve the first stage. Finish shaping the molding by using a block plane with razor-sharp iron, files and sandpaper. (*Note:* You can substitute the Surform Shaver hand rasp for the block plane with great success.)

installing the moldings

When the moldings are shaped and smoothed to your satisfaction, they can be installed on the three required edges (there is none along the back edge). To do it, predrill lead holes through the moldings or you will split them. Use 1-in. No. 18 brads and glue to affix the moldings.

predrill hole for nails

Like the original, all joinery here is with nails and glue. To prevent any chance of splitting, predrill lead holes for the nails. You actually need two different-size holes for your nails. They should slide freely through the first piece, and then be driven into the leadholes in the second.

We used fewer nails than in the original because it is apparent that many of them were driven over the years to correct loose or split boards (see photo). You do want *some* nails to show and give it an antiqued look; in these spots use 3d or 4d common nails. Set the heads slightly below the surface. The balance of the fastening is done with almost-invisible 4d finishing nails.

the tray

We used mahogany to fashion our tray and laid it out as shown to suit the author's tools. The interior members can be resized and reshaped to suit the use to which you will put the tray. Assemble the tray using glue and 4d finishing nails. Once again, take care to align the pieces correctly and predrill to prevent splitting. Finish by locating and installing the shelf cleats on the case members.

Sand all parts before assembly, finishing up with 150-grit abrasive, and assemble the box. The next day, attach the lid to the case using the pair of 1-in. hinges set in mortises as shown.

homemade corner irons

The corner "irons" are, in reality, cut from 28-gauge sheet metal. You can cut and shape them at this time, but *do not* install them yet.

It is important that you notice that these pieces of "hardware" are *not* cut perfectly even. We copied the "off" sizes, shapes and locations of the originals exactly. After cutting the pieces, file off any burrs and bore the holes for the escutcheon pins. After bending the corner pieces, paint them with flat black latex (after neutralizing the sheet metal with vinegar).

Finish shaping the escutcheon plate for the "keyhole" and temporarily position the plate on the box. Mark the wood for the keyhole, remove the plate and gouge out the keyhole. Since you won't actually install a lock, you needn't bore through for any hardware. Gouge it out with a small chisel or knife, and paint the hole black.

use commercial handle

We made a look-alike handle by using a commercially available handle and cutting the backplate from 28-gauge sheet metal. The photographs show how closely the reproduction resembles the original.

The box shown was finished by staining with

MATERIALS LIST—OPEN TOOLBOX

Key	No.	Size and description (use)
A	2	½ x 6 x 23″ pine (side)
B	2	½ x 5¾ x 12″ pine (end)
C	1	¾ x 9¼ x 21¹⁵⁄₁₆″ pine (centerboard)
D	1	¾ x 10 x 18⅝″ pine (bottom)

MATERIALS LIST—LIDDED TOOLBOX

Key	No.	Size and description (use)
A	1	½ x 13⅛ x 22″ cherry (lid)
B	1	½ x 13⅛ x 22″ cherry (bottom)
C	2	½ x 11 x 22″ cherry (front/back)
D	2	½ x 11 x 12⅛″ cherry (side)
E	1	½ x 1⅞ x 23″ cherry (front trim)
F	2	½ x 1⅞ x 13⅛″ cherry (side trim)
G	1	⅝ x ¾ x 23½″ cherry (front molding)
H	2	⅝ x ¾ x 13⅞″ cherry (side molding)
I	2	½ x ½ x 20″ cherry (cleat)
J	2	½ x ½ x 12⅛″ cherry (side cleat)
K	2	¾ x 1 x 13⅛″ cherry (skid)
L	1	½ x 11⅜ x 20¼″ mahogany (tray bottom)
M	2	½ x 2½ x 20¾″ mahogany (tray front/back)
N	2	½ x 2½ x 11⅜″ mahogany (tray side)
O	2	½ x 2½ x 10⅞″ mahogany (divider)
P	2	½ x 2 x 6¼″ mahogany (divider)
Q	1	28-ga. x 3 x 4″ sheet metal (escutcheon plate)
R	6	28-ga. x 1½ x 4¾″ sheet metal (corner plate)
S	2	28-ga. x 2⅝ x 4¼″ sheet metal (back plate)
T	2	1¾ x 3½″ Brainerd No. 0234 chest handle
U	2	1 x 1¾″ Brainerd No. 6175 butt hinge
V		4d finishing nails
W		¾″ roundhead escutcheon pins cut to ⅜″

Carver Tripp maple stain thinned about 50 percent with turpentine. After dusting off the piece, apply the stain with either brush or rag. Let the stain set several minutes, then wipe off all excess. Allow the box to dry overnight.

Next day, after wiping the box with a tack cloth, seal with a coat of clear (water white) shellac thinned 50 percent with denatured alcohol. Allow the box to dry overnight. When dry, sand lightly with 180-grit paper wrapped around a cushioned sanding block. When it's smooth, dust off and wipe with a tack rag.

You can now attach the flat black "hardware." Fasten the corner braces and all three escutcheon plates using brass escutcheon pins. We used ¾-in. pins, which we nipped to ⅜-in. length using a diagonal cutter. The escutcheon pin heads must also be touched up with the flat black latex paint.

Install the handles over the plates using the screws (that come in the package) into predrilled holes. When all the hardware is in place—and the black paint is absolutely dry—apply a coat of varnish to all parts as it comes from the can. Allow the piece to dry thoroughly before using.

making the open box

The open box is easier to recreate. However, that doen't mean sloppy work is acceptable. Do it the professional way: Start by rough-cutting the six boards to approximate, but slightly over, sizes.

When all parts are cut, you can lay out the angles accurately, using a bevel square. Start by laying out the angles for cutting the ends of the sides. Cut the ends of both sides at the same time, or use a clamped stop block on your radial-saw table so that both sides will be identical in length. Next, repeat the procedure to cut the miters on the ends of the endpieces. Again, cut both at one time or use a clamped stop block. Once the endpieces are cut, you can use your bevel square to transfer the angle so that the bottoms of the sides and ends will be ripped parallel to the bottom board.

At this stage, tack-fasten the boards together to check all bevel and miter cuts. Make adjustments if necessary; overall size, after all, is not critical.

Remember that you will need bevel cuts on all four edges of the bottom piece, and along the edges of the end boards where they butt the side pieces. These are easily determined with the pieces tack-joined. When sides, ends and bottom are fitted to your satisfaction, sand all boards smooth, finishing up with 150-grit abrasive paper.

assembling with glue and nails

Assemble the case, using carpenter's glue and 3d common nails. Again, do it professionally and first assemble the box using a bare minimum of 3d *finishing* nails and clamps. You will need a pair of mitered boards, for use as pads, with each clamp. These let you draw the boards tightly together. When the box is assembled and clamped, set it aside to dry. The next day, remove the clamps and add the 3d common nails. Set all nailheads slightly below the surface.

When the box is assembled, use your bevel square to lay out the centerboard (handle). Make a test cut in scrap and, when satisfied with the angle joint, lay out and cut the board itself. The hand-hold cutout is centered on the board and can be made quickly by boring a 1-in.-dia. hole at each end and finishing the cut with either sabre or coping saw. Sand the board and install it in the case using carpenter's glue and 3d common nails.

don't overdo distressing

The original box is quite battered and distressed. We deliberately held the distress marks on the reproduction to a minimum. Overdistressing is often the mark of a neophyte finisher. A few dents or bangs here and there with a ball-peen hammer, perhaps a gouge or two with a carver's chisel, the exposed nails, plus a few punctures with awl or file tang will do.

Dust the box off and wipe it with a tack rag. Then, to ensure an even stain finish, apply boiled linseed oil to all exposed end grains. Immediately apply the oil stain of your choice and wipe off excess.

Set the piece aside to dry overnight. Next day, sand lightly with 180-grit paper; dust off and wipe with a tack rag. Apply a coat of varnish thinned 50 percent with turpentine. Let the box dry 24 hours.

Next, using an artist's pointed brush, apply burnt umber pigment from a tube, thinned as needed with turpentine, to all nailheads and to small distress marks (punctures). The idea is to simulate years of accumulated dirt. Allow the umber to dry overnight, sand the piece lightly with 220-grit paper, dust and wipe with a tack rag.

Finish by applying a coat of varnish as it comes from the can.

To achieve a hand-rubbed, waxed look, we used Pratt and Lambert's satin finish varnish on the boxes shown.

INITIAL CUTS are made with the workpiece firmly held down with clamp and left hand. The hand is removed from the photo above for photo clarity.

■ YOU MIGHT NOT BELIEVE you could cut perfectly true circles with a radial-arm saw. This jig lets you cut circles as large as 32-in. diameter.

Rout the dadoes and grooves in the ¾-in. birch plywood for the pivot and clamp tracks—deeper cuts first, then the cuts for the strap-iron runners.

Circle cutter for a radial saw

By C. E. BANISTER

Round over the edges of the strap iron with a fine-tooth file. Attach pivot runners with countersunk flathead wood screws and clamp runners with flathead machine bolts and Teenuts.

Bore holes for the Teenuts in the pivot track and install the nuts. Cut the slot in the pivot slide and drill the hole for the 8d finishing nail. Insert the nail in the hole and solder. Varnish and then install the clamp and pivot slide.

Secure the base to the sawtable with C-clamps. Make initial cuts with the workpiece held firmly by the clamp and your left hand. After each cut, rotate the piece about 60° for the next cut. After two full rotations, remove clamp and hold the piece firmly by hand as you rotate it into the blade that is locked in position.

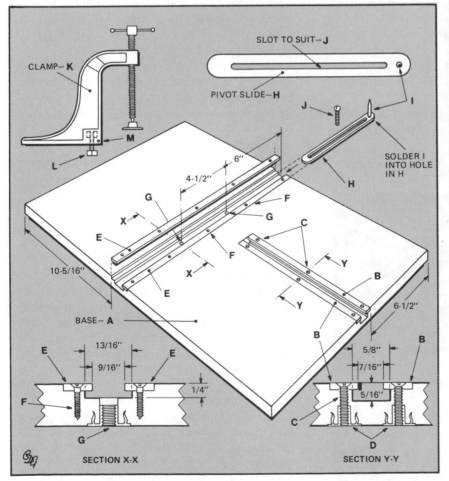

EVENLY CUT circles are produced in a few minutes. Final cuts are made without clamp and work held by hand.

MATERIALS LIST—CIRCLE-CUTTING JIG

Key	No.	Size and description (use)
A	1	¾ x 16½ x 25½″ birch plywood (base)
B	2	⅛ x ½ x 11¼″ strap iron
C	6	No. 8 x ¾″ fh machine bolt
D	6	No. 8-32 Teenuts
E	2	⅛ x ½ x 16½″ strap iron
F	10	No. 6 x ⅝″ fh wood screws
G	2	¼ x 20 Teenuts
H	1	3/32 x ¾ x 7″ strap iron
I	1	8d finishing nail, cut ¾″ long
J	1	¼-20x7/16″ stovebolt
K	1	3″ Jorgensen hold-down clamp (Adjustable Clamp Co., 411 North Ashland Ave., Chicago, IL 60622)

Misc.: Urethane varnish

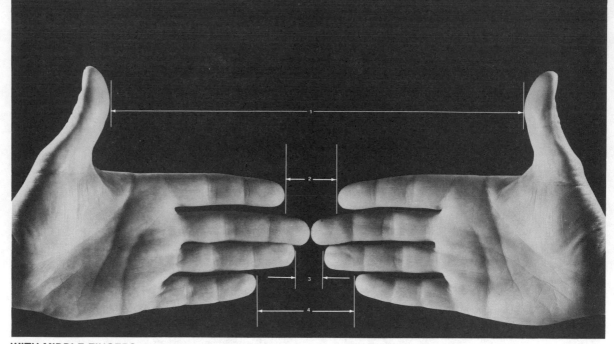

WITH MIDDLE FINGERS touching and thumbs stretched, measure 1, 2, 3 and 4 for your hands.

You're the rule

by **RUSSELL JAMES**

■ WHAT DO YOU DO when you need a quick measurement, but don't have a ruler handy? What if close is good enough, but the consequences of eyeball measurement are less than appealing? Here's a solution: Take the time to "calculate" some of the handiest measurements around—those of your own body.

You can start with your hands. Place them over a ruler (palms up, thumbs stretched, middle

BUTT YOUR little finger to an edge and make three more measurements (see the text).

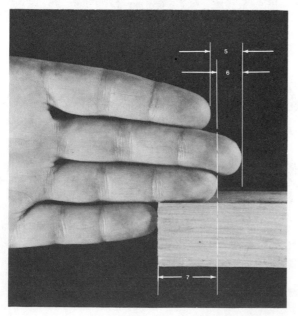

fingers touching) and note the dimensions between all opposing fingertips (see 1 through 4).

In examples 5, 6 and 7, use your little finger as a stop and record measurements from the edge of a board to each tip; also the difference between tips. This works just as well if you place your hand flat. Simply catch the fingernail of your little finger below the edge of what you're measuring.

A similar principle operates for Nos. 8 and 9. The middle finger is the stop and by changing knuckles you get two quick reference points. Of course, dimensions on "biophysical rulers" vary depending on the individual. So experiment—find those most valuable to you. With practice, you can be accurate within $\frac{1}{16}$ in. with no trouble.

Your palm also provides valuable measurements, such as those obtained from the creases between finger joints. I know a shopworker who uses a combination of 10 through 14 when sorting accumulated screws and bolts. Even when rulers are available, he finds that his fingers are quicker. He'll even make pencil marks on knuckles for those few increments he doesn't have "on hand."

Larger measurements are also available. The length of your outstretched arm from armpit (or tip of nose) to your middle fingertip is particularly useful, as is the distance between tips when both arms are stretched wide.

Other horizontal measurements come from

BY PLACING fingers as shown you'll have a "protractor" with 60° angle and perpendicular line.

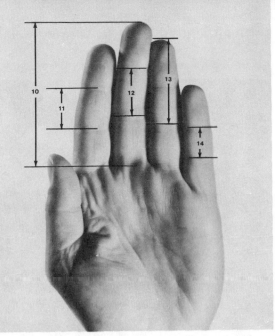

AT LEAST five dimensions are available by simply placing your hand down, palm up.

holding one or both elbows out to your side with your hands on your waist. When both elbows are spread, you can quickly approximate the width of such things as doorways and save the headache of trying to move something big through too small an opening.

For vertical measurements, try the distance between the floor and the tip of your nose, and don't forget to make an adjustment when you change your shoes. The same notion applies to the distance from the floor to your belt buckle or chin.

The possibilities are limitless. Even diameters can be judged with your personal ruler. The difference between tubing sizes can be readily determined depending on which knuckle the tubing jams on when slid over the finger. For example, ½-in. tubing jams on the first knuckle of my little finger, ⅝ in. jams on the second knuckle and ¾ in. clears both.

Larger outside diameters can be known by the combination of thumb and finger that will most nearly encircle them. For still larger diameters, both hands together could supply a ballpark figure.

You can use your hands for close approximations of often used angles (No. 15). Make a triangle of your fingers as pictured and press it against a table edge. The line that intersects where both fingertips and knuckles meet is perpendicular to the edge of the table, thus giving a 90° angle that is surprisingly accurate. In the process, an equilateral triangle is formed, giving the 60° angles shown.

Finally, by making the old V for victory sign with my middle and first fingers, I get a 45° angle. Of course, these angles and some other measurements mentioned might be something that you'd never use. But, unlike your tape measure, they will always be with you.

MAKE a "gun" of one hand, using the forefinger as the barrel. Fold your middle finger at the third knuckle (left) and then at the second (below). On the hand shown we got 3¼ in. and 1½ in., respectively.

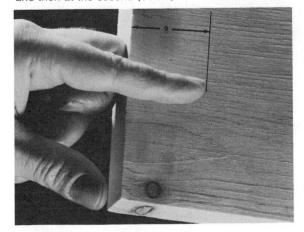

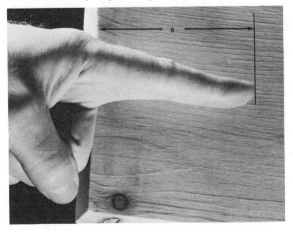

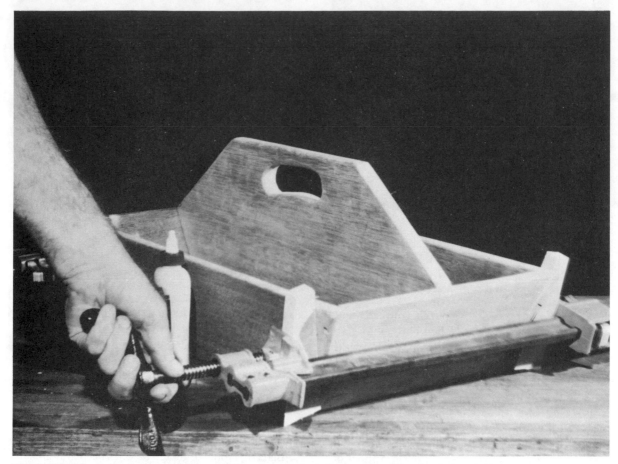

NEAT JOINTS are the unmistakable mark of a competent craftsman. Even the simple butt joint shouldn't be sold short; it's often used effectively in such projects as this antique toolbox reproduction.

You can master fine wood joinery

By ROSARIO CAPOTOSTO AND HARRY WICKS

■ THERE ARE A number of important steps in every woodworking project—from purchasing the stock through planning, cutting, sanding and finishing. But it's safe to say that quality of the joints is as important as any other phase of woodworking.

You may be a master of fine finishes, but a beautiful, hand-rubbed look will not conceal sloppy joinery. Nor will it strengthen the piece. The fact is, poor joinery is the major reason for failure (deterioration) of homebuilt (and commercially manufactured) furniture.

five important joints

Though there are countless joints to suit every conceivable joinery problem, the plain truth is that you will probably use five joints most of the time. The most commonly used joints include:

■ Butt.
■ Rabbets and dadoes.
■ Dowel.
■ Lap.

We will cover all of these joints in this article. You will learn the basics of joinery and some professional tips to use in your projects.

mastering joinery

In simplest terms, professionals learn by practice. And practice is the quickest route to craftsmanship for you, as well. You can use scrap materials to perfect your skills with the more advanced joints—those that call for deft work with a chisel, for example. If you work at joints only when you're faced with making one for a project, mastering joinery will take you time, at best, and it may elude you completely, at worst.

In the long run you'll save time if you practice diligently on scraps.

Take advantage of the professional tricks offered on these pages. As every craftsman knows, they are mastered by experience and by working with other skilled woodworkers.

points to remember

Here are a couple of basic points to remember:
■ The butting members of a joint should be smooth. The very smoothness of mating pieces increases the resistance to pull apart. Think of the last time you tried to separate two pieces of glass. Chances are you had to *slide* one off the other—you couldn't *pull* them apart.

■ Never load a joint with glue. Students are always shocked when we demonstrate just how little glue a professional uses in a joint. Apply the glue to both surfaces, then spread it thin with a clean stick, dowel, or brush. Excessive glue will *not* make the joint stronger. In fact, it can actually result in a weaker joint.

Too much glue also ensures considerable glue squeezeout, which is sure to ruin the looks of your handiwork. Even though you may not see

HOW TO MAKE BETTER BUTT JOINTS

THIS IS a typical butt joint, with one member simply abutting the other. Here, one piece is placed to project slightly to give an architectural shadow-line. The nails are driven at an angle for strength.

SCREWS GIVE an even stronger butt joint than nails—but glue is still used. To hide screwheads, counterbore holes to accept dowels. If looks don't matter, turn screws into countersunk holes.

SCREWS INTO end grain provide minimal holding power. Insert a dowel (partially installed here for clarity) to eliminate any chance of screw pulling out of joint.

THERE ARE many methods—plus commercial hardware—for strengthening a butt joint. A shopmade block such as this is installed using nails or screws through predrilled holes. Or you can use metal corner braces or irons.

YOU CAN USE a plywood gusset on a butted corner if appearance is inconsequential and its surface mounting won't interfere with function of the case. Outside edges must be perfectly square (90°), and aligned with abutted pieces to ensure a square finished project. Use glue and ringed nails.

ANOTHER version of a wooden corner block: Because this one has longer legs it gives greater stability. Shape allows easy installation.

MAKING RABBETS AND DADOES

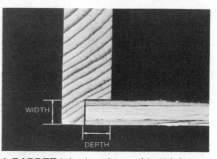

A RABBET joint is a form of butt joint, but its L-shape gives it greater strength. The edge rabbet width is equal to the thickness of the stock to be inserted into the rabbet; the depth can be anywhere from one-third to three-quarters of the stock which is being rabbeted. For this example, ½-in.-thick plywood is joined to ¾-in. stock, so rabbet was cut ½ in. wide by ⅜ in. deep.

WITH FENCE moved away from blade, saw notch is clearly shown. This stunt lets you "bury" part of the dado head in the "fence."

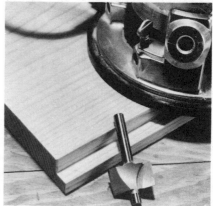

TO MAKE A dado with hand tools, first cut width lines to desired depth with a fine backsaw. Then use a sharp chisel to clean out interior portion.

USING A router and a rabbet-cutting bit is the fast and easy way to make a rabbet. Make certain cutter is sharp. In soft woods you should make at least two passes; make the first pass with cutter set for half depth. On hardwood, cut it in approximately three or four passes with the cutter set for one-quarter depth on first pass.

TO CUT a rabbet on table saw, always make edge cut first. This way you'll have maximum support for workpiece.

MAKE SECOND CUT with rabbet edge *away* from fence. For both cuts, blade should be elevated just to clean out corner of cut, and no more.

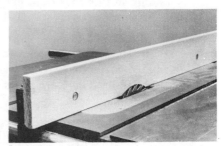

YOU CAN CUT a rabbet in one pass by mounting your dado head set on table saw. For safety, add wooden auxiliary fence, as shown here, to the rip fence. Position it with no more than half of the wood over the lowered cutters. Start the saw and slowly raise the head of the dado until you have cut a semi-circular notch.

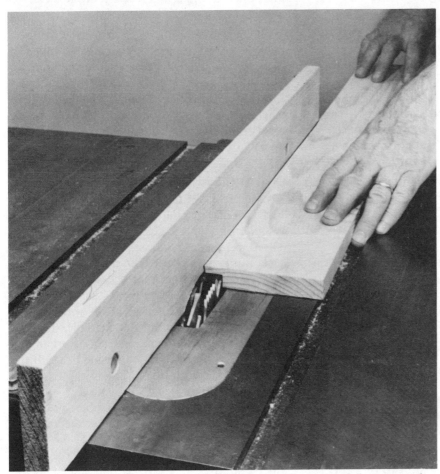

WITH THIS METHOD of making a rabbet in one pass, the work is fully supported and hands are away from the cutters. Use a pusher stick to complete the cut. For photo clarity, the blade guard is removed from saw in these pictures.

TO CUT a blind (stopped) rabbet you must add a wooden auxiliary fence with a pair of start and stop blocks clamped to it; notice the shape of start block. By rounding off the front corner, you automatically create an aid to help you lower workpiece (arrow) onto the spinning blade.

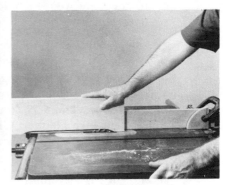

BOARD IS pushed through until it comes to rest against a stop block. At this point you should either turn off the saw and wait for blade to stop or back workpiece up a few inches and carefully lift it off. Don't attempt to lift board off table the same way it was lowered on to the spinning blade.

fine wood joinery, continued

the glue squeezeout, it seals the wood to prevent stains and finishes from penetrating.

about butt joints

Because the butt joint is the simplest of all, many beginning woodworkers sell this type of joint short. There are times when a butt joint is quite adequate.

For example, in cabinetmaking, cases are often joined using reinforced butt joints (see photograph on page 106). And butt joints are extremely common in household carpentry as long as they are executed precisely in craftsmanlike fashion.

butt joint disadvantages

A case can be made against butt joints, of course; the biggest disadvantages are:

■ Because of the minimal contact area (glue surface) between members, a butt joint is one of the weakest joints in woodworking.

■ Because a butt joint leaves end grain exposed, it is not the best looking option in joinery.

Thus, it is obvious that the woodworker must consider the pros and cons of a joint on every project he tackles. You would not, for instance, use a butt joint and leave end grain exposed on a fine piece of walnut furniture. On the other hand, you will often use butt joints when recreating early American furniture, especially the primitive type created by the settlers.

making butt joints work

■ In almost every case, you should beef up a butt joint by adding a corner strengthener. You can make adequate wooden braces or you can use commercial corner braces.

■ An end butt joint is the weakest of all because one of the joining pieces is end grain (as in the toolbox on page 106). One good stunt is to thin your carpenter's glue slightly with water and to precoat the end grain. The wood will suck up the thinned glue like a blotter. When it's dry, you can proceed with the joint, using the glue as it comes from the bottle.

■ Though edge-joining (gluing up two or more narrow boards to create a wide one) is usually done using dowels into the edges, there are times when the dowels can be eliminated. If the wide board will be contained on all four sides in a rabbet, for example, you can frequently do an adequate job by using corrugated fasteners or Skotch Connectors.

glue and clamp

The usual technique, after spreading a scant amount of glue on the mating surfaces, is to align the boards and hold them rigid with a number of bar clamps until the glue dries. Next day, the clamps are removed and the glued-up board is placed on a solid, flat surface, hidden side up. The corrugated fasteners are driven into the board to span the joint and close it permanently.

If the board ends will be concealed in a rabbet, it's also a good idea to drive in a corrugated fastener at each end—into the end grain—spanning the joint.

a weaker joint

The important rule to remember is that corrugated fasteners should be used only where they will not be seen. Don't think that the resultant joint is as strong as a doweled joint; it isn't.

Study the pictures on page 107 showing six typical butt joint applications. The rules depicted are basic for butt joints and should be added to your woodworking techniques. Remember that a nail driven at an angle, for example, holds better than one driven straight in. Also remember that, generally, you should bore lead (pilot) holes to avoid splitting, even in softwoods, because you are usually working near the end of a board.

about glue blocks

A glue block of one type or another should be used to reinforce a butt joint's glue line whenever possible. For thick stock the glue block can be shaped like those shown on page 107, but for thin stock, it is generally better to use a strip of wood for the length of the joint (because the screws used are so short). A glue block can be used outside the joint, if placing one inside will interfere with the case's operation. For example, the joint between a cabinet side and an overhanging countertop could require an outside block. If the block were placed inside, it might interfere with drawer operation.

Finally, if more than two members are being butt-joined, it is often possible to create an interlocking joint by careful placement of the pieces. If three boards join to form a corner, the corner will be stronger if each board is joined to the other two.

about rabbets and dadoes

A rabbet is an L-shaped cut made in one board to receive another. Whether the rabbet runs with the grain or across the grain, it is called a rabbet.

Because a rabbet increases the gluing surface

of the pieces being joined, the joint is considerably stronger than a butt joint. A typically good use for a rabbet joint is in mounting a cabinet's back panel.

nomenclature

Dadoes and grooves are U-shaped cuts made across the face of a board. If the cut is across the grain, it is called a dado; if with the grain, it is called a groove. As with the rabbet cut, the width of the cut matches the thickness of the piece being inserted into the dado. The depth is generally one-half the thickness of the piece being plowed. In some cases, the dado is cut deeper, but be aware that this can weaken the joint.

Though a dado gives a strong joint, the general criticism is that it isn't an attractive joint. Thus, when using dadoes in a cabinet, the usual practice is to add stiles and rails to hide the plowed joints. Dadoes and grooves, like rabbets, increase the strength of the joint because of the greater gluing surface.

cutting a rabbet

When there are just one or two rabbets to cut, it is generally done using a combination blade on the table saw, and a two-step cut.

For safety reasons, it's important that you always follow the sequence shown in the photos on page 109. Done this way, the workpiece has maximum support and there is less chance of an accident with the saw.

However, when you have a number of repetitive rabbets to cut, you can speed up the job considerably by installing your dado head set on the table saw. Make certain you add the wooden auxiliary fence, as shown, so the cut can be properly made (with the edge being cut next to the fence).

Most shops create such fences and install them on the saw fence, using flathead machine bolts and wingnuts. The hardware is kept with the fence; the fence is stored on the wall when not in use.

using hand tools on rabbets

A rabbet can be shaped using a handsaw with the workpiece clamped in the bench vise. In general, it is best to use a stiff-bladed backsaw for accuracy of cut.

Accuracy is a must, so also use a clamped-on guide for the saw to ride against. Make the first cut, then rotate the work in the vise to make another cut to clean out the rabbet.

Some craftsmen prefer to make the first cut with a saw, then clean out the waste with a razor-sharp chisel. No matter which way you choose to work, you must make all the cuts with great accuracy if you are to achieve craftsmanlike joints.

Similarly, dadoes can be cut using hand tools. Again, the width lines are cut to the desired depth using clamped-on guides; then, the waste is carefully cleaned out with a chisel (see the photo, page 108).

stopped or blind rabbet

A stopped or blind rabbet joint is not visible at the ends. It can be done either of two ways:
■ You can make your rabbet cut through the board, then fill the ends with carefully cut filler strips, after the boards are joined.
■ You can make a stopped cut on your table saw, as shown in the photos on page 109. To do this, you must locate the start and stop points for the board being cut.

The easiest way to do so is to crank the blade to cutting height and hold a piece of scrap alongside the blade. You can see with fairly good accuracy just where the start block should be placed so the cut will start at the desired point, and where the stop block should be placed to stop the cut where wanted.

Position the blocks and clamp them securely to the fence. Make a test cut in scrap and adjust the blocks if necessary. When you're satisfied with locations, you can cut the actual workpieces.

The rounded portions left at the start and finish of the cut are then cleaned out (squared) with a chisel, tailoring the work to suit the board entering the rabbet.

tips for making stopped cuts

We have probably made thousands of blind rabbet cuts, but it wasn't until the photography session for this story that we came up with the idea of rounding over the start block, as can be seen in the photo. The rounded section makes it safer and easier to lower the board being cut.

To make the blind cut, start the saw and hold the workpiece firmly against both the fence and the start block with its outboard end held well above the blade. Keeping fingers away from the blade, slowly lower the workpiece into the spinning blade until it rests flat on the tablesaw surface. When it does, slowly push the work forward until the far end contacts the stop block.

removing the cut piece

There are two methods for removing the cut piece: 1, You can back it up slightly with blade spinning, carefully raise the far end clear of the

MAKING JOINTS WITH DOWELS

DOWELING IS THE surest way to strengthen a joint in wood. The type shown is commercially prepared with glue-escape channels machined in and chamfered at both ends. Joint here uses hidden (blind) dowels.

blade and lift it off, or 2, you can turn off the saw and wait until the blade stops before lifting it off. In either case, work carefully.

Chances are you will turn to doweling more than any other method when you want to beef up a joint's strength. Dowels can be used in almost any joint from butt to mitered—the techniques for using them remain basically the same. The important thing is to master the basics. Once you get fundamentals under your belt, the more sophisticated joinery techniques will come easily during your practice-with-scrap sessions.

working with dowels

If you intend to seriously pursue woodworking to build your own furniture, cabinets and the like, you must master dowel joinery. In the beginning, you can work with dowel centers (in fact, these are often the handiest tools in the shop, even after you may have more advanced

equipment on hand). However, as your workshop production increases, so will your need for the quicker and more accurate doweling jig.

The usual practice with dowels is to select a diameter that is about half the workpiece thickness: It should *never* be greater. Thus, for example, you would use a ⅜-in. dowel with ¾-in. stock; a ¼-in. dowel with ½-in. wood, and so on.

commercially made dowels

The easiest way to use dowels is to buy the commercially made versions (see photo, page 112). These are 3 in. long, chamfered both ends, and come with escape air and glue channels routed in. (The chamfered ends make it easier for you to insert the dowel.)

If you have a lot of doweling to do, you can hold down cost somewhat by buying dowel rod by the 3-ft. length and cutting lengths to suit the job. If you choose this course, remember to cut

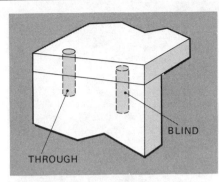

DOWELS IN butt joint make it considerably stronger. Through dowel is stronger of the two, but blind dowel is used to make joint invisible from the front.

DOWEL CENTERS are an inexpensive—yet accurate—way to ensure perfectly aligned mating holes for dowels. Always locate and bore holes in end grain first (see text). Then butt work against a straightedge, as here, slide piece to be marked (arrow) against the centerpoints and press the boards together firmly.

WITH HOLES accurately marked, they can be bored in the second piece to complete the joint.

OR, USE a dowel jig—the authors' preferred method for handling a dowel joint. To start, clamp parts to be joined securely in vise. Then use a square and a pencil to mark the dowel locations on the edges of both boards.

NEXT, LOCATE hole centers, using a combination square. Here, on ¾-in. stock, square's blade projects ⅜ in. Make certain hole centers on both boards are marked from the same surfaces; that is, surfaces that line up.

BORE HOLES using appropriate bit in portable drill and a doweling jig. Position jig with its registration mark in line with first line drawn. Properly positioned bit guide will ensure that hole is bored at center of the cross marks. Make certain that the jig is rotated 180° in order to bore the mating hole.

IF YOU MUST bore a number of dowel holes along the centerline of long boards, using a portable drill and a guide such as the Portalign tool makes the task much easier—and you can be sure of on-target holes. Next, dowel centers will be used to locate the dowel holes on the board to be edge-joined to the board shown in the photo.

TECHNIQUE OF MAKING AN EDGE LAP JOINT

EDGE LAP actually consists of a dado cut made across a board edge, rather than its face (often called a notch). If you are making just one or two joints, start by making the shoulder cuts, then make several saw kerfs in between, as shown here. Finish the cleanout with a chisel. If you have a lot of edge laps to cut, it's faster to make the notches by mounting a dado head on the saw and making one pass.

the glue-escape channels and to chamfer the ends. We do the first by raising the table-saw blade a scant amount (maybe 1/32 in.) and feeding the rod in, before cutting pieces to length. Cut about half the rod, lift it off the saw, then repeat for the remaining half length. Finally, cut the pieces to length.

Chamfering can be done with a sander or plane, or very quickly in a pencil sharpener.

aligning dowel holes

Obviously, if the dowel holes aren't aligned, the two pieces of board they are in won't be, either. For that reason, always do your marking from the same side of the board. For example, mark what will be the underside on the two boards being joined—then do the measuring for center for both boards from the *same finish surface*. This way, should your mark be off a scant amount on the first board, it will be off the same amount—in the same direction—on the second. This is especially important when working with dowel centers, or a doweling jig.

using dowel centers

After locating dowel hole positions on the first board, bore the dowel holes. Then insert the appropriate-size dowel centers into the newly-drilled holes, and press the two boards together. Make a light match mark before separating the two boards. Remove the board and bore holes in the second edge.

The holes should be bored first in the end grain when joining an end grain to another edge, since an end grain doesn't have a uniform surface; that makes it likely the center point will hit a hard or soft spot and move the mark ever so slightly. When this happens, of course, the resulting joint won't be flush.

tap in the dowels

Apply glue sparingly to the dowels and insert them into the holes in one of the boards. You'll probably have to tap the dowel lightly with a mallet to get it halfway home. Using a brush or small-diameter stick, apply glue to the remainder of the board edge—and remove all excess glue from around the dowels. Align the two boards and join them by applying pressure with clamps.

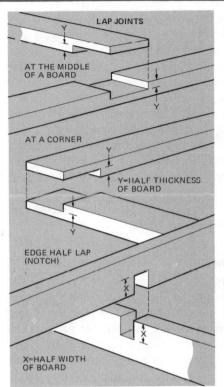

LAP JOINTS

AT THE MIDDLE
OF A BOARD

AT A CORNER

Y=HALF THICKNESS
OF BOARD

EDGE HALF LAP
(NOTCH)

X=HALF WIDTH
OF BOARD

USING SQUARE and the stock itself, mark width of notch on first piece at the desired location. Repeat this step on the mating piece of wood.

NEXT, EXTEND combination square to a length equal to half of the width (of boards to be notched) and lock it in place. Then use the square to mark the depth of cut on all of the pieces to be cut. Accuracy is a must.

THESE ARE the three most commonly used lap joints. Surface lap joint lacks holding power and, if strength is important, should be reinforced with hardware. The edge lap (or interlocking) joint is solid by itself.

YOU CAN CUT notches by hand, using a fine crosscut saw or backsaw. Clamp the workpiece in a vise and use a simple, U-shaped wooden block as a guide to keep saw on a straight cutting line when you are making the two end or shoulder cuts.

USE SHARP chisel, with its bevel edge facing waste side, to remove material from notch. In soft woods, you can rap the chisel with your hand; for hardwoods, mallet taps are best. Chisel out only a small section of scrap at a time.

WHEN THE NOTCH is almost fully cleaned out, test-fit the pieces to avoid overcutting and sloppy fit. Use chisel or file to clean out additional material.

WELL-EXECUTED edge laps produces a joint that is nearly invisible, with no gaps between boards and edges that are flush.

TO NOTCH edge lap with table saw, affix a small piece of masking tape to table in front of blade. Elevate blade to equal notch depth and make test cut in scrap. Then, holding test piece firmly against miter gauge, back latter up and turn off saw. Use a sharp pencil to mark blade position.

MAKE THE two outside cuts first, using tape registration marks as your guide.

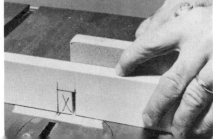

MAKE REPEATED passes over spinning blade to remove waste.

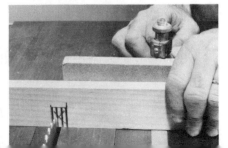

Bar clamps are best when edge-joining boards and scrap wood should always be placed beneath a metal clamp's jaws to prevent damage to the workpiece.

Often, edge-joined boards have a tendency to "curl" or bow. You can prevent this with clamps and additional boards *across* the bow. Apply clamp pressure until you can spot slight glue squeezeout along the glue line (joint) and set the work aside to dry for 24 hours.

using a doweling jig

With one of these, you can become an expert with dowels in less time than you might imagine. There are several types of doweling jigs available; the one shown on page 113 is the authors' favorite.

To use the jig, you first lay out the hole locations with a square, as shown on page 113. Use a pencil with a very fine point, or a scratch awl. Then place the jig on the workpiece after aligning its registration mark with the mark you just made on the wood. When it is aligned, lock the jig in place with its clamping device.

Next, the appropriate-size bit guide is lined up and locked in place. (In the example shown, the ⅜-in. guide is in place on the jig because we wanted to bore ⅜-in. holes.)

Measure the distance from workpiece edge to top of jig and add 1¹⁄₁₆ in. to determine the drill bit's total depth of penetration. Put your depth stop on the bit at that point—a masking-tape flag works fine—and stop drilling when the flag touches the top of the jig.

Since the jig is, in effect, a round tunnel that your bit must follow, you will get the most accurate holes using spur or brad point bits. These aren't as fast drilling in wood as spade bits are, but the results will be more accurate because the bit is in close proximity to the guide.

several professional tips

■ Always use at least two dowels in a joint to gain maximum strength. A pair also prevents the joint from pivoting.

■ Make certain you use only hardwood dowels. The commercial type available at lumberyards and home centers will be either birch, maple or hickory.

■ Keep your dowels in a dry, well-ventilated place. If you work with a wet dowel it will shrink as it ages and, consequently, will cause an unwanted loose joint.

about lap joints

Webster's New World Dictionary describes a lap joint as "a joint made by lapping one piece or part over another and fastening them together." And that, in simplest terms, is exactly what a lap joint is. There are many variations, however.

The most common lap joint is the surface lap, such as those found in a garden trellis. A surface lap joint is not strong; the contact (glue) area won't resist twist or lateral stress. For this reason, it's the usual woodworking practice to create half-lap joints, as shown in the drawing on page 115. Here, the wood parts are notched to half-thickness so the joint will be an interlocking one, and the surfaces will be flush.

full lap joint

Occasionally, you'll need to use a full lap, generally when one of the parts is thinner than the other. The seat cut (dado) is made in the thicker piece to accommodate the thinner piece. Thus, for example, if you want to join a ½ by 3½-in. member to a length of 5/4-in. stock, you would cut a 3½-in.-wide dado to a depth of ½ in. in the 5/4-in. lumber. As with a half lap joint, a full lap should also produce members that are flush when they are joined.

An end lap occurs in framemaking (i.e., door) and the rabbet cuts are determined using the mathematics shown in the drawing on page 115.

cutting an end lap joint

When cutting a frame lap joint (rabbet), always make the shoulder cut first, then the cheek cut. The workpiece should be clamped in a vise and, to ensure accuracy, you can clamp a depth stop block to the saw. In general, you should leave the line when making a joint—you can always take some more off with a sharp chisel. Too much removed, however, means that the resulting joint won't be flush.

Rotate the workpiece in the vise to make the second (cheek) cut. Repeat the steps for the second member. Test the parts for fit and, if necessary, clean out additional stock from mating cheeks for a flush joint.

To cut end laps on a table saw, you can use a combination blade and two cuts. Again, make the shoulder cut first, using your miter gauge. Then turn the stock on edge and use the rip fence to make the cheek cut. Work carefully when making a cheek cut and keep the part being cut out away from the fence (to ensure the stock riding the table throughout.)

use a tenoning jig

It is better and safer to use a tenoning jig to make the cheek cut when using a conventional blade. With one of these, the work is securely clamped and there is no chance of kickback. In fact, if you own a tenoning jig, you can make an end-lap rabbet cut in one setup by using a dado head and elevating the cutters to desired lap width.

If the stock being joined in your end lap joint is wider than 2½ in., use a dado head, rather than a conventional blade, to make the cut.

To do it, install the dado head set on the saw and set its cutters to project the desired distance. Using your miter gauge, make the shoulder cut first, then carefully make repeat overlapping passes over the cutters to clear out the remainder of the joint.

more professional tips

■ When creating a notch or dado with a table saw—whether using blade or dado head set—it's not uncommon to have saw ridges remain on the cheek. Since these must be cleaned out later with a chisel to ensure a tight joint, cut a hair less than required.

■ Professionals always keep stock of the same size and dimension on hand for test cutting and fitting. Use this stock for testing all saw settings, and so on before cutting your expensive, project material.

half laps

There are many variations of half lap joints, the simplest of which is shown in the drawing on page 115—the half lap at the middle of a board.

Here, in both members, the dados are cut to equal the stock's width and half its thickness. The cutting can be by hand or with power, as shown in the photo on page 114.

edge half laps

These are the same as a conventional half lap except that the cutting is done in the board edges, rather than on the surface. As a result, the dados are much narrower and deeper. Frequently called notches because of this shape, the joint produced is a strong interlocking one. This is a conventional assembly technique in certain projects—that is, egg-crate or wine-rack, construction.

Again, the shoulder cuts are made first, then the area between is cleaned out. The shoulders can be cut using a handsaw and a miterbox, or the work can be clamped in a vise. The cutout should be carefully marked, using a square as shown, but, if you don't trust your ability to stop sawing at a marked line, clamp a depth stop to the saw.

After making the shoulder cuts, make one or two additional kerfs in the field (see photo, page 114), then clean out the notch with a sharp chisel. To do it, position the work on a flat, solid surface and hold the chisel with its bevel toward the waste area. Give the handle a sharp rap with the palm of your hand to clear the waste. Finish clearing the notch, using the chisel with a paring action.

edge laps on the table saw

Edge laps are particularly easy to cut on the table saw if it's equipped with a dado head set. If you are cutting the notches for a project requiring many members—such as a wine rack—you can save time by ganging the marked members together and cutting them all at once. Remember to clamp the pieces securely so they can't shift during the cutting step.

about joints in general

■ Always use a quality glue in your joints. Apply the glue sparingly, and *never* spread it on too thickly.

■ Before gluing, make certain you test-fit the parts. Put the pieces together and clamp them "dry" to locate problems. A lap joint should have tight shoulders and the members must be flush. If you must join a great number of parts that have been notched, you can avoid confusion during final assembly by making light pencil match marks during your dry assembly.

■ Whenever possible, use hardware (screws or nails) for additional joint strength. Though the lap joint is a considerably stronger joint than the plain butted joint, it too can use some help in the form of screws or nails.

■ If you do produce a less than perfect joint, all is not lost. If you plan to paint the project, you can fill small voids, using a paste consisting of fine sawdust mixed with white glue. Or, use a quality wood filler such as UGL's Wood Patch.

For projects to be stained, you won't get off so easily. If the sloppy joint is just a hairline loose, you *may* be able to conceal it using a wax putty stick (of the type intended for wood paneling) after the piece has been stained and varnished, or some other finish has been applied.

But, as a woodworker, you should always remember that the quality of the joints in your projects is a true measure of your skill as a woodworker.

Tips on chain-saw maintenance

Lumberjack Dave Geer, a perennial
chain-saw contest winner, shows
how he keeps his chain saw humming.
The same techniques will keep
your saw in top shape

■ KEEPING CHAIN SAWS running properly is a growing concern of many homeowners who are turning to wood as an alternative source of heat. What better person to turn to for chain-saw tips than a professional lumberjack. So, we asked Dave Geer, a consistent chain-saw cutting champ, to share his tips for keeping a chain saw in tiptop shape.

Often featured on network television programs, the 56-year-old Geer is probably one of the best known lumberjacks today. A regular competitor in Homelite's Tournament of Kings world saw-cutting championship held in Charlotte, NC, each year, he is presently staging Dave Geer Lumberjack Shows across the country.

In Dave's opinion, the three most important rules to follow when getting ready to use a chain saw are: 1. read the homeowner's manual and the manufacturer's instructions; 2. tighten all screws and bolts; 3. make sure the chain is properly filed.

In Photo 3, the correct procedure for mounting the chain is demonstrated. Saw owners must learn the technique when assembling a new saw for the first time. It's a good idea, however, to disassemble chain and guide bar when trans-

porting the saw over long distances, or before storing, so it is a technique to remember. After the guide bar is mounted, straighten out any kinks in the chain and lay it out in a loop. Then, feed the chain into the grooves, as shown.

A good instruction booklet contains the information necessary to understand saw chain tension adjustment, as shown in Photo 4. Chains become warm or even hot when they are used, and you have to take this into account when tension adjustments are made.

Keeping your chain in good cutting condition makes sawing easier and safer, while prolonging the life of the saw. Photo 5 shows the first step in the sharpening process.

The raker, shown in Photos 6 and 7, controls the depth of the cut and acts like a runner guide for the cutting edge.

If you find a dirty air filter when checking the power head (Photo 9), tap the loose dirt free and then rinse out finer dirt with a nonoily petroleum solvent.

Finally, like all professionals, Dave cautions everyone to practice chain-saw safety rules. Always maintain good balance and never work when you are tired.

1 Reading the instruction manual is one of the three most important rules in chain-saw use and maintenance. Safety hints are included.

2 Remove two hex nuts from mounting studs and remove drive-case cover. Check this area regularly to make sure nuts are tight and parts clean.

3 When assembling saw after storage, see that chain-drive tangs are set properly in guide-bar grooves. Work from sprocket to nose.

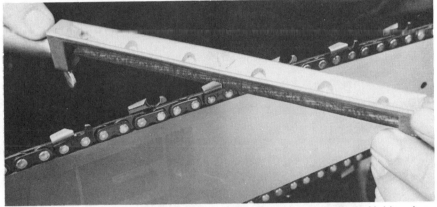

4 Dave lifts the chain with right hand to check tension. Tension screw is then adjusted with a screwdriver. Tension should be adjusted before each use.

5 Use a file holder to maintain a 35° filing angle when filing saw teeth. Holder also keeps file at correct height. Keep file level and stroke in one direction only.

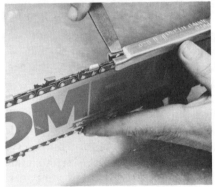

6 Use a depth-gauge jointer to true up chain's depth gauge (rakers). Fit jointer over the chain with slot toward bar nose, and file flush.

7 Viewing guide bar and chain in Photo 6 from the other side, the front side of the raker is then rounded over for a good sliding action.

8 Pull starter rope to check for proper recoil-spring action. Spring adjusts easily if necessary. Keep the air intake louvers clean.

9 Start power-head maintenance with a check of the air filter. Make sure filter and area around carburetor are clean. Seat filter properly.

10 Screwdriver points to an area near combustion cylinder where carbon accumulation may occur. Remove muffler and clean away carbon.

11 Check the sparkplug first when starting troubles occur, as a fouled plug is usually the cause. Clean plug by brushing or scraping.

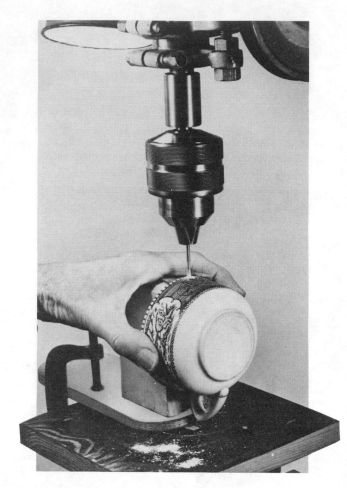

How to drill hard materials

By WALTER E. BURTON

■ A NEW WORLD opens up for many craftsmen when they discover ways of drilling in hard material. Suddenly, a variety of new projects are possible, as more materials become available for the craftsman's use.

abrasive-grit drilling

An inexpensive method of making a hole in glass, china or similar material is to grind it through with abrasive particles, preferably on a drill press. The bit can be made from rods of aluminum, copper, brass or even a headless nail. As these bits have tubular cutting ends, they are known as "core-type bits." The desired diameter is usually milled in a lathe from a rod, then the bit is center-drilled to form a recess in which cores develop from the material being drilled.

Granular abrasive is used between the material and rotating drill. It is the abrasive that does the actual cutting. Abrasive is usually aluminum-oxide or silicon-carbide grains of 80- to 120-grit size. Types of abrasive include loose grains produced by abrasive manufacturers, value-grinding compound (such as Permatex water-mixed), aluminum-oxide or silicon-carbide grains from "sandpaper." Whatever the abrasive or its source, it is usually mixed with water to make a "soup."

Drill-press speed should be low or moderate for core-type bits. Raise the bit every 10 seconds or so to permit fresh soup to flow over the cutting area. When the hole is almost through, control the feed pressure carefully to prevent chipping on the underside. Don't become discouraged if this method seems exasperatingly slow. Drilling rate depends on such things as hardness of the material being drilled, grit characteristics and drill rpm.

carbide-alloy drills

A typical masonry drill that's available commercially consists of a steel shank tipped with a flat piece of tungsten carbide. These bits have two cutting edges at a broad angle to each other. So-called "glass drills" are of similar construction, but the carbide pieces are shaped like an arrowhead, the tip angle being smaller (sharper) and the web thinner at the point.

When using carbide-alloy bits, support the glass on a firm surface, such as wood or hardboard, and clamp it securely. Keep the carbide cutter lubricated; a few drops of turpentine serve as a good lubricant. Run the press at moderate speed, and feed the bit carefully to prevent overheating and possible glass breakage. Although the bit can pass easily through the glass, there's a chance that it will cause chipping around the hole as it emerges. To decrease this possibility, turn the glass over as soon as the drill tip emerges (set the depth stop first) and finish drilling from the second side.

diamond bits

For drilling small, hard gemstones and the like, I recommend diamond-studded bits. A typical set of Micromite drills includes 1-, 1¼-, 1½-, 2- and 2½-mm sizes. Retail price for the set is about $20. They always should be used wet, with the workpiece being wholly immersed in water or a special drilling fluid.

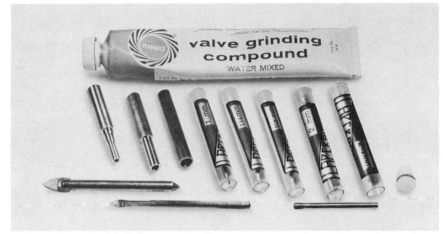

MAKE YOUR OWN BITS like the three at upper left, or buy diamond bits (in plastic tubes) and tungsten-carbide bits (in foreground). Valve-grinding compound holds the abrasive grit when drilling.

BRASS BITS are made on a metal-working lathe. A center hole is being drilled ½ in. deep in a ¼-in.-dia. brass rod. Core bits of this type cut slowly.

A ³⁄₁₆-IN.-DIA. hole is drilled in the bottom half of a glass jar using a brass bit and abrasive compound.

THIS ¼-in. tungsten-carbide bit mounted in a drill press can easily drill through ¼-in. plate glass in several minutes.

DRILLING in stones is done with the Dremel variable-speed Moto-Tool and drill-press stand (No. 210).

Sometimes a dam is constructed around the workplace to hold the fluid. This dam is formed with a caulking material (such as Mortite) or anything else that will make a water-retaining cup.

A small, variable-speed hand grinder is suitable for driving diamond bits in the workshop. The manufacturer of Lapcraft Micromite diamond drills, however, has suggested that they be powered by a Dremel variable-speed Moto-Tool mounted on its drill-press stand. When drills are handheld, it is difficult to drill in small, hard objects with precision, but a drill press does make it easy.

To master the technique of using diamond bits, apply pressure carefully to the workpiece until the bit "bites." Then the bit will run without jumping or crawling sideways. Drilling pressure is increased until the drill really starts cutting, as indicated by the appearance of cloudiness in the fluid. Be careful not to apply too much pressure. If the motor slows down, reduce pressure at once: Prolonged pressure can overheat and damage the drill bit. The bit should be backed out frequently—say, every 10 seconds or less—so fluid can refill the hole to cool the tip and clear away loosened solid material.

As in all shop work, take precautions—wear safety glasses while drilling and gloves while handling glass and glass particles.

SOURCES—DRILLING MATERIALS
Carbide glass drills: Edmund Scientific Co., 7082 Edscorp Bldg., Barrington, NJ 08007.
Tungsten-carbide drills and solid carbide for steel: Ash & Co., 5100 Grand River, Detroit, MI 48208; Brookstone Co., Brookstone Bldg., Peterborough, NH 03458.
Diamond drill bits, diamond core drills, drilling fluid and Dremel Moto-Tool drill press: The Lapcraft Co., Box 389, 195 West Oletangy St., Powell, OH 43065.
Aluminum-oxide and silicon-carbide abrasive grain: Carborundum Co., Niagara Falls, NY 14302; the Norton Co., Worcester, MA 01606.

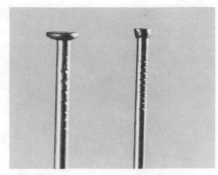

BASICALLY, two types of nails are used in house carpentry—the common nail (left) and finishing nail. Latter features cupped head for easy setting.

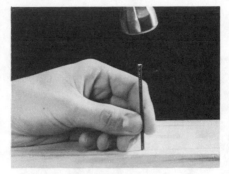

TO DRIVE A finishing nail, grasp it between thumb and index finger and start nail with several light taps.

NEVER drive a finishing nail home with hammer. Instead, stop driving nail when it is about ⅛ in. above the wood surface.

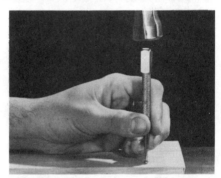

POSITION ¹/₃₂-in. nailset in head's dimple and set nail with one or two sharp raps. Hold the set securely so that it won't "dance" out of nailhead and cause damage to the wood.

WRONG WAY to install long run of baseboard—with square-cut ends simply abutted. Careless joinery is sure indication of poor workmanship.

INSTEAD, MAKE joints in long runs using a miter. Use miterbox for accuracy.

FIRST STRIP has open miter.

APPLY GLUE to the miter surfaces and then install second piece.

SECURE MITER joint with 3d (1¼-in.) nails through the joint.

A pro's tips on finish carpentry

By HARRY WICKS

■ MANY OF THE LITTLE TASKS that a homeowner does in the course of do-it-yourself projects go unnoticed. If your work happens to be a bit careless on such jobs, it makes little difference. But that isn't the case with finish carpentry.

The finish carpentry that you are most likely to encounter as a homeowner will involve "trimming out" a room. This includes the installation of those moldings and trim that are intended to

CLOSE THE finished joint tightly, and it will stay that way.

DOOR CASING (trim) should be set back a uniform distance from jamb edge; ¼ in. is the usual reveal. Mark setback in several places.

CUT MITER at one end of casing, then mark casing length from inside corner. The length of the casing includes the ¼-in. reveal.

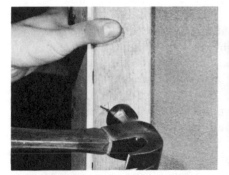

TO INSTALL DOOR (and window) casing, use 4d finishing nails through thin edge into jamb, and 6d nails through thick edge into stud. Nails should be spaced about 10 to 12 in. apart.

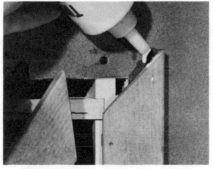

TO GUARANTEE that miter joints will stay closed, install as follows. Cut header casing to suit span between vertical casings. Then apply white glue sparingly to mating surfaces.

NEXT, BORE slightly undersize lead holes through joint. The bit that you select should provide a tight fit for the finishing nail that follows.

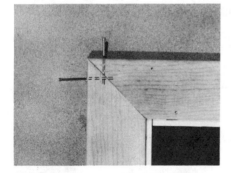

SECURE JOINT with two 6d finishing nails. Set the nails with nailset.

CORRECT door-trim detail at floor. Door casing extends to floor and baseboard trim abuts the casing.

TO KEEP an outside corner miter closed, as in a baseboard, first apply glue to miter. Then secure it with 4d finishing nails. If you plan to stain and varnish the trim, remove all traces of glue.

conceal joints and framing details, and give the room a finished appearance. Such work also includes the application of baseboards, door and window casings, outside corner guards, ceiling moldings, chair rails and the like.

use the right tools

■ **Hammer**—For finish work, many professional carpenters prefer to use the lighter 13-oz. hammer; I do, myself. But if you are doing trim work that requires hefty finish nails (10d or heavier), you should switch back to your 16-ouncer, especially when you're using the nailset.

■ **Saw**—Buy a top-quality crosscut saw and keep it razor sharp. When cutting trim, for instance, the saw should have little, or no, set.

■ **Square**—Purchase a first-rate combination square and give it the treatment that accurate measuring tools deserve.

How to use a sabre saw

By HARRY WICKS

■ THE TASKS SHOWN on these pages are jobs that make owning a sabre saw a must. Making cutouts is a frequent need in the shop, as well as in household carpentry. Once you've mastered good sabre-saw technique, you will make better cutouts faster than you've ever done before.

A frequently asked question is, "Which sabre saw should I buy?" I answer the same way that I do for all tools—portable or stationary: "Choose the tool that will handle the jobs you expect to do." For example, if you plan to use your sabre saw primarily for around-the-house carpentry tasks—where you can expect lots of cuts in walls and ceilings—I'd recommend a lightweight version, so your arms won't tire.

But if you will use a sabre saw in the shop most of the time, as I do, pick a heftier tool with a good-sized shoe. This will allow greater control and accuracy when cutting on the workbench or over a pair of sawhorses.

For many homeowners who plan to use the tool occasionally, a sabre saw in the $40 to $60 range should suffice.

cutting straight lines

For rough work, cuts can be made freehand. However, because of the vibration caused by the reciprocating blade, you are well advised to use some sort of guide against which the saw shoe can bear when making any straight cut requiring accuracy.

If the straight line is within the capacity of the rip guide that came with your saw, use it whenever possible (photo at top of this column). You will notice that the guide is designed to engage the workpiece edge *before* the blade enters the edge.

It's a good idea, when using the rip guide, to hold it against the work edge with one hand. If you let the saw travel into the waste area too frequently, you may have trouble picking up and following that line later—even with the guide.

For straight cuts on the interior of a panel of plywood, you can use a tacked-on wooden strip. To eliminate any chance of bowing, use a 4d finishing nail every 12 in. or so. Mark the guide's location from the cutting line in a number of places and pull the straightedge to it as you nail your way down the line.

To cut a perfect circle, you should know about a couple of professional tricks:

■ Though your first inclination may be to insert a fine-tooth woodcutting blade, don't. The blade to use for a circle cut is a rough-cutting wood blade with a heavy tooth set. The reason is that this blade will cut sufficient clearance for making the turn accurately. Cut outside the line so you'll have stock to sand smooth.

■ Second, cut with the maximum saw strokes per inch. To do it, use a fast saw speed and a slow feed.

WHEN MAKING a straight cut near an edge, use your rip guide. Position guide so kerf will be on waste side of line. This way, if saw leaves work edge, it will drift into waste.

IF HOLES in workpiece don't matter, use a wooden strip tacked on with 4d finishing nails. To do it, mark location of guide every 12 in. along work, then pull the strip to each mark as you tack-fasten. Fasten well to prevent bowing.

IF YOUR SABRE SAW makes bevel cuts, the straightedge guide *must* be clamped on the side toward which the saw pulls during a bevel cut. Use a rough-cut blade and a slow feed. To avoid any chance of injury to the hand holding the board in front of the saw, clamp entire setup to sawhorses that work straddles.

WHEN THE WORKPIECE can't be marred, use a wide board (which won't bow) and C-clamps, as shown here.

TO MAKE plunge cut, tip saw onto front edge of shoe, then start motor.

SLOWLY—with tool held securely— lower the moving blade into the waste.

THIS BLADE is designed to let you cut right up to a vertical or horizontal surface. It's useful for cutting flooring up to a wall or countertop.

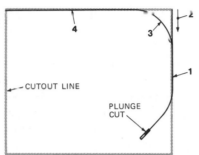

WHEN BLADE is fully into work, with saw shoe flat, cut toward one of the cutout lines (1) and then cut straight into the corner. With blade moving, back the saw up (2) and turn corner (3). Step 4 simply repeats step 1 and so on.

WHEN CUTOUT is dropped, reverse saw 180° and cut out triangular-shaped corner pieces. Note that workpiece straddles either 2x3s or sawhorses for blade clearance and maximum support.

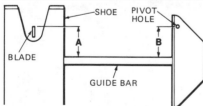

THE RIP GUIDE that comes with this saw features a drilled hole so that the guide can be used to make circles. The pivot point (nail) must be lined up with the *front* edge of the blade, as shown in the drawing above.

STOP THE SAW periodically when cutting circle so workpiece can be shifted on its support. The saw blade should cut only the work, not the supports.

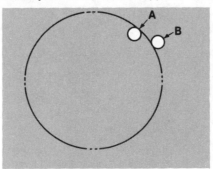

IF CUTOUT OPENING must be perfect, bore entry hole A. For a neat disc, start with entry hole B.

PERFECT CIRCLE needs nail hole at center filled and sanded and its edges smoothed; then it's ready for finishing.

FOR BEST RESULTS when cutting a circle, use a rough blade with a heavy set. Push the saw with a slow feed rate and, if your saw has variable speed, set it to the fastest cutting speed to obtain the maximum strokes per inch.

PM experts test four new tools

New, exciting tools that serve a variety of functions come on the market all the time. Here we take a look at just how well some of these tools performed in actual workshop sessions, under on- the-job conditions, by PM craftsmen. We tried to find out if these tools were really worth the money

SANDER/GRINDER ACCESSORY

■ THE ProEdge, a handy attachment for your sander/grinder, makes sharpening chores easier and helps to assure accurate results. It is particularly useful for sharpening those tools that have a curved cross section, since it allows you to rotate the tool on its axis while you are grinding.

The accessory consists of a special platen (metal plate which provides a hard backing for the grinding belt) and an adjustable tool support. Both parts can be quickly attached to most sander/grinders. However, the unit will not fit models that are manufactured by Foley. Specify the make of tool you have when ordering the sharpening attachment.

The platen, against which the grinding belt rides, is shaped to allow both flat and hollow grinding. The tool support arm has a toolrest with a depression for centering tool handles. It can be adjusted to produce any degree of bevel desired. The conveniently indexed arm provides a means to regrind or touch up previously sharpened tools.

The ProEdge attachment is available from Prakto Inc., Box 1023, Birmingham, MI 48012, for about $50 postpaid. This includes six belts and lube wax. The stropping belt with compound is about $15 postpaid.

—*Rosario Capotosto*

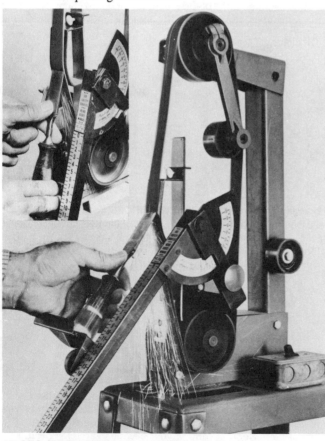

EDGES ON CHISELS, gouges, parting tools are easy to hone. Grind hollow bevels against platen curve (inset).

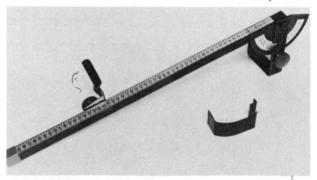

ACCESSORY FITS most sander/grinders.

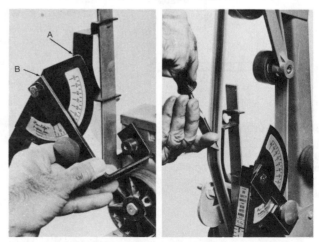

MOUNT BRACKET to pulley arbor (left). When stropping, point cutting edge in direction of best movement.

POWER MITERBOX

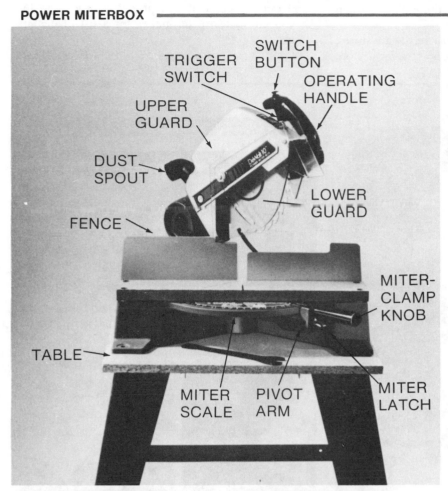

VERSATILE miter saw can produce very smooth cuts (A) when you use a sharp blade and slow feed. For fast job you can switch to coarser rip blade with fast feed (B).

SPECIFICATIONS—POWER MITERBOX

Model: 7717
Motor: 10.5 amps., 120 v.a.c.
No-load blade speed: 5500 rpm
Blade: 10-in. diameter
Blade arbor: 5/8-in. diameter
Capacity: 3 5/8-in. height; 4 1/4-in. width
Positive miter stops: 0°, 22 1/2°, 45° (right and left)
Cord length: 8 ft.
Weight: 34 lbs.
Price: About $249
Manufacturer: DeWalt Div., Black & Decker Inc., 715 Fountain
   Ave., Box 4548, Lancaster, Pa. 17604

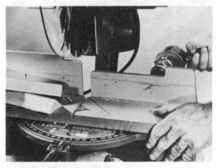

FOR CUTTING crown and cove moldings, make jig shown. Rip 45° spacers, mark fence, bore for screws.

USE CUTOFF from spacers and a clamp to hold jig while you install screws to hold spacers to fence.

WITH BOTH pieces in place, it's a snap to cut accurate, neat-looking miters on crown and cove moldings.

■ SINCE MY WORKSHOP is already equipped with a healthy 10-in. radial saw, I really questioned the value of adding a power miterbox to it. (A radial saw, of course, readily cuts miters.) After trying one out, though, I found that it's a welcome addition.

The saw is a precision tool that takes the frustration out of miter cutting. The angle-measuring scale on the machine is calibrated in half-degree increments, making it possible to cut a 1/4° setting. To do so, you simply move the pivot arm so its center mark is between two 1/2° graduations and lock it there.

The miter latch has detents at 0°, 22 1/2° and 45°, right and left (the most common miter angles). You swing the pivot arm to the desired angle detent and lock it in place by rotating the miter clamp knob.

The power miterbox handles in craftsmanlike fashion. It's well made and, with reasonable care and attention, should give many years of first-rate service. The blade brake makes the tool extra safe; the blade stops almost immediately when trigger switch is released.

The tool is available at many hardware stores, home centers and lumberyards. If a local store doesn't stock it, it can probably order one for you; or write to the maker for a list of dealers near you.

—*Harry Wicks*

LARGE-CAPACITY BAND SAW

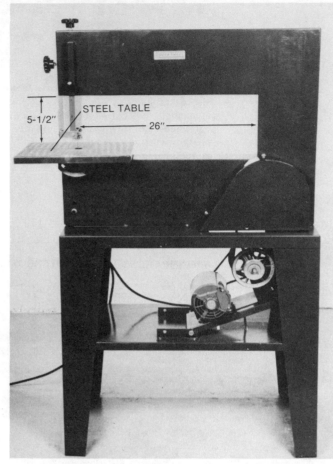

STEEL TABLE

5-1/2"

26"

UNIT CAN halve 4-ft. panels and cut large, irregular shapes.

BLADE-ADJUSTMENT KNOB

BLADE TENSIONING KNOB

6" DRIVE WHEELS

BLADE GUIDES

UNUSUAL four-wheel design allows deeper throat than possible with two-wheel saws. Top knobs are for blade adjustments.

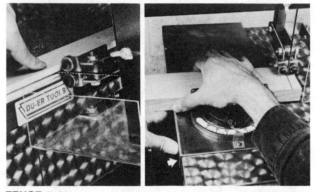

DU-ER TOOLS

FENCE (left), when used for resawing, allows no play to correct tracking. L-shape miter gauge rides table edge.

■ A BAND SAW really broadens your woodworking capabilities. But if you're setting up a shop on a tight budget, it is an unrealistic purchase. One economical alternative is one of the

SPECIFICATIONS—B-26 BAND SAW

Throat: 26 in.
Depth of cut: 5½ in. (6 in. with plastic guard removed)
Saw dimensions: 18 in. wide × 30 in. high × 36 in. long
Table construction: Reinforced sheet steel
Table size: 16 × 16 in.
Blade sizes: ⅛ to ½ in. × 109 in.
Drive wheels: 8-in. diameter
Price: $364.90 for complete machine with stand, ⅓-hp motor; $49.95 for jackshaft reduction gear for metal cutting.
Shipping weight: 148 lbs.
Accessories: Table extension, B-241; miter gauge, B-242; rip fence, B-243-H; stand, W-264 (welded) or B-264 (bolted).
Manufacturer: Du-er Tools, 5448 Edina Industrial Blvd., Minneapolis, Minn. 55435

SHOP-MADE saw dolly improves stability by widening base.

DOLLY DETAIL

1-1/2 x 1-1/2 x 34"
(2 REQD.)
FASTEN WITH
NO. 10 x 2" FH
SCREWS AND GLUE

3/8" PLYWOOD,
SIZE TO FIT
INSIDE STAND
LEGS; FASTEN
WITH 6d FINISHING
NAILS AND GLUE

1-1/2 x 1-1/2 x 22"
(2 REQD.)

4"

2" BED CASTER
(4 REQD.)
FASTEN WITH
NO. 8 x 1-1/2"
RH SCREWS

1/4"-DIA. BORE (4 PLACES)
BORE MATCHING HOLES IN STAND FEET
AND FASTEN WITH FOUR 1/4"-DIA. x 2"
CAPSCREWS, NUTS AND WASHERS

small portable band saws that have become quite popular lately. If you have the space, however, a large-size, low-priced tool might suit you. Three features recommend the one shown here:

■ It's a large-capacity unit.

■ A six-pulley transmission system allows multiple operating speeds. You can change over quickly from speeds of 860 ft. per minute (fpm) for cutting wood to 160 fpm for cutting metal and plastic.

■ The price is right. This saw costs significantly less than saws of equivalent capacity.

There are compromises, however. I found the miter gauge, fence and blade guides awkward to use and adjust. The tilting table is not as rigid as that found on saws that have cast mounts. Finally, you must undo 14 wingnuts if the blade requires changing or rubber wheels need to be reattached.

—*Joseph R. Provey*

Note: Since our test, the manufacturer has informed us that a heavy-duty, cast table will be offered and that the miter gauge will ride in a groove. In addition, the housing door has been made easier and faster to open.

BENCH GRINDER

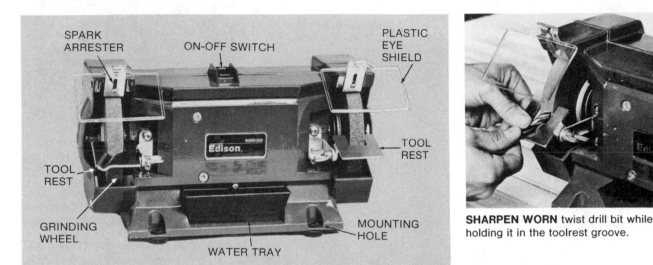

THE 6-IN. bench grinder has two wheel stations, comes with built-in motor.

SHARPEN WORN twist drill bit while holding it in the toolrest groove.

SQUARE screwdriver tip after reshaping blade by holding on rest, touching wheel.

CONVENIENT water tray allows frequent quenching to prevent loss of temper.

SPECIFICATIONS—BENCH GRINDER
Model: 6-in., No. T 660216-A
Housing: Die-cast aluminum
Weight: 22¼ lbs.
Speed: 3450 rpm
Electric: 115 v.a.c.; 8 amps.; UL-listed
Grinding wheels: Fine and coarse (included)
Price: $80
Manufacturer: BenchMark Tool Co., 2601 Industrial Dr., Jefferson City, Mo. 65101

■ I RECENTLY TESTED a steady, fairly quiet bench grinder and found it handy for typical household grinding tasks.

The grinder is effective for sharpening various tools and, when used with a wire wheel, for cleaning rust off garden tools.

The toolrests adjust easily or they can be removed to obtain proper bevels or access to the wheels. Safety features include a spark arrester and eye-shield assembly. Fenders minimize the danger of a shattering wheel.

—*Joseph R. Provey*

Eight new yard tools

USED AS a cart (left) or dolly (below left), the MK II Tote Machine garden cart saves time and effort, has a welded tubular-steel frame with 9½x26x34-in. polyethylene bucket and carries up to 300 pounds. It's about $90 at garden centers or from Slacan, Division of Slater Steel Industries Ltd., Box 152, Buffalo, NY 14209. The optional accessories include: an extension bar for high loads, a garbage bag holder and a tie-down strap. It's handy for all kinds of gardening chores.

YOU CAN REDUCE a wheelbarrowful of prunings and twigs to as little as one-tenth its original bulk with the Quickrich shredder, according to its maker. The hand-powered machine shreds wet leaves, hedge clippings, cabbage stalks and twigs up to ⅜-in. diameter. A wooden rammer safely feeds the blade, which is set inside a slotted tube. The blade cuts cleanly against the tube slots. It's about $83 from Rotocrop Inc., 604 Aero Park, Doylestown, PA 18901.

THE 20-IN. self-propelled Model B726 mower by Ryan (left) features a controlled discharge, baffled 14-ga. steel housing and 3.5-hp Briggs & Stratton four-cycle, vertical-recoil-start engine. The rear-wheel-drive mower has fingertip height adjustment to five positions and wheel-assembly reinforcing in the housing. It's about $245. Write to Ryan Lawn-Care System, Outboard Marine Corp., Galesburg, IL 61401. They'll send you information on dealers in your area.

TORO'S newest electric mower (above) is the first to use monofilament cutting lines instead of a steel blade. Besides cutting a 20-in. swath, the lines extend ¾ in. beyond the wheels so you can trim around objects. Two counter-rotating discs (above right), each having two cutting lines, are powered by separate motors. As the lines wear, a lever feeds out new line and cuts it to the proper length. It's $220 from Toro Co., 8009 34th Ave. S., Minneapolis, MN 55420.

A LIGHTWEIGHT, three-pound string trimmer from Bolens attaches to all of that firm's electric-start riding mowers and garden tractors. The trimmer, which rides along on its own carrying bracket on the machine, is simply hooked up to either the solenoid or battery, depending on the vehicle model. The 12-volt trimmer cuts a 9-in. swath and has a 20-ft. straight cord and a 10-ft. coiled cord. You tap the trimmer on the ground to activate the automatic line feed when needed. The Bolens trimmer is about $67 from FMC Corp., Outdoor Power Equipment Div., 215 South Park St., Port Washington, WI 53074. Write to them for further details on this trimmer/mower combination.

THE CHEW CHEW lawn vacuum not only picks up leaves and clippings, but mulches and bags them in one operation. The machine reduces lawn debris to one-eighth its original volume, the maker claims. The self-propelled, 5-hp unit has a 10-bushel capacity. Attachments include a shredder-hopper for shredding branches, a 10-ft. flexible hose for vacuuming hard-to-reach spots and a blower to herd debris into piles for easy pickup. The Chew Chew lawn vacuum retails for about $900. Further information on the Chew Chew can be obtained by writing the manufacturer, Lambert Corporation, 519 Hunter Ave., Dayton OH 45404.

THIS LIGHTWEIGHT, front line tiller is designed for suburban farmers with small tilling, mulching, weeding and composting jobs. It has a four-stroke, 2-hp Honda engine and a transportation wheel to insure good mobility. For easy in-use handling, the 20½-in.-wide tines stop turning once the clutch lever is released. The tiller is made by American Honda Motor Co. Inc., Power Products Div., 100 West Alondra Blvd., Gardena, CA 90247. It sells for about $280.

THIS COMPACT TRACTOR has an 11-hp Briggs electric-start engine and a five-speed transmission. The rear bagger has five-bushel capacity and fits Wheel Horse B-series tractors with tunnel-design mowers. Two removable containers collect clippings. A transparent tube allows a visual check of clipping flow. The tractor is about $1335, mower $390 and bagger $200 from Wheel Horse, 515 W. Ireland Rd., South Bend, IN 46614.

Your chain saw powers this winch

By R. JOSEPH

■ IT'S QUITE A FEELING to be able to haul up to 8,000 pounds by pulling the trigger of a chain saw. That's what you can do with this winch designed to be powered by a chain-saw head.

Such a tool is ideal for hauling firewood from places where your truck won't go. It would also be invaluable for stream or pond cleanup, dragging elk or deer out of a canyon, pulling a truck out of mud or a ditch, tightening fences and pulling machinery onto trailers.

WINCH POWERED by a chain saw pulled these two 16-ft. logs 150 ft. up a ravine.

CHAIN at end of the cable is looped and secured around the log that is to be moved.

BEFORE USE, a chain is fastened to the winch clevis (inset) and secured to a tree.

UNIT HOLDS 150 ft. of ³⁄₁₆-in.-dia. aircraft cable or 250 ft. of ⅛-in. cable.

SPECIFICATIONS—CHAIN-SAW WINCH

Construction: Tenzalloy aluminum
Capacity: 8,000 lbs. with snatch block
Weight: 20 lbs.
Prices: Winch with fair-lead and choice of cable (³⁄₁₆ in. or ⅛ in.), $365; snatch block, $15.35; ⅛-in. × 250-ft. cable, $48; ³⁄₁₆ × 150-ft. cable, $42
Manufacturer: Fred A. Lewis Co., 40 Belknap Rd., Medford, Ore. 97501

THE WINCH can be used only with a chain saw having an accessible drive sprocket.

BRAKE
AIRCRAFT CABLE
ANCHOR CLEVIS
GEAR HOUSING
CHAIN-SAW HEAD

SAW SPROCKET

This compact, easily transported welding kit is ideal for small welding jobs around the house. Gas is low in cost and widely available

REPAIRING the broken leg support of a chair is a job easily handled by the Tote-Weld. The complete kit, including gas cylinders, comes in a sturdy plastic carrying case as shown above.

Light-duty welding rig

By BOB BERGER

■ TOTE-WELD is a light-duty, easily portable outfit. Made by Mapp Products, a division of Airco Inc., the outfit weighs only 30 pounds, and has a sturdy plastic case with a comfortable handle.

Unlike many other welding rigs, this one is ready to use as soon as you connect the hoses and regulators. It comes with a 20-cu.-ft. refillable oxygen tank and a 1-pound Mapp gas disposable cylinder.

Mapp gas may not be as familiar to home workshoppers as acetylene, but it has some important advantages. The gas smells—or more aptly, it stinks—so there's little possibility of a leak going unnoticed. Mapp gas cylinders are safe against shock. In the manufacturer's evaluation studies, full cylinders were dropped, hammered, and even blasted with dynamite, but none of the cylinders exploded, according to the company.

In my opinion, the best thing about Mapp gas is its wide availability and low cost. I bought a cylinder for $5.49 at a local discount department store. Because the fuel is easy to get, I don't keep a large supply on hand.

Putting the Tote-Weld through its paces proved that it can do the job despite its small size. As delivered, it can cut up to ⅜-in. steel plate and weld ³⁄₃₂-in.-thick steel.

The Tote-Weld is carried by welding supply houses only. Check your classified directory for a dealer carrying Mapp products.

About $200, the Tote-Weld includes torch, welding and cutting tips, tanks of oxygen and Mapp gas, regulators for each hose, spark lighter, goggles, brazing flux, rods and manual.

TORCH IS WELL balanced and has a comfortable grip. Oxygen is fed to work by pressing the button.

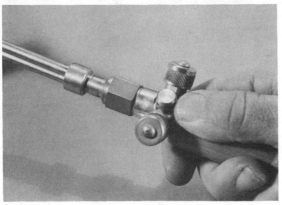

TOOL IS USED to make diagonal cut in angle iron. Kit includes cutting tips for steel to ⅜ in. thick.

Secrets of towing with a compact car

■ WHEN SMALL CARS and big gas bills arrived several years ago, there was fear that trailering was going to be a casualty. Then it looked as if towing a camper to the hills, or a runabout to the lake, might become just a pleasant memory. But now we are learning compact cars can be

recreation vehicles, too—with an important difference.

Recently, we tested an interesting assortment of small cars pulling various trailered boats. The good word is that every rig worked well—because we paid special attention to details: Safety

By BILL MCKEOWN

Coleman camper, with canoe and motor, is easily towed behind a Plymouth Reliant. Dodge Omni pulls a full VersaTrailer.

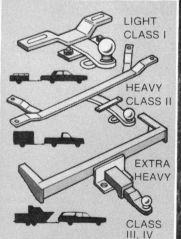

LIGHT
CLASS I

HEAVY
CLASS II

EXTRA
HEAVY

CLASS
III, IV

Hitches in Class I are for trailers under 2,000 pounds. Class II is under 4,000. Classes III and IV tow rigs under 10,000 pounds total.

Over a ton of Glastron-Carlson and motor proves no problem for 4wd Eagle.

An aluminum DuraCraft bass boat with 25-hp and trolling motor is easy for AMC SX/4.

Jeep Scrambler had no trouble launching and hauling 1,420-pound Larson Wild Fire rig.

A Grumman 4.6, rigged at 1,020 pounds, rolls behind Reliant.

Aluminum scores again as a 680-pound Fisher 15 rig climbs a steep ramp with Ford Escort

New options and accessories can make the difference between safe and scary trailering

factors, load matching and performance features must be considered more carefully.

We checked out 10 cars from Detroit manufacturers.

From American Motors we had an Eagle wagon, SX/4 and Jeep CJ5. All three vehicles had the 4.2-liter Six under the hood.

From Chevrolet we used two Citations, one with 2.5-liter Four and the other with 2.8-liter V6 and towing package. A third Chevy was a Chevette with 1.6-liter Four.

From Ford there was a Fairmont with 3.3-liter Six and an Escort with the 1.6-liter Four.

From Chrysler we had a Plymouth Reliant with 2.6-liter Four and a Dodge Omni with 2.2-liter Four.

We tried the cars with a number of boats of various sizes.

We packed a Zodiac inflatable and 7.5-hp Evinrude into a Coleman VersaTrailer. That combo weighs in at about 500 pounds.

We tried a 15-foot aluminum Fisher—with 15-hp Johnson mounted—on a Gator trailer—680 pounds.

AIR LIFT, inflated inside rear coil spring of a compact car, helps to prevent sagging.

On the heavy end, we went to 3,540 pounds with a Cobia Odyssey cruiser, powered by an OMC sterndrive. That one we hitched to the four-wheel-drive AMC Eagle.

We had no trouble driving at speed, or muscling the boats up and down launching ramps. Trouble-free towing is easy when you understand the following rules:

■ Match of tow load to car and driving conditions comes first. It should be figured out before you buy your rig, and must be more exact than ever before.

The weight a compact can handle is determined by size, power and type of car, plus the routes that you will drive. It is also estimated by

EVEN A STERNDRIVE cruiser—nearly two tons with trailer—can be towed by a four-wheel drive car.

ONCE LIFTED and bolted into place, the load-distributing arms of the equalizing hitch level the load to both the front and back wheels.

IN ADDITION to the load-leveling of the hitch, sway bars secured below the trailer tongue will prevent the rig from excessive fishtailing.

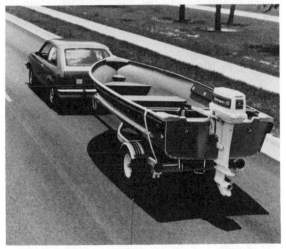

A SMALL CAR towing a light aluminum boat needs a Class I hitch (under 2,000 pounds).

COMPACT'S cargo capacity can expand with Le Trunk. It's made by U.S. Trailer of Livonia, MI.

USE OF TRUCK scales is the only accurate way to figure the weight of the car, rig and gear.

■ The type of driving you do and the routes you follow are going to be important. Frequent hauling of a heavy trailer at maximum speeds over hills and deserts to a steep launching ramp can strain your compact, overheat it and possibly wreck it. Offroad running across rugged terrain may punch away at springs and shocks. Lugging up steep slopes and spinning wheels in sandy spots could cook your engine and transmission oil and put added burdens on drivetrain and brakes. Bucking whipsaw gusts from passing trucks and pushing through strong winds can make steering difficult and dangerous with a heavyweight in tow.

Hitting the road for an occasional easy run over flat roads to a level campsite or launching hoist is a different towing matter. Though your car dealer and manufacturer aren't likely to admit it, a certain amount of safety factor is usually figured into their rules for towing. But the smaller your car, the more critical the limits can be. You can possibly get away with occasional overloading, but the days of casually hooking up a trailer to a makeshift bumper hitch disappeared with the arrival of smaller cars and engines.

■ A car manufacturer's "tow package" used to be a possible option. Now it should be considered essential, if available. Again, ask before buying. Not many "RPOs" (regular production options) can be added later on without difficulty and considerable expense.

If you have a choice, consider a large engine, a high engine-to-wheel axle ratio, automatic transmission, heavy-duty suspension and radiator, power brakes and steering, heavy-duty battery and generator, equalizing hitch and platform mount and a trailer-wiring harness. You might also think about how much time you'll spend on the road and opt for tinted glass, cruise control, luggage rack, dash instruments, tilting steering wheel, reclining seats, spotlights and high-intensity running lights, airconditioner, CB radio and the rest.

With trailer in tow, you may find driving much easier and more comfortable at lower (and more economical) speeds. That will make trips longer, and you're likely to appreciate how much less tiring it is, for example, to drive with closed windows shutting out traffic noise and wind buffeting, as you can with airconditioning.

Your transmission will often heat up during heavy driving with a trailer in tow. An extra radiator to cool it is not usually a predelivery option, but is an important aftermarket item to consider, and can be installed by your dealer, at a garage, or at home if you are a good mechanic. Side mirrors and other trailer accessories are easy do-it-yourself installations. Only the attachment of hydraulic trailer brakes that are cut into your car's brake lines should be left to the experts.

■ Balance and level ride is particularly important for your smaller car. Weight on the rear of a light car tends to lift the front wheels, endangering steering control for any vehicle and reducing traction for the popular models with front-wheel drive. Choice of the proper load-balancing hitch, plus rear spring booster or air shocks will help. Supplies and luggage stored in the back of the car and in the boat or trailer behind can also ruin level balance and cause a rear sag.

Tongue weight on the hitch ball should be 10 percent of the trailer load, and total weight of loaded car and trailer should be checked on a truck loading scale. Luggage, passengers and gear in the car and trailer can make the total weight soar. Never level an overloaded trailer by moving gear back to lighten the tongue weight. This is dangerous.

■ The equalizing hitch is engineered to lever weight forward through the chassis and distribute the trailer load to the front wheels as well as the rear. Trailers of any weight can use it, and those of 2,000 pounds and up (Class II and above) should always use it. Sway bars can be added to help reduce fishtailing. Reese, Draw Tite, Eaz-Lift and Valley Tow-Rite are among the makers of these clever devices, with custom models for most small cars. You can fit them on or they can be installed by trailer dealers like Hitch World, a new U-Haul division with over 1,000 branches around the United States and Canada. Accessories such as wiring harnesses and transmission coolers are also available.

■ Trailer brakes are essential for small-car towing of larger rigs, and some compacts require their use. Surge brakes are the simplest; they automatically slow the trailer as the car decelerates. Electric brakes fitted to a trailer allow control by the car driver.

Acceleration with a small car is going to be slower and passing will be trickier, but using a small car to tow a lightweight trailer or boat need not cramp your style.

So, go by the book. Refer to the owner's manual, and check with the manufacturer if you don't think the manual gives you the answers. You need to work out those details before you buy the car, take delivery and hitch up.

the manufacturer, and you'd better find out what he allows before you void your warranty.

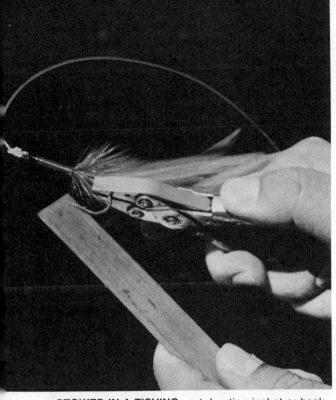

STOWED IN A FISHING vest, hunting jacket or back-pack, a file like the Red Devil No. 3915 paint-scraper sharpener can be pulled out when needed to put a fast edge on fishhooks or tools.

Putting an edge on sportsman's tools

Here's a sharp method for making a point or sharpening a blade afield. Using dull tools is dangerous. A small file can restore sharpness wherever you happen to be

By BOB STEARNS

■ AN EXTRA-SHARP POINT can make all the difference in hooking a bony-mouthed trophy, but hooks and gaffs aren't the only edged and pointed tools that are essential outdoors.

A wide variety of knives, axes, hatchets and machetes also play an important role. Yet many sportsmen don't seem to know about the new techniques that can make sharpening easier.

No competent fishing guide or charter-boat skipper would set off without the means for re-sharpening hooks, gaffs and fileting knives. Nor would a professional hunting guide be caught in the woods without a keen blade and an implement to sharpen it. Yet many anglers fish with dull hooks, or go afield with a knife barely capable of skinning out warm butter.

And how do you chop firewood with a dull ax? With great difficulty and considerable danger. Not only are dull cutting tools ineffective, but they can bounce or skid away from the impact point. It's easy to get careless with a dull edge and try to overcome poor cutting by applying extra pressure. The result can be a nasty cut. Blades can be honed on a wheel or large stone at home, but that's often not practical afield or offshore, and hooks need special treatment. Here's what has worked for me.

Unquestionably, the best tool for sharpening

fishhooks is a file. Hooks usually don't come from the manufacturer as sharp as they should be, and the same sometimes applies to knives and axes. The right file cuts metal faster than any stone, even a diamond-dust hone. The file also shapes cutting edges along the sides of the point, something that's almost impossible with any stone.

You'll get arguments about the most effective shape of a point. Popular with professional guides and knowledgeable anglers are the diamond shape, triangular cut, spear point and round shape. All except the round have sharp cutting edges along the sides of the hook point that enable it to push its way through tough bone and cartilage. I like the diamond, since four cutting edges should be better than three, and use it on all hooks except those too small to accept four cutting edges. Then it's either a spear point or round shape (if it's so small that any shaping would weaken it).

How sharp is "sharp"? Long ago, a charter-boat skipper advised that the best way to test a hook is with your fingernail, not the tip of your finger. If the point isn't sharp enough to "hang" on the hard surface of the back of your nail when sliding it across with only slight pressure, then it certainly isn't sharp enough to "hang" inside the hard mouth of a fish.

HOW SHARP? Slide the point of the fishhook lightly across your fingernail. If it snags, it will catch fish.

GLUE to the back of your fishing-pliers holster a small sheath to hold a tungsten ignition-point file.

FOR PUTTING a piercing point on a gaff, you may find strokes toward the tip work the best.

IN THE FIELD, with no whetstone available, the tiny ignition-point file can resharpen a knife blade.

the best hook sharpener

Some years ago, famous outdoorsman Lefty Kreh discovered the ideal hook sharpener: a Red Devil No. 3915 file, from the Red Devil Co., Union, NJ. This particular file was designed for sharpening the tough blades of paint scrapers. It's at most hardware stores for around $4, and occasionally in tackle shops. Dick Schotter, director of engineering for Red Devil, describes the No. 3915 as a "machinist general-purpose" model, capable of filing almost anything.

Unlike other files, it's unusual in appearance—rectangular rather than tapered—8¼ inches long by ¾ inch wide, and with both surfaces flat. Because it has a large tang (handle), it's easy to grip firmly and apply with lots of pressure. The fine teeth can cut anything short of an extremely hard-tempered knife blade; even on this you can touch up nicks if the knife was properly sharpened.

Even tougher is the tiny file I carry in a sheath glued to the underside of my fishing-pliers holster. Called an "ignition" or "tungsten" point file (the Nicholson No. 02381 is an example), this mini costs only about a dollar.

I also keep one in my fishing vest, plus several spares in the tackle box. It's 5¼ inches long by ⁵⁄₁₆

inch wide. I usually break 1½ inches off the 2¼-inch tang, leaving a ¾-inch handle. Slipping a length of small-diameter rubber or plastic tubing over this makes a good handle.

This ignition-point file can sharpen small hooks, right down to a No. 20 dry fly. Because it is designed for use on tungsten—a very hard metal—it will also smooth the toughest steel in any knife blade.

The files mentioned are ideal for the outdoorsman because they're lighter and more compact than a sharpening stone, and virtually unbreakable, as well. However, they can't produce quite the ultimate, even sharpness that's possible at home with a good stone. For cutting tools, the best approach is to carefully sharpen all tools before setting out. Then use the files to restore sharpness and smooth rough edges dulled with use, as well as point up hooks.

Because a file works best when the pressure stroke is toward the work, you must push the file forward against the sharp edge. Don't try to make a stroke using the full length of the file's cutting surface. That puts your hand too close to the edge of the knife or ax. Apply pressure during the forward stroke only, unlike sharpening a hook. Dragging the file back across the edge

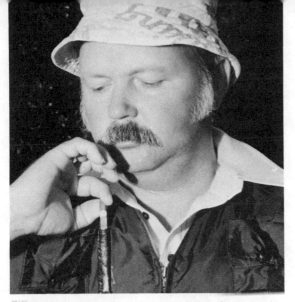

FIT A SPARE ignition file into a pocket of your vest. Break off tang and tape the handle.

VERSATILE rectangular file sharpens knife quickly. Use short strokes to keep fingers from blade.

you're trying to sharpen will only dull it. Lift the file off the blade completely until you're ready to start the forward pressure stroke. Apply only enough pressure to feel the file cutting the metal evenly. Too much pressure may clog the file's teeth.

With a stone or file, count the number of strokes and use an equal number on each side of the blade. If possible, watch an expert like Al Buck, famous for his Buck knives, demonstrate sharpening at a sportsman's show. Note the thin angle he holds between blade and stone. It may appear that he uses a back-and-forth motion, but actually his pressure stroke will be as the blade cuts toward the stone; pressure is relieved and the blade floats back on the return stroke.

Only water is likely to damage a file seriously. If it's put away wet, rust is certain to appear in a few days; salt water can cause rust overnight. Some anglers make a simple leather sheath for their file, and keep this well oiled.

I do the same with the sheaths for my tiny ignition-point files, and have found I can usually get a full year's use out of each one this way.

In an emergency, you can sharpen a soft-steel knife or ax somewhat with a lot of things. Try a hand-sized flat rock, a brick or a chunk of concrete if nothing better is available. But for the sharpest—and safest—results, use a Carborundum or Arkansas stone for basics and pack away a file right now for knives and hooks afield.

SKILLED HAND of knifemaker Al Buck, of Buck Knives, strokes the edge *toward* the stone for a keen blade.

EVEN A ROCK will serve as a makeshift whetstone. Using a dull knife or ax requires dangerous extra pressure.

SEVERAL popular cutting shapes for hooks are shown.

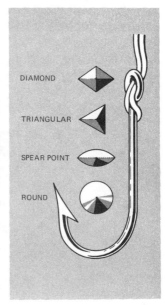

DIAMOND

TRIANGULAR

SPEAR POINT

ROUND

1 Mounted on the $12.75 Rhode Rack Ultra rear carrier are Velocipac rear carrier bags, $56.

2 The Hanna Pro Helmet, $38, is recommended for BMX biking.

3 Zefal Hp tire pump, for $12.75, is designed for the high pressures of bicycle tires.

4 Velocipac Bar bag, $32, mounts on the center bar out of the way, but convenient for the rider.

5 Cannondale Cycling Gloves, $15, have padded palms of leather.

6 The $300 Veltec Pacer 2000H handlebar meter monitors the rate of a rider's heartbeat, distance pedaled in miles or kilometers, speed and elapsed time.

7 The 25-pound $395 Bickerton Portable folds to fit carrying bag.

New for better biking

■ A LOOK AT today's improved bikes and gear tells why the sport continues to grow. And a preview of the pedal-powered streamliners may be a forecast for the budget transportation of tomorrow.

Specialty machines for touring, for speed, for commuting, for

BIKE TRAILER that can carry a lot, the Blue Sky has optional seats with safety belts and other extras that push the $165 price up to $250.

trails and mountains, for bicycle motocross, for kids, and just for cruising are all being developed. Some bike builders believe new streamlining can lower the wind resistance of that major cause of drag—the rider—and are designing special enclosures. Bikes can now top the legal speed limit for cars, with engineer Al Voight's Huffy Vector tricycle recording 56.66 mph over a short course, and covering 36.94 miles in one hour. Huffy, America's largest bicycle manufacturer, considers the Vector a prototype of commuting models for the future. A 15-speed Wind model is currently in production, and Huffy is developing an Aerowind model with aerodynamic improvements.

Folding, take-apart and collapsible cycles stow in a closet, car trunk, boat or plane. The lighter the bike, the higher the price: You can get a 40-

Bicycle built for one—or two

■ THERE'S A BICYCLE manufacturer in Oakland, CA, turning out not only old-fashioned high wheelers, but also a brand-new type of bike, the convertible tandem.

Two bicycle enthusiasts, Mel Barron and

A SPECIAL center section on Rideable's folding bicycle can accommodate a seat, handlebars and crank which easily convert a two-wheeler for one into a tandem for two.

Diana Hoffman, founded Rideable Bicycle Replicas Inc. in 1975 to reproduce copies of 19th-century high wheelers. Then in 1981, Mel designed and patented the convertible tandem.

The convertible tandem promises to fill a need. If you've ever owned a conventional tandem, you know that riding one can be lots of fun *when* and *if* you find a partner. But partners aren't always available, so most tandem bikes tend to spend long periods gathering dust.

Rideable's convertible tandem, though, gives you a choice. Any time you can't talk someone into going for a spin, simply remove the tandem's center section and go biking alone.

The removable center section contains the forward seat, sprocket, and handlebars. In roughly two minutes, using only a screwdriver

SHIMANO claims that its new cluster gear and rear hub give smoother, easier shifts.

pound foldup for about $150, but a neat, 23-pound Pocket Bike goes for $1,000. (All prices were in effect at the time this was written).

Today's cyclists have specific demands and a number of specialized bikes are the result. Junior racing, off-road travel, distance runs and short shopping trips all rate special machines.

BMX bikes are used by youngsters for the pedal-power equivalent of dirt-track motocross. From a starting grid about 10 feet high, the track narrows into a series of jumps and bumps, straightaways and banked-berm turns that challenge the riders over a quarter-mile course. Off-shoots from BMX include events down rugged hills on "thrasher" bikes and acrobatic rides on bikes called "tricksters."

Kids who don't graduate to mopeds often try mountain bikes—light, balloon-tired, trail-rider specials with high crank-to-ground clearance for off-road backpackers. A tamer version, also with conventional handlebars, is the 'round-town cruiser. And for distance pedaling, there are the lightweight, multigear tourers, cousins of the racing machines.

Helmets, bags, speed-distance-heartbeat monitors are some modern refinements. Over a dozen trailers are on the market and assorted improvements in gears and gadgets are available.

and pliers, anyone can pull out this center section, reconnect the front and rear halves, and ride off into the sunset.

You convert the gear mechanisms from tandem to single mode by undoing one chain link, removing the forward chain, unscrewing a short length of rear brake cable, and releasing two crank/thumb-screw pads on the frame. You then reattach the fore and aft frame pads and you're off.

Rideable's 20-inch tandem weighs less than 50 pounds and stores neatly in car trunks, boats, aircraft, RVs, closets and other small compartments. The bike can be purchased with seat posts of different heights for adults or children. Both sets of pedals freewheel independently, so if one rider wants to rest, he can. The tandem, which retails for about $375, comes in red, blue or white, and includes a toolbag. It'll be available soon. For more information write to Rideable Bicycle Replicas Inc., 2433-47 Telegraph Ave., Oakland, CA 94612.

high time for high wheels

Rideable is the only company in this country that builds old-fashioned high wheelers on a regular production basis. The firm currently offers two different-sized reproductions of 19th-century British high wheelers. These bikes were called penny-farthings because, at the time, the penny was a large coin and the farthing a small one—like the wheels of the bicycles. In Rideable's case, the front or "ordinary" wheels are 38 or 48 inches in diameter and the rear ones are 16 inches.

High wheelers were all the rage before 1874, when "safety" bicycles came into vogue. And it's true that high wheelers were neither terribly safe nor practical. But Mel Barron modified the design slightly by setting the seat lower on the frame for easier mounting and pedaling. The front fork is also a bit wider, as is the front axle, for better riding stability.

Some penny-farthings go to hobbyists and collectors. Since genuine high wheelers sell for $1,000 to $5,000, a collector might buy a $600 copy for enjoyment.

The 38-inch Rideable high wheeler lists for $599 in standard black; the 48-incher is about $25 more.

Goggles with powered fan

Plastic face mask

Neoprene ski suit

Aluminum poles with built-in shock absorber

Automatically retractable bindings

Aluminum honeycomb skis with split tail

Lever-action boots

RETRACTABLE BINDING (top—"locked" off ski for photo) uses sophisticated cable linkage to break away and snap back. Boot with "shock absorber" was designed by Porsche engineers.

Ski gear—straight from science fiction

The take-me-to-your-leader look reflects the state of the art in safer downhill gear, while the new trend toward all-terrain skiing moves in on the cross-country sport.

By JOHN ROSS

■ ONE LOOK at the current costumes and accouterments of skiing is enough to convince anybody that Darth Vader has just stepped down from the silver screen for a chase scene on skis.

Even the people whose lifts whisk skiers up to the mountaintops have some surprises in store. Trail patrols at several resorts, for example, carry hand-held radar guns to catch speeding skiers on the slopes. And one forward-thinking ski resort—world-famous Jackson Hole in Wyoming—even goes

INTEGRATION of binding and boot may be the next step in ski-tech hardware. The system shown is an experimental unit that is not in production yet.

Form-fitting racing suit

No-wax skis with variable fish-scale bottom surface

Fiberglass or graphite reinforced poles with cross-country baskets or rakes

Lightweight, all-plastic binding

Runner-shoe boots with notched heel

SKI BOTTOMS (below, left) incorporate no-wax surfaces; newest is the mica type (left), but fish-scale has found wide acceptance. Pole baskets have been radically altered—some into ''rakes.'' New lightweight, narrow bindings give full flex, while heel plate locks into boot for downhill steering control.

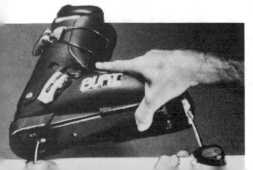

epoke 900

nowax

as far as to slap tickets on offending skis standing outside the base lodge during lunch breaks. The "ticket" in this case signifies that the skier's bindings appear to be deficient.

Downhill skiing's vital link in a package of necessary components is the binding. This curious contraption is as complicated as it looks because it must perform conflicting functions: The binding has to release whenever the forces of skiing (or falling) might cause injury—hence the terminology "release binding." It must also do what its name says—bind the skier to the ski. This latter function, referred to as retention, is obviously as critical to skiing as release.

Two basic types are available: the models that have separate release attachments for ski boots at toe and heel, and some less conventional designs that fit the boots to plates held onto the skis in a way that allows the plates to release with the boots. In general, the greatest possible number of release directions in toe/heel bindings, are three (left and right at toe; upward at heel), while with plate bindings, more release directions are possible.

Most plate bindings share the need with all toe/heel types for a means of keeping a released ski from sliding away downhill. The answer is a ski brake—"runaway straps" are unsafe and obsolete—which automatically deploys spring-loaded prongs at right angles to each ski's running surface when the boot disengages from the ski. The prongs catch in the snow and hold the ski.

A ONE-PIECE ski/boot? Kneissl produced this mock-up to show skiers that the idea has real possibilities.

retractable bindings

But the operating principle of the newest, most advanced plate binding does away with the brake by eliminating the need to get back into the bindings each time they release. It's a *retractable* ski binding, with two cables, one forward and one rear, extending from inside the plate and running on a system of tension-producing aluminum idler wheels.

The cables allow almost limitless angles of release. And when the force causing the binding to release is relieved, the ski simply *snaps back* of its own accord and fully engages with the plate to which the boot is attached. This recoiling device, dubbed the Burt binding by its American inventor, Burton Weinstein, is undoubtedly the state-of-the-art mechanism at this writing.

Recently, a major European binding manufacturer, named Marker, showed the world its prototype of an electronic binding, which raised,

among other queries, the as-yet-unanswered question: "What if the batteries go dead?"

At the moment, several binding makers at work designing electric models are mum about specific components. They do say that the use of tiny computer chips to calculate the resolution of forces acting on the binding is almost a certainty.

In the meantime, as work proceeds on various prototypes in secret, the ski business is buzzing about another fascinating concept: integrating the binding with the boot. But any boot/binding combination has certain clear-cut obstacles to overcome. Carrying around ski-release systems in the soles of footwear exposes them to severe wear not normally found in skiing.

One major ski manufacturer recently stirred up a blizzard of interest in the concept of integrating the ski boot and binding with a molded mock-up of what such a combination might look like. Meanwhile, Burt International already has a prototype of its binding contained in a boot (photo on page 147), a package that is intended for production in about five years.

Ski boots have already undergone radical departures of their own and have come a long way since Robert Lange's company introduced the first plastic-shell ski boot in the mid-1960s. The most apparent and consistent progress in ski-boot design has been the rise of the boot top.

This year's models will actually reach the upper extremities of the calf muscle. Not merely special boots for racing, these "knee-high" models have flexibility enough for intermediate skiers. Why so high? The higher the boot, the greater the leverage on the ski edges, but that's not the whole story. Experts also say these radical new boots can reduce the fatigue of skiing, relieve foot pressure and permit better blood circulation for more warmth.

Today's ski boots are impressive examples of evolutionary engineering, especially in terms of adjusting their fit. Rear-entry designs, adjustable spring-loaded buckles, and exterior screws and levers that change the inner contours are almost common. One brand-new boot has a built-in air pump to fill bladders positioned at the ankles. And mechanically adjusted forward flex and forward lean are both available on certain of the new boot models.

The revolutionary new boots shown in our photo on page 146 are called "lever boots," and they come with shock absorbers fitted to the levers. This rear-entry model from Kastinger in Austria has a long extension that fits against the front of the lower leg and rises almost to the knee. This lever is held in place by a loose-fitting cuff. The idea is to produce the leverage of high-top boots. In addition, there's an automotive-type, spring-loaded shock absorber between the lever and the toe (designed, incidentally, by Porsche car engineers).

The working principles of this lever boot, patented by an American engineering professor named Dan Post, include tapping the natural rotary motion of a skier's lower leg when making a turn and transferring it, through the lever, to the skis. The result is said to be greater edging (steering effect) from less effort and little body motion. Also, the shock-absorber strut allows free hinging between the upper and lower boot.

Among the more exotic ski developments are graphite-fiber reinforcing for strength; aluminum honeycomb, channeled fiberglass and acrylic-foam cores for lightness; plus various construction, impregnation and lamination methods, using materials like Kevlar for stiffness.

The latest design breakthrough in skis, however, is even more radical than the departure in the materials from which they are made: An American ski designer has actually changed one aspect of the basic shape of the ski. A V-shaped section has been cut out from the tail of a new production ski from Hexcel Sports, an innovation that designer Hub Zemke says reduces skidding.

The tail has traditionally been the stiffest part of the ski. But the greater flexibility of the narrow, V-cut tail sections when edging reportedly enhances the carving effect of the edges and reduces the chances of their not holding, particularly in packed, icy or rutted snow.

poles apart

When it comes to the shape of a ski-pole shaft, it has to be straight and true, right? Wrong. If you've watched a downhill race recently, you've undoubtedly seen the bent pole that the top competitors ski with these days. The aerodynamic configuration allows the pole, in effect, to wrap around behind the skier for decreased wind resistance.

This swept-back shaft is used almost exclusively in racing, but many other advances in poles are suited to recreational skiing. The standard grip, for instance, is giving way to a platform-type grip with an enlargement at its base, which the hand can push down against.

The newest concept is a shock-absorbing handle employing a sturdy spring inside the platform grip. This innovation from a family company started by Ivor Allsop helps relieve the jolts and jars of poling.

At the business end, pole baskets have gone from simple rings (that can snag) and snowflake patterns (that can't) to unusual cones, wedges, umbrellas and discs that reduce drag, both in and out of the snow.

While sharp pole tips are now being blunted to prevent injuries, the Scott pole company has a metal disc basket with a turned-under edge which replaces the tip altogether.

Advances in ski tech are not restricted to primary equipment. Accessories and clothing on the market today offer examples of intense technical ingenuity and a flair for the futuristic. In the category of electronic gear, for instance, today's skier can be wired from head to toe.

Stereo tape players that have headphones and special packs for skiing, electric gloves and socks, and even wearable ski-boot warmers are all available.

dry your damp boots

Emergency signal transmitters for skiing out-of-bounds are also becoming more prevalent. A very practical electrical device that's new this year is Allsop's plug-in boot tree that dries damp ski boots overnight.

Other varieties of powered skiing apparatus include Smith's ski goggles with a tiny, built-in fan powered by a battery on the elastic headband to prevent fogging.

There are bumper blocks that mount on ski tips to prevent even a novice's skis from crossing and tangling up.

Among the useful newer wrinkles is polypropylene long underwear that readily passes moisture out, but doesn't absorb it. In outerwear, such so-called "wicking" materials as Gore-Tex and Klimate, which make use of a breathing, bonded membrane, are revolutionizing the creation of warm, waterproof ski clothing.

Several manufacturers of diving wet suits are laminating closed-cell neoprene rubber between thin layers of nylon and Lycra for superwarm ski suits.

The tremendous level of technological development in downhill skiing equipment over the past 30 years or so has been equalled by cross-country skiing in a much shorter period.

from hickory to fiberglass

Hickory wood skis have given way almost completely to livelier fiberglass models. Some make use of composite materials and construction methods similar in sophistication to those of Alpine skis. These supple, skinny skis are almost as springy as archery bows.

However, unlike downhill skis, the critical area of experimentation and innovation has been the running surface, because of the necessity to alternately grip and glide.

A whole assortment of synthetic bottom coatings and running-surface configurations have been developed. Some—such as Trak's original fish-scale design—need no waxing in order to achieve both traction and slide. Improvements have been made on these patterned bottoms which now make use of different scallop shapes in different areas of the bottom. Other waxless bases have also come into being; the most efficient of these may be the mica bottom.

natural movement

Narrow, lightweight, high-performance skis are now mated with slender, lightweight bind-ings, some made entirely of space-age plastics. They are either 50 or 38 mm wide at the toe, as opposed to the former standard of 75 mm. The narrow bindings that couple with toe extensions built into the boots are intended to provide the most natural, unrestricted and efficient movement of the skier's legs while running in a prepared snow track.

Cross-country boots have been keeping pace with the technical advances in bindings, evolving to the point where many low-cut models made of synthetic materials look more like running shoes than ski boots.

In the plethora of poles on the market, widely available X-C shafts made of carbon-fiber graphite are strong, flexible and unbelievably light. The racing influence which stresses lightness and efficiency has transformed pole baskets into a mysterious assortment of shapes including saucers, rakes and even butterfly wings.

downhill, X-C are merging

One innovation that shows just how far the sport has come is the development of heel-holding devices (see photo on page 147). Normally the heel of the X-C boot must lift up as an essential part of striding on skis. But when sliding downhill, an X-C skier needs the stability for turns and stops that results when boot heels are laterally fixed.

Making grooved boot soles to fit into matching plates that perform the heel-holding function is a major step for one of the largest companies in the field. It may not be long before the downhill skier in the Darth Vader suit, speeding through a radar trap at one of the major ski resorts, will be wearing cross-country skis.

SOURCES—SKI EQUIPMENT

Allsop Inc. (Alpine poles), Box 23, Bellingham, Wash. 98225.

Burt International Inc. (Alpine bindings), 8 South Smith St., East Norwalk, Conn. 06855.

Fitzwright & Sine Manufacturing Co. (gopher neoprene downhill skiwear), 17919 Roan Place, Surrey, B.C. V3S 5K1.

Flying Aces of America (Alpine skier's hat), 530 South Barrington, Suite 110, Los Angeles, Calif. 90049.

Hexcel Sports (Alpine skis), 750 South Rock Blvd., Reno, Nev. 89502.

Kastinger U.S.A. Inc. (Alpine boots), 15533 Northeast 90th, Redmond, Wash. 98052.

Norfell Inc. (cross-country poles), Tracy Rd., Chelmsford, Mass. 01824.

Nortur Inc. (cross-country skis), 2000 East Century Circle, Minneapolis, Minn. 55441.

Scott U.S.A. (face masks), Box 1478, Clearfield, Utah 84016.

Sport Optics (Smith Alpine goggles), Box 11, Ketchum, Idaho 83340.

Sunbuster (cross-country skiwear), 15115 Northeast 90th, Redmond, Wash. 98052.

Trak Inc. (cross-country skis, boots, bindings, poles), 187 Neck Rd., Ward Hill, Mass. 01830.

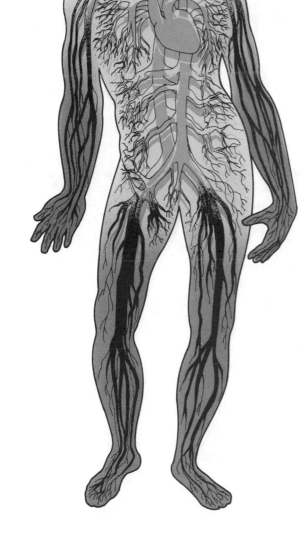

CRUCIAL for keeping you alive, veins and arteries of the body core can withdraw blood from your extremities to warm the vital organs.

New ways to fight the chill that kills

Now, improved clothing, techniques and treatments can save your life in the cold

By BILL MCKEOWN

IT WAS A SUNNY, windy day of late fall when the two brothers started their hike. The temperature was a brisk 48° F.—the kind of weather that might be found almost anywhere in the country—and the boys worked up a sweat as they followed a trail uphill through the woods. They were sliding down the far side of a mossy ledge, four hours out and ready to turn and head back, when Pete, 17, fell and twisted his leg under him. They couldn't tell if it was a sprained or broken ankle, but it was obvious that he wouldn't be able to make it back home. Younger brother Fred left Pete his cotton jacket and started downhill to get help.

Night brought a driving wind with rain squalls, and there was no sign of Pete when four friends with a folding stretcher came looking for him several hours later. Apparently, Pete had headed down to look for shelter and had fallen in a shallow, but icy stream in the dark. Their flashlights showed where he had crawled out on the far side, but then his trail seemed to wander and they lost it. During the night, as they searched, the temperature never dropped below freezing, but by morning, when Pete was finally found, his body was stiff and lifeless. His grieving friends recognized it as another case of death from "exposure" as they carried him back down.

That was four years ago, but the added tragedy is that, from what we now know, Pete's life might have been saved.

Doctors call it hypothermia, and the diagnosis is made when a low-reading thermometer, preferably rectal, goes down to 94° F. or below. Death comes when the body cools below about 80° F.—the temperature of a mild summer day. Well before that, the body may become stiff, the pulse disappear, and the skin appear gray. Proper and rapid treatment, in a hospital, if at all possible, is essential.

The condition of hypothermia, we now know, can occur almost anywhere at almost any time—to an athletic mountain climber caught in a rainstorm, a sailor who falls overboard in water

WIND-CHILL CHART

WIND SPEED	ACTUAL TEMPERATURE (°F)					
	40	20	0	− 20	− 40	− 60
	EQUIVALENT TEMPERATURE (°F)					
CALM	40	20	0	− 20	− 40	− 60
10	28	4	− 24	− 46	− 70	− 95
20	18	− 10	− 39	− 67	− 96	− 124
30	13	− 18	− 48	− 79	− 109	− 140
40	10	− 21	− 53	− 85	− 116	− 148

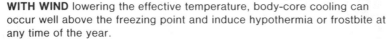

☐ LITTLE DANGER   ☐ INCREASING DANGER   ☐ GREAT DANGER

WITH WIND lowering the effective temperature, body-core cooling can occur well above the freezing point and induce hypothermia or frostbite at any time of the year.

BODY TEMPERATURE (°F)

°F	
98.6	SHIVERING, SENSATION OF COLD
93	MUSCLE RIGIDITY, LOSS OF MANUAL DEXTERITY
86	UNCONSCIOUSNESS
79	DEATH
75	

AS BODY temperature drops, significant symptoms may indicate critical cooling. Hypothermia begins below 94° F. At temperatures below 80° F., the cold victim dies.

under 70° F., or an alcoholic passed out on the cold sidewalk of a city.

Symptoms may start with shivering and drowsiness. Lack of coordination, irrational actions, slurred speech, and finally unconsciousness may follow. It's very important to watch for these subtle signs before they can advance.

Army-developed clothing

The most extensive study of new methods and equipment to combat the cold has been done by the U.S. Army Research Institute of Environmental Medicine at Natick, MA. Here they have tested, and in some cases created, the clothing designed to keep GIs comfortable anywhere in the world, and they have worked out the rules for using it properly. Even a warmth measurement has been devised: One CLO equals the body-heat retention of one standard suit of clothes; the Army-issue of layered uniform for cold conditions provides up to 4.6 CLO.

With recruits from city and country, snowbelt and tropics, the Army teaches them to remember the acronym COLD. C stands for cleanliness of clothing. It is important to wash garments to remove the grease and grime that clogs fabric airspaces and reduces insulation. O is a reminder to avoid the overheating that causes sweating, damp clothes and chills that follow as moisture lowers skin temperature. Clothing should be opened before sweating begins, or removed layer by layer. Several light garments are better than one heavy one.

L means loose clothing, with space for insulating air layers between. D refers to the importance of keeping dry. (Wet cold, according to the Army, is usually defined as temperatures above freezing during the day and down to 14° F. at night.) Snow should be brushed off—not rubbed into the fabric—to avoid dampness. Clothing should be aired and dried whenever possible.

synthetics for warmth

New synthetic polypropylene underwear has been found to be particularly effective in wicking away warmth-stealing sweat from the body. One civilian equivalent is the Lifa brand from Helly-Hanson, originally tested by Norwegian fishermen. Wool clothing, unlike fabrics such as cotton denim, supplies warmth retention even when it's wet. Fiber pile, also made from synthetic yarn and now available from various sources, doesn't hold water and helps it evaporate. Mittens made of preshrunk boiled wool, such as the Dachstein type, have a tighter weave and are worn alone or under waterproof outer shells for added protection.

Feet are difficult to keep warm, so several methods can be combined. While plastic bags can be fitted over socks as vapor barriers, the wet warmth may eventually turn cold. Socks that wick away wetness are preferred by many outdoorsmen. Foot powder can also be used to keep feet dry. Boots should be loose enough to fit comfortably (European lasts often taper too much and cramp the toes).

To keep the cold ground under boots from robbing foot warmth, plastic inserts can be fitted inside, beneath your socks, as added insulation. Remember that body thermostats in the head and neck control temperatures throughout the entire body. Put on a warm cap and added blood to the feet will make them feel warmer as well.

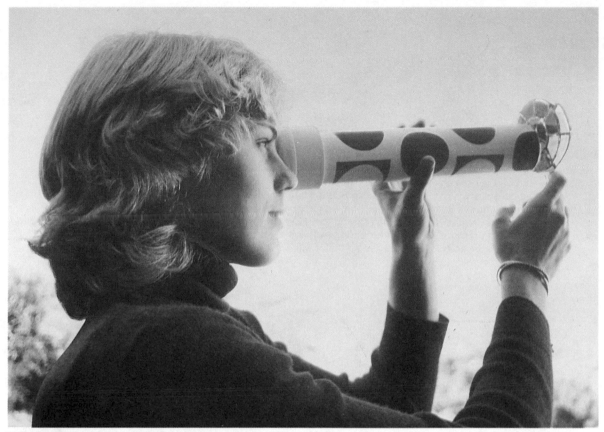

THE KALEIDOSCOPE provides endless entertainment for a person of any age. A slight turn of the stained-glass wheels creates infinite variations of brilliant color, as shown by photos (below) taken through the tube.

Dazzle everyone with this kaleidoscope

■ PUT THIS color-filled tube to your eye, and in seconds you'll see countless patterns of fiery red, sunny amber or icy blue. You can use up to 18 different colors and patterns of glass in the ka-

leidoscope. The greater the number of colors you use, the more vibrant the designs.

The kaleidoscope tube is a 1-ft. piece of plastic plumbing pipe (A) with an end cap (B). Bore the

By DAN A. ROBERTSON

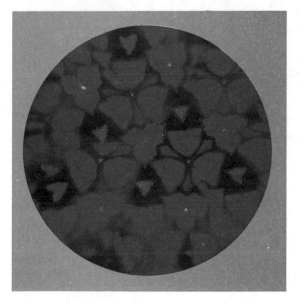

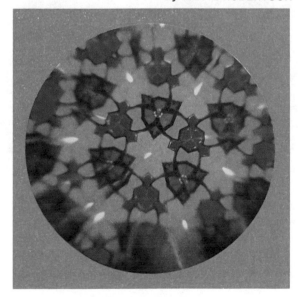

MATERIALS from top: 2-in. inside diameter plastic pipe and end cap, soldering iron, 50/50 solder, stained-glass scraps, copper spacers, bolt, washers, wood strips, wood block, mirror strips, acrylic circles, glazier pliers, pattern for stained-glass wheels, glass cutter and copper foil.

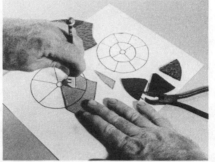

IF YOU CAN see through the glass, lay it on the pattern and score inside the inked lines with a sharp, oiled glass cutter. If the glass is too dark, cut a paper pattern for each piece and lay it on top of the glass so that it will act as cutting guide.

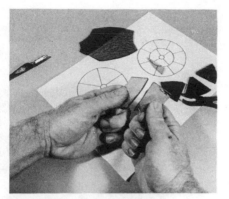

SNAP GLASS immediately after scoring it, using a downward and outward motion. Use pliers to break off small pieces. Rub edges of two pieces together to dull any sharp spots.

CAREFULLY center copper foil on edges of each piece of glass and wrap it tightly. Then smooth foil with dowel. Foil won't stick to greasy glass.

AFTER POSITIONING glass pieces on pattern and fluxing copper foil, run a bead of solder along edges, using a 60- to 100-watt iron. Then solder a piece of copper tubing in center as a spacer.

ASSEMBLE revolving unit; it consists of two glass wheels, acrylic disc, a wood block, bolt and nut.

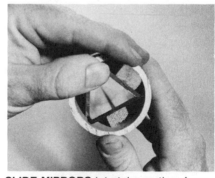

SLIDE MIRRORS into tube so they form a triangle, mirror side facing inward. Wood strips that hold mirrors should fit snugly, but be careful not to scrape any of the backing off the mirrors.

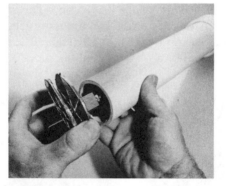

CEMENT end cap and acrylic eyepiece to one end of tube, and cement the glass assembly into the other end. Clean parts before assembly.

MATERIALS LIST—KALEIDOSCOPE

Key	No.	Size and description
A	1	2" i.d. (2⅜" o.d.) × 12" plastic plumbing pipe
B	1	2" i.d. plastic end cap
C	2	⅛ × 1⁹⁄₁₆ × 12" mirror
D	1	⅛ × 1¾ × 12" mirror
E	2	⅛ × 2⅜"-dia. clear-acrylic disc
F	2	½ × ¾ × 12" wood strip
G	1	½ × ¾ × 10½" wood strip
H	1	½ × ¾ × 1" wood block
I	2	¼ × ⅜"-dia. copper tube
J	1	No. 8-32 × 2" machine bolt
K	1	³⁄₁₆" i.d. nut
L	4	³⁄₁₆" i.d. washer

Misc.: 1 roll of ¼-in.-wide copper foil tape, 1 roll of 50/50 or 60/40 solid-core wire solder, 18 pieces of colored stained glass, glass cutter, pliers, oleic-acid flux, flux brush, cutting oil, 60 to 100-w. soldering iron, PVC solvent cement, epoxy resin cement, contact paper, inked wheel pattern.

eyehole in the center of the cap and smooth the edges with fine (180-grit) sandpaper or steel wool.

Draw a full-size pattern of each color wheel on paper with a dark felt-tip pen. Lay a piece of stained glass over a section of one color wheel, with the smooth side of the glass facing up. Dip a sharp glass cutter into cutting oil or kerosene, then press the cutting wheel onto the glass along the inside of one of the inked lines. When you make the score, you should hear a slight hissing as the cutter travels over the glass, scratching a faint line into the surface. *Never* go over a scored line twice, however, or your cutter will quickly become dull.

If the glass you're using is so dark that you can't see the inked pattern through it, make a duplicate pattern on stiff paper. Cut out the pattern pieces and lay one on top of the glass to guide your cutter.

To make a quick break, form fists with both hands and grip the glass so your thumbs straddle the score line with fingers under the glass. Move your hands in a down-and-out motion to snap it.

Wash the glass with detergent and hot water, dry it, and then wrap copper foil around the edges of each piece so edges are centered on foil. Smooth foil with a dowel or pencil.

Lay the foil-wrapped glass on the pattern to check for fit. Then brush the copper with oleic-acid flux and solder the pieces together with 50/50 or 60/40 solid-core wire solder. Solder spacers (I) into the center of each wheel. Next cut the three mirror strips (C and D). Make the scores on the glass side, not on the silvered side. Then snap off the strips as you would any other glass.

Cut two clear-acrylic discs (E) to seal the ends of the tube. In one of the discs bore a ¼-in.-dia. hole with a center that is 7/16 in. from the edge. To secure the mirrors inside the tube, cut three wood strips (F and G) and wood block H. Bore a 5/16-in.-dia. hole through H.

Make sure all glass, mirror and acrylic parts are clean. Then cement the acrylic disc without the hole to one end of the tube. Slip end cap B in place. Slide the three mirror strips into the tube in a triangular shape, mirror sides facing inward. Carefully slide the wood strips in place. Position wood strip G under mirror D.

Slide the parts onto machine bolt J in the order shown above and secure nut K with epoxy resin. Apply epoxy resin to the open rim of the tube and to the wood block where it will be in contact with the tube. Position the wheel assembly and tape disc E in place until the epoxy hardens.

As a final touch, you might decorate the kaleidoscope with self-adhesive vinyl cut into simple shapes.

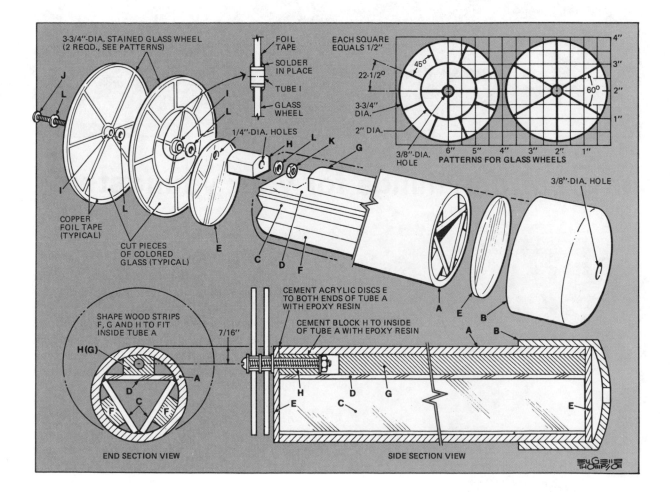

1

Four great playthings for your youngsters

2

■ ONE OF THE more rewarding aspects for the active home work-shopper is building things for children.

The reward is two-fold: First, you get to share the joy that is triggered by the giving of toys such as those pictured on this page. The second is the smug satisfaction of being a "hero" (that only the builders of kids' furniture ever get to know).

On these pages we have rounded up four fun projects to keep you and your children busy. We built three of them in the PM workshop—and tested the prototype digger at length—before we photographed the projects for publication.

3

4

1 PM'S BOY-POWERED digger works beautifully—just like the real ones—and will give the user hours of fun.

2 SLEEK MODEL RACER is easy to make: body is cut from a scrap piece of 2x4. Mag wheels are created using a hole saw; the roll bar is a U-bolt.

3 HERE'S A PLAY center to wow pre-schoolers (and older youngsters). It has a play TV, bulletin board, chalkboard (top), and place to make up (above).

4 DOLL CRADLE is reproduction of 18th-century cradle. Ours is handcrafted of mel-low pine with varnish finish.

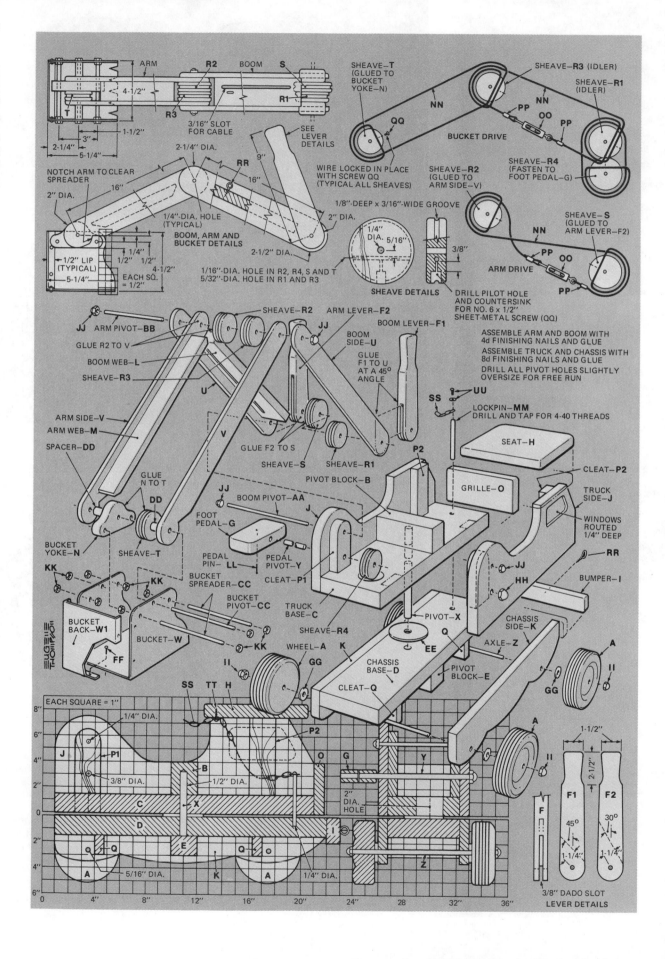

ARM

R2   BOOM   S

4-1/2"

R3

R1

3/16" SLOT
FOR CABLE

1-1/2"

3"

2-1/4"

5-1/4"

T

SHEAVE–T
(GLUED TO
BUCKET
YOKE–N)

SHEAVE–R3 (IDLER)

SHEAVE–R1
(IDLER)

NN

NN

QQ

PP
OO
PP

BUCKET DRIVE

WIRE LOCKED IN PLACE
WITH SCREW QQ
(TYPICAL ALL SHEAVES)

SHEAVE–R2
(GLUED TO
ARM SIDE–V)

SHEAVE–R4
(FASTEN TO
FOOT PEDAL–G)

NOTCH ARM TO CLEAR
SPREADER

2" DIA.

16"

RR

16"

9"

2-1/4" DIA.

1/4"-DIA. HOLE
(TYPICAL)

BOOM, ARM AND
BUCKET DETAILS

2" DIA.

2-1/2" DIA.

1/8"-DEEP x 3/16"-WIDE GROOVE

1/4"
DIA.   5/16"

NN

PP   OO

ARM DRIVE

PP

SHEAVE–S
(GLUED TO
ARM LEVER–F2)

1/2" LIP
(TYPICAL)

5-1/4"

1/4"
1/2"   1/2"

4-1/2"

EACH SQ.
= 1/2"

1/16"-DIA. HOLE IN R2, R4, S AND T
5/32"-DIA. HOLE IN R1 AND R3

SHEAVE DETAILS

3/8"

DRILL PILOT HOLE
AND COUNTERSINK
FOR NO. 6 x 1/2"
SHEET-METAL SCREW (QQ)

JJ   ARM PIVOT–BB

GLUE R2 TO V

BOOM WEB–L

SHEAVE–R3

ARM SIDE–V

ARM WEB–M

SPACER–DD

GLUE
N TO T

BUCKET
YOKE–N

SHEAVE–R2

U

V

SHEAVE–S

GLUE F2 TO S

SHEAVE–T

DD

JJ   ARM LEVER–F2

BOOM
SIDE–U

BOOM LEVER–F1

GLUE
F1 TO U
AT A 45°
ANGLE

SHEAVE–R1

P2

SS

UU

LOCKPIN–MM
DRILL AND TAP FOR 4-40 THREADS

SEAT–H

CLEAT–P2

GRILLE–O

TRUCK
SIDE–J

WINDOWS
ROUTED
1/4" DEEP

ASSEMBLE ARM AND BOOM WITH
4d FINISHING NAILS AND GLUE
ASSEMBLE TRUCK AND CHASSIS WITH
8d FINISHING NAILS AND GLUE
DRILL ALL PIVOT HOLES SLIGHTLY
OVERSIZE FOR FREE RUN

PIVOT BLOCK–B

BOOM PIVOT–AA

J

JJ

FOOT
PEDAL–G

PEDAL
PIN–LL

PEDAL
PIVOT–Y

CLEAT–P1

TRUCK
BASE–C

SHEAVE–R4

RR

JJ

HH

BUMPER–I

KK

KK

BUCKET
SPREADER–CC

BUCKET
PIVOT–CC

PIVOT–X

EE

Q

CHASSIS
SIDE–K

AXLE–Z

A

BUCKET
BACK–W1

BUCKET–W

KK

WHEEL–A

GG

K

CHASSIS
BASE–D

PIVOT
BLOCK–E

CLEAT–Q

II

GG

II

FF

II

SS   TT   H

EACH SQUARE = 1"

8"

1/4" DIA.

6"

P2

J   P1

4"

B

O   G

Y

A

2"

3/8" DIA.

1/2" DIA.

2"
DIA.
HOLE

0

C

X

II

1-1/2"

2-1/2"

2"

D

I

F

F1   F2

E

45°

30°

4"

A

5/16" DIA.

Q   Q

K   A

1/4" DIA.

Z

1-1/4"

1-1/4"

6"

0   4"   8"   12"   16"   20"   24"   28"   32"   36"

3/8" DADO SLOT

LEVER DETAILS

BOY-POWERED DIGGER

■ THIS IS AN IDEAL project for the craftsman who wants to build an exceptional toy for his youngster. The digger works beautifully and provides hours of fun and exercise for its proud young owner.

Utilizing a cable and sheave mechanism, the arm and boom are precisely operated with hand levers, while the attitude of the bucket for loading and dumping is controlled with a foot pedal. The young operator uses both hands and feet to operate the machine, which works fine in sand, sawdust, or snow.

making the sheaves

Start by making the boom mechanism and sheaves. Lay out and cut the six pulleys and sheaves from ¾-in.-thick hardwood with a band saw. One easy way to mount the stock in the lathe for turning is to bore a ¼-in. center hole in each blank and use a ¼-20 machine screw turned into your tapered screw center after removing the existing screw. Turn the outside diameter of the sheave blank true, then turn a groove ³⁄₁₆-in. wide by ⅛-in. deep for the cable. Round-over both edges of the sheave. Smooth up the face, leaving

CABLE GROOVE in sheave is turned so it will accommodate two turns of cable.

THROUGH-HOLES in sheaves are bored parallel to diameter.

BOOM AND ARM are assembled with axles and sheaves in place temporarily.

RECESSES ARE routed in truck sides to simulate windows.

TRUCK is for outdoors so assemble with waterproof glue, finishing nails.

TIRE FACES and treads are turned on lathe; note dead center support.

ALUMINUM parts for the bucket were formed on small bending brake.

BUCKET PIVOTS on end of arm; spacers on rod keep bucket centered.

SHEAVE rotational positions and attitude relationship are critical.

the center slightly thicker than the edges for clearance. Sand and finish with varnish, then remove the stock from the lathe.

Enlarge the center hole on all sheaves to achieve a running fit on the ¼-in. axles. To do it, use a ⁹⁄₃₂-in. bit. Watching the bank of sheaves turning is part of the enjoyment that the young operator derives from using this toy.

Bore holes through the sheaves from groove to groove parallel with the diameter, *but offset slightly to miss the axle holes.* These holes should be ¹⁄₁₆ in. in the small and one of the medium sheaves, and ⁵⁄₃₂ in. in the large and three of the medium sheaves. Bore the holes *across the grain* for strength. Drill and countersink for sheet-metal screws at right angles to the cable holes for locking the cable in the sheave where needed.

the boom arm

Cut the boom pieces from the ⅜-in. exterior plywood as shown. Tack the pieces together in groups of two. On your jointer (or with a hand plane) make an overall ¼-in. taper on the width of both stacks. Lay out the ¼-in. holes, spaced 16 in. on center. Scribe the rounded ends with a compass, then cut and sand the rounded ends of the stacks. Bore the ¼-in. axle holes, then disassemble the stacks and round all edges of the boom and arm sides with a router and rounding-over bit.

Next, lay out and cut the operating handles. Cut a ⅜-in. dado slot in both handles to fit the plywood sides of the boom. Bottoms of the dadoes must be made at appropriate angles. The boom handle is glued to the ⅜-in. plywood at a 45° angle.

The arm-operating handle straddles the right-hand boom stringer with a 30° limit cut at the bottom of the slot.

If you are using a circular saw, clamp the handle to a scrap of plywood at the appropriate angle to kerf the slot. Round edges with a router, bore the ¼-in. holes and glue the handle to the boom stringer. Using waterproof glue, fasten the largest wheel to the side of the arm-operating straddle lever.

Study photos and drawings and complete gluing operations before you assemble the boom, arm and bucket. Reinforce with ¼-in. dowels.

Make the web for the boom and arm of 1-in. stock. Slot one web where the cables must cross, as shown. Assemble the boom and arm parts with waterproof glue and brads, with axles temporarily installed for alignment. Disassemble axles and paint boom/arm parts, then reassemble.

making truck sides

Stack two pieces of ¾-in. stock and lay out, band saw and bore holes as shown on page 158. Round all edges with a router and rounding-over bit except the sides adjoining the roof and front grille, and inside the bottom edge. Rout ¼-in.-deep recesses to simulate cab windows.

Assemble strengthening cleats to the bottom and sides, using waterproof glue and nails. Assemble in the same way the blocks for the pivot rod through the base and vertical cleats inside the truck sides at trunnion and cab. Rebore the ½-in. hole for the body pivot not quite through the block.

From ¾-in. stock, cut out the grille, front bumper, two chassis skirts, two skirt spreaders

---

MATERIALS LIST—BOY-POWERED DIGGER

Key	No.	Size and description (use)	Key	No.	Size and description (use)	Key	No.	Size and description (use)
A	4	1¾ × 5″-dia. hardwood (wheels)	N	1	¾ × 2 × 4″ hardwood (bucket yoke)	DD	2	⁵⁄₁₆″-i.d. × 1¹⁄₁₆″ metal or plastic tube (spacers)
B	1	2 × 2½ × 5½″ hardwood (pivot block)	O	1	¾ × 4 × 7″ pine or hardwood (grille)	EE	1	½″-i.d., 3″-o.d. leather washer
C	1	1½ × 5½ × 20″ hardwood (truck base)	P1	2	¾ × 1½ × 5″ pine (cleats)	FF	5	⅛″-dia. cold rivets
D	1	1½ × 5½ × 21″ hardwood (chassis base)	P2	1	¾ × 1½ × 6″ pine (cleats)	GG	4	⁵⁄₁₆″-i.d. flat washers
E	1	1½ × 2 × 5½″ hardwood (chassis pivot block)	Q	2	¾ × 2 × 6″ pine (chassis cleats)	HH	1	⅜″ pushnut
			R	4	¾ × 2½″-dia. hardwood (sheave)	II	4	⁵⁄₁₆″ pushnuts
F1	1	1 × 2 × 10″ hardwood (boom lever)	S	1	¾ × 3″-dia. hardwood (sheave)	JJ	4	¼″ pushnuts
F2	1	1 × 2 × 10″ hardwood (arm lever)	T	1	¾ × 2″-dia. hardwood (sheave)	KK	1	¼-20 hex nut
G	1	1 × 2¾ × 5″ hardwood (foot pedal)	U	2	⅜ × 2½ × 18⅜″ plywood (boom side)	LL	1	8d finish nail cut to 1″ (pedal pin)
H	1	1 × 7½ × 8″ hardwood (seat)	V	1	⅜ × 2¼ × 18⅛″ plywood (arm side)	MM	1	¼″-dia. × 4″ steel rod (lockpin)
I	1	1 × 1¾ × 8″ pine or hardwood (bumper)	W	1	³⁄₃₂ × 3¼ × 13½″ aluminum (bucket)	NN	1	¹⁄₁₆″ steel airplane cable (20 ft.)
J	2	¾ × 7½ × 20″ pine or hardwood (truck sides)	W1	1	³⁄₃₂ × 3¼ × 5½″ aluminum (bucket back)	OO	2	Turnbuckles
			X	1	½″-dia. × 5″ steel rod (truck pivot)	PP	4	Double-hole swedges
K	2	¾ × 3½ × 21″ pine or hardwood (chassis sides)	Y	1	⅜″-dia. × 5″ steel rod (pedal pivot)	QQ	6	No. 6 × ½″ sheet-metal screws
			Z	2	⁵⁄₁₆″-dia. × 11½″ steel rod (axles)	RR	2	½″ screw eyes
L	1	¾ × 2¼ × 13⅜″ pine or hardwood (boom web)	AA	1	⅓″-dia. × 1½″ steel rod (boom pivot)	SS	1	16″ sash chain with snap hook
			BB	1	¼″-dia. × 3½″ steel rod (arm pivot)	TT		No. 8 × ½″ rh screws
M	1	¾ × 1½ × 13⅛″ pine or hardwood (arm web)	CC	3	¼″-dia. × 5″ threaded steel rods (bucket and pivot spreaders)	UU		4-40 × ½″ rh screws and washers

and foot pedal. The seat should be of 1-in. hardwood with the grain running across the truck. Round all corners and edges where appropriate, and assemble parts with waterproof glue and finishing nails. Imitation lights and grille ornaments were added on the prototype.

the wheels and bucket

Band saw four 5-in. blanks from 2-in. stock. For turning, glue sandpaper to a wood faceplate to act as a friction drive. Place a blank against the sandpaper and bring up the dead center to engage the compass detent at the center of the blank. Turn the tire and face of the wheel, then bore the 5/16-in. axle hole. Paint the tires black, the wheels as you prefer.

Aluminum sheet 3/32-in. thick is available at scrap-metal yards or duct-fabrication shops. Lay out bucket parts according to the drawing. Cutting can be done on a band saw as aluminum is softer than the woodcutting blade.

Drill 1/4-in. holes for the yoke rods. Bending is done on a small brake clamped to the circular-saw table. You could do a suitable job with a machinist's vise and hammer. Make the bends and assemble the back to the bucket with cold rivets.

Assemble the bucket to the yoke with two 1/4-in. rods threaded at both ends. The front rod has nuts on the inside of the bucket and on outside faces to prevent collapsing and spreading. Bucket sides at the front rod must be slightly sprung to install the front rod with internal nuts in place.

Assemble the yoke to the end of the arm with 1/4-in. rod threaded at both ends, a tube spacer and washer on each side of the yoke, and nuts on the outside at rod ends. Mushroom rod ends slightly to keep nuts tight. Assemble the arm and boom with 1/4-in. rod and pushnuts. Assemble the boom to trunnions on the truck with 1/4-in. rod, pushnuts, washers and spacers.

installing the foot pedal

Make the foot pedal 2¾ in. wide by 5 in. long from hardwood stock 1 in. thick. The pedal controls the attitude of the bucket. Even when boom and arm levers move, a consistent position of the pedal holds the position of the bucket. Changing the bucket attitude responds well to movement of the pedal.

Drill the pedal through its width for the 3/8-in. rod that will pass through the lower part of the truck trunnions and accept the hardwood pedal on one end. Tap the rod into the pedal flush with the edge, then pin it with an 8d finishing nail in a

hole drilled through pedal and rod. Looking toward the rear from the front, pass the rod through the right trunnion and slip on a 2½-in.-dia. sheave. Pass rod end through the left trunnion and install a pushnut. Do not pin sheave to the rod until the cable is run.

Determine cable lengths by running string through and around the sheaves. Looking aft, the shorter cable on the right connects the sheave glued to the operating lever with that glued to the arm, operating the arm. The longer cable interconnects the four sheaves on the left—pinned sheave on the foot-pedal rod, two idlers at ends of the boom and small sheave glued to the bucket yoke. This controls the bucket attitude. Use string as guides to cut cable lengths.

Airplane cable of 1/16-in. diameter should be found at an industrial hardware store. Pull cable loosely around the sheaves and through locking holes, and adjust sheaves by rotating them to allow proper turning leeway. Start at lowest sheaves, leaving 10 or 12 in. of cable loose for turnbuckle attachment under boom.

Tighten lockscrews (sheet-metal screws with points ground flat) at these lower sheaves before final routing of the cable. Attach cable ends to the turnbuckles with double-hole swedges (crimp-on cable clamps) appropriate for 1/16-in. cable (an industrial hardware store should have them). Here, a swedging tool was made with holes drilled in a flat bar, and a hacksaw cut made through the centers of the holes.

Check and adjust sheave rotational positions for leeway in movement and cable tightness before you tighten the lockscrew on the outboard sheave. If cable holes in any sheaves are too large, insert one or two short pieces of cable in the hole. Adjust arm lever to arm position before locking it. Repeat the procedure for the bucket-control cable from foot pedal. Holes in idler sheaves must be large enough for two thicknesses of cable. Attach swedged loops to turnbuckles, tighten cables.

finish assembly

With parts prepainted and truck-boom assembly completed, pivot the truck body to the chassis. Cut a pivot pin from ½-in.-dia. steel rod, to a length just short of the depth of both holes plus the washer. A waxed leather disc was used on the prototype; metal discs will serve as thrust washers. A small chain anchored by a screw under the roof has an end snap hook to engage a screw eye on the boom. It acts as a snubber to lock the boom in traveling position.

SLEEK MODEL RACER WITH ROLL BAR

■ CUT THE WHEELS out of a piece of 6/4 pine stock. As this stock measures 1⅜-in. thick, boring from both sides is required because the typical hole saw penetrates only ¾ in. deep.

Cut the body from a piece of 2x4. Use a band saw or a rip handsaw to cut the long taper. Drill ³/₂₆-in.-dia. holes for the lagscrew axles and ⁵/₁₆-in.-dia. holes for the roll bar. Drill the axle holes from both sides unless you have a long drill bit.

Paint the wheels and body. Select a suitable plastic bubble from a hardware package and carefully remove the backing. The bubble shown contained brads mounted on cardboard. Cut a cowl from ⅛-in. plywood or stiff cardboard, sized to fit over the bubble flange. Paint it, then nail it into place.

For a sporty touch, apply striping tape of a contrasting color.

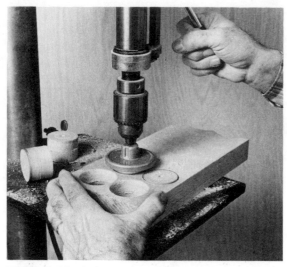

USING A 2-in. hole saw in a drill press, you can cut the racer wheels from 6/4 stock.

MATERIALS LIST—RACER

Key	No.	Size and description (use)
A	1	1⅜ × 3½ × 13" 2×4 fir (body)
B	4	1⅜ × 1⅞"-dia. 6/4 pine (wheels)
C	1	Plastic bubble from hardware package (canopy)
D	1	⅛" plywood (cowl)
E	1	⁵/₁₆ × 2½" U-bolt (roll bar)
F	8	⁵/₁₆" i.d. washer
G	4	¼ × 2½" lagscrews
H		Striping tape (as reqd.)

SAND WHEELS and check for fit. Accessories include U-bolt, plastic bubble.

VINYL STRIPING tape has pressure-sensitive backing. Strips come precut.

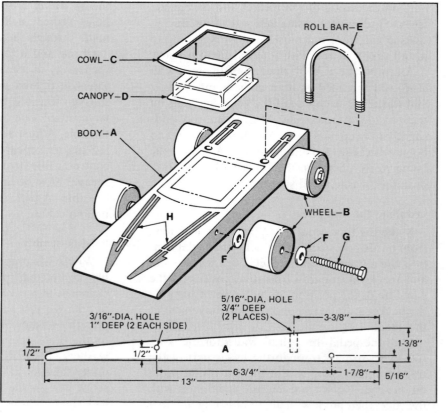

COWL—C

CANOPY—D

ROLL BAR—E

BODY—A

WHEEL—B

H

F   F   G

3/16"-DIA. HOLE 1" DEEP (2 EACH SIDE)

5/16"-DIA. HOLE 3/4" DEEP (2 PLACES)

3-3/8"

1/2"   1/2"   A   1-3/8"

13"   6-3/4"   1-7/8"   5/16"

PLAY-CENTER TV FOR YOUNGSTERS

■ CUT THE PLYWOOD to size, then draw three rectangles for the cutouts. Draw three straight lines the length of the top and side of the smaller opening and the side of the large opening. Drive in one nail at each end of these lines. Place the flexible guide against the standing nails, then deflect it ½ in. at the center and trace the line.

Bore 2-in.-dia. holes tangent to the outline to form the round corners and make the cuts with a sabre saw.

Carefully cut the ½-in.-wide slots at the bottom of the board and in the tops of the base pieces to produce neat interlocking joints.

Sand and paint all the parts before assembly. Use a chalkboard paint on the hardboard. Use flathead screws with finishing washers to attach the hardboard and bulletin board. The shelf is attached last. We used Amerock T-594 knobs for the TV "controls."

Self-adhering plastic clothing hooks are attached to the Homasote bulletin board.

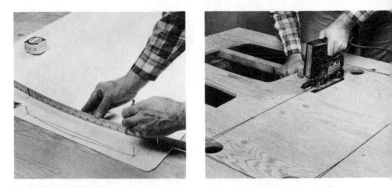

FLEXIBLE RULE is used to draw the pattern for curved cutouts (left). Rule is deflected ½ in. at center. Holes (right) made with a 2-in. hole saw form corners of the cutouts.

MATERIALS LIST—PLAY TV

Key	No.	Size and description (use)
A	1	½ × 48 × 52" plywood (frame)
B	2	½ × 12 × 24" plywood (foot)
C	1	½ × 3 × 19" plywood (shelf)
D	2	½ × 4 × 5" plywood (shelf end)
E	2	½ × 1 × 5" plywood (shelf cleat)
F	1	½ × 19 × 38" cork-faced Homasote (bulletin board)
G	1	⅓ × 19 × 23" chalkboard
H	2	⅞ × 44" wood outside corner-guard molding (frame edging)
I	1	1⅛ × 19" wood outside corner-guard molding (shelf edging)
J	1	8 × 10" mirror
K	1	24" shade with brackets
L	3	Dial knobs, Amerock T-594
M	1	No. 6 countersunk washers
N	14	¾" No. 6 fh screws
O	4	⅞" No. 6 fh screws
P	16	1" No. 6 fh screws
Q	1	4d finishing nails
R	4	Coat hooks (self-sticking plastic type)

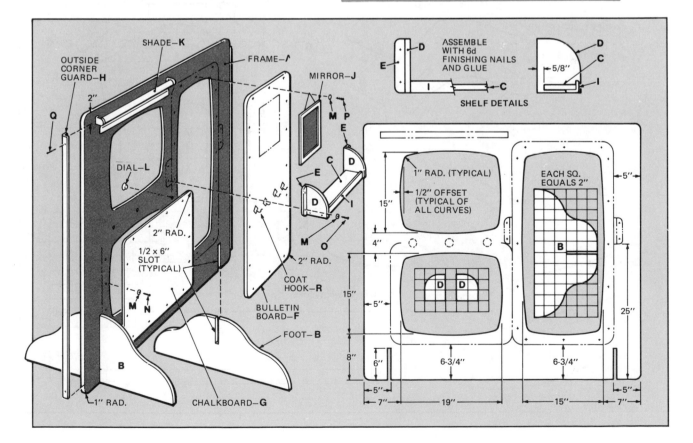

A 7° BEVEL is cut along both edges (left). Note that, after you have cut one side, board must be flopped before cutting second edge to insure that bevel angle is properly positioned. 35° bevel on top of cradle sides is cut (right) after pieces have been separated.

MATERIALS LIST—DOLL CRADLE

Key	No.	Size and description (use)
A	1	3/4 × 10 3/4 × 22 1/2" pine (bottom)
B	1	3/4 × 11 1/4 × 13 11/16" pine (headboard)
C	2	3/4 × 11 1/4 × 22 1/2" pine (sides)
D	2	3/4 × 3 1/2 × 18 3/8" pine (rockers)
E	1	3/4 × 6 3/4 × 9 3/4" pine (footboard)
F	1	3/4 × 3 3/4 × 11 1/4" pine (canopy support)
G	2	3/4 × 5 9/16 × 6 7/8" pine (canopy side)
H	1	3/4 × 5 3/4 × 6 7/8" pine (canopy top)

Misc.: 6d finishing nails and glue.

18TH-CENTURY DOLL CRADLE

■ SELECT A PIECE of a warp-free 1x12 pine and draw on the cradle sides. Make the bevel cuts along both edges of the board before cutting out the sides so you will have a straight edge to ride the fence. Cut the 35° bevel on the tops, then smooth all exposed edges except the bevels.

Next, cut the footboard, headboard, canopy support and rockers. Then cut the canopy parts to size with the appropriate bevels. Sand before assembly.

To assemble, glue and nail the sides to the footboard and headboard, using 6d finishing nails. Attach rockers to the bottom, then join the bottom to the sides. Attach the canopy support and the canopy pieces. Set all nailheads and fill.

We obtained an antique finish using ordinary stain. Apply a diluted coat of sanding sealer, let it dry, then sand lightly. Next, wipe on a satin stain and stroke it lightly with a cloth to produce a grained effect. Allow twice the normal drying time, then finish with polyurethane varnish.

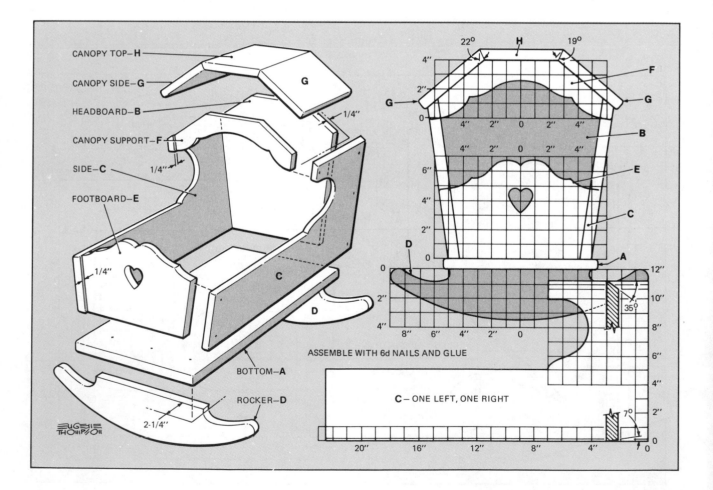

Playcubes—
easy as 1, 2, 3

By PAUL LEVINE

■ STORAGE HAS always been a problem in our house. These attractive storage seats offer a partial remedy to the where-to-put-it problem by concealing many odds and ends. Topped with fabric-covered foam rubber, they also serve as extra seating when needed.

Each of the cubes, designed by architect Martin M. Bloomenthal, has a numeral graphic on its side. You might build a cube featuring your youngster's age or initial.

The basic box is constructed of 1x12-in. clear pine with a plywood bottom and top. Begin work on the cube by cutting the side panels (A, see drawing) with mitered sides. Plow dadoes to accept the top cleats (E) and cut rabbets for bottom (C).

Next, use a table saw to cut grooves for the splines (D). Shape the numeral on the side panel with a router and straight cutter. To do it, first make a template of ⅛-in. hardboard using a numeral on the facing page. The finished numerals are 9¾ in. high. However, the template must be larger to allow for the difference between the bearing and the cutter diameter. I used a ¼-in. straight mortising bit and a ⁷⁄₁₆-in. router template guide, so the template is ³⁄₃₂-in. larger all around than the finished numeral.

rout the numeral

Clamp the template rigidly to a side panel. Adjust the router so its cutter will rout the numeral to a ⅜-in. depth *in the side panel.* Remove

CREATE A TEMPLATE out of ⅛-in. hardboard that will suit your router shoe (see text). Clamp it to the workpiece for routing the numerals or letters.

SINCE ROUTER cutter leaves rounded corners, you will need to use a chisel and hammer to make the square shapes. Then sand the cutout.

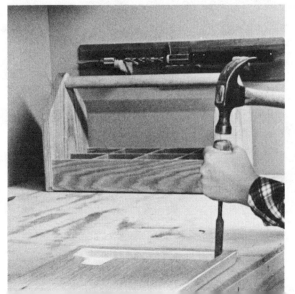

the template and chisel corners square.

After cutting the bottom (C) and the corner splines (D), assemble the box with glue and clamps. Set it aside to dry. The next day, beef up joint strength by using 6d finishing nails spaced 6 in. apart on alternate sides of the miter joint. Set the nails. Cut top cleats (E) and base (F) and glue parts in place. Cut the wood top (B) so it fits loosely and removes easily for access. Bore a ¾-in.-dia. finger hole at the center.

Apply wood filler as needed and sand the cube with 120-grit abrasive paper. Dust and wipe with a tack cloth. Brush on two coats of 3-lb. cut white shellac, the first coat thinned 50 percent with denatured alcohol, the second coat brushed on as it comes from the can. If desired, paint the numeral.

Cut out a cushion of 2-in.-thick foam rubber. Sew a suitable fabric slipcover to complement the cube.

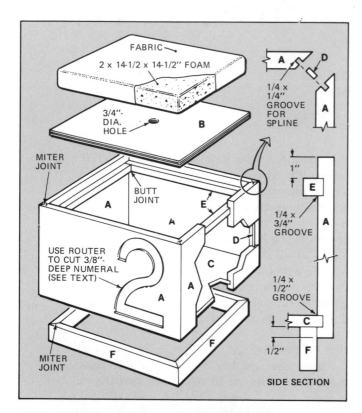

MATERIALS LIST—PLAYCUBES

Key	No.	Size and description (use)
A	4	¾ × 11¼ × 16″ clear pine (side panels)
B	1	⅜ × 14⅜ × 14⅜″ plywood (seat top)
C	1	½ × 15 × 15″ plywood (bottom)
D	4	¼ × ½ × 11¼″ plywood (splines)
E	4	¾ × 1 × 14″ pine (top cleats)
F	4	¾ × 2 × 14½″ pine (base strips)

Misc.: White glue, ⅛″ hardboard for template, 6d finishing nails, wood filler, 3-lb. cut shellac, prime coat, paint, cushion fabric and 2 × 14½ × 14½″ foam rubber.

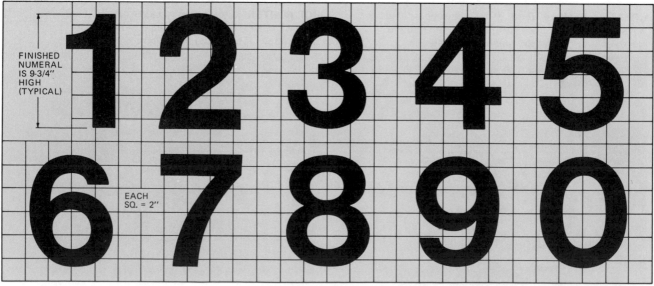

AS SHOWN ABOVE, the play tower can easily accommodate four youngsters or more.

Build this play tower with a chain saw

■ THERE CAN BE little doubt that many chain-saw owners bought their tools for no other task than cutting firewood. It's true that a small but powerful chain saw makes relatively quick and easy work of cutting up a cord of firewood. But the tool can also be used for many project-building tasks.

The project shown on these pages was developed jointly by Homelite, a prominent maker of chain saws, and *Popular Mechanics*. Our aim was to create an attractive, useful project that could be built using very few tools besides the chain saw.

The challenge we gave designer David Stiles was to come up with a functional back-yard play structure, built of sturdy members to assure a long life. Master craftsman Rosario Capotosto took the designer's sketch and created the structure shown, working out all construction details as he went. The result is the easy-to-follow plans on the following pages.

The basic structure is made of 2x4, 2x6 and 4x4 pressure-treated stock. (The actual measurements are given in the materials list.) We recommend that you use pressure-treated stock (Wolmanized was used in the structure shown) where members are in contact with the soil, because this lumber is both water- and insect-resistant. If you prefer, use cedar posts and conventional fir 2x4s and 2x6s. To prevent rotting, apply at least three coats of a wood preservative.

ROOF IS covered with handsome cedar shakes. It has a wide overhang to provide shelter from showers.

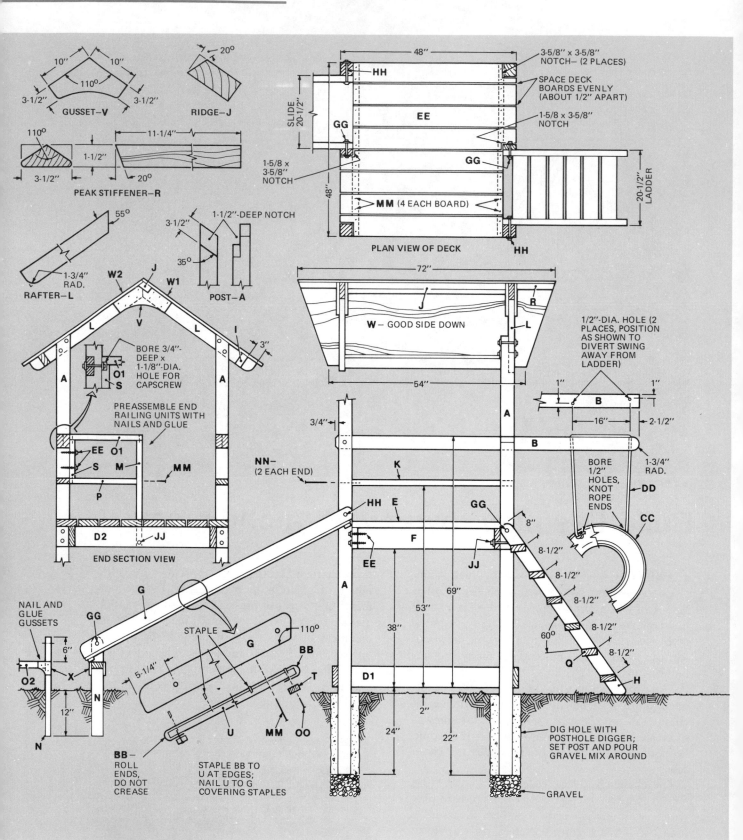

GUSSET–V

10''   10''
110°
3-1/2''   3-1/2''

RIDGE–J
20°

110°
1-1/2''
3-1/2''   20°
11-1/4''

PEAK STIFFENER–R

55°
1-3/4'' RAD.

RAFTER–L

1-1/2''-DEEP NOTCH
3-1/2''
35°

POST–A

W2   J   W1
V
L   L   I   3''
A   A

BORE 3/4''-DEEP x 1-1/8''-DIA. HOLE FOR CAPSCREW
O1
S

PREASSEMBLE END RAILING UNITS WITH NAILS AND GLUE
EE   O1
S   M   MM
P

D2   JJ

END SECTION VIEW

48''
HH
SPACE DECK BOARDS EVENLY (ABOUT 1/2'' APART)
3-5/8'' x 3-5/8'' NOTCH– (2 PLACES)
1-5/8 x 3-5/8'' NOTCH
SLIDE 20-1/2''
GG   EE
GG
48''
1-5/8 x 3-5/8'' NOTCH
MM (4 EACH BOARD)
20-1/2'' LADDER
HH

PLAN VIEW OF DECK

72''
J   R
W – GOOD SIDE DOWN
L
54''

1/2''-DIA. HOLE (2 PLACES, POSITION AS SHOWN TO DIVERT SWING AWAY FROM LADDER)

1''   B   1''
16''   2-1/2''
A   B
BORE 1/2'' HOLES, KNOT ROPE ENDS
1-3/4'' RAD.
DD
CC

3/4''
NN– (2 EACH END)
K
HH   E
EE
F
EE
A
GG
JJ
8''
8-1/2''
8-1/2''
8-1/2''
8-1/2''
60°
Q
8-1/2''
H
69''
53''
38''
D1
2''
24''
22''
DIG HOLE WITH POSTHOLE DIGGER; SET POST AND POUR GRAVEL MIX AROUND
GRAVEL

NAIL AND GLUE GUSSETS
G
GG
6''
X
O2
N
12''
N

STAPLE
G
110°
5-1/4''
BB
T
U   MM   OO

BB– ROLL ENDS, DO NOT CREASE

STAPLE BB TO U AT EDGES; NAIL U TO G COVERING STAPLES

chain-saw joinery

Before starting, make certain that the chain is sharp. Begin by making the 35° angle cuts at the top of each post. Wear safety glasses and clamp the work firmly to your sawhorses. A chain saw does have muscle, and you don't want the posts shifting about during cutting.

Next, make the 35° shoulder cuts in the posts.

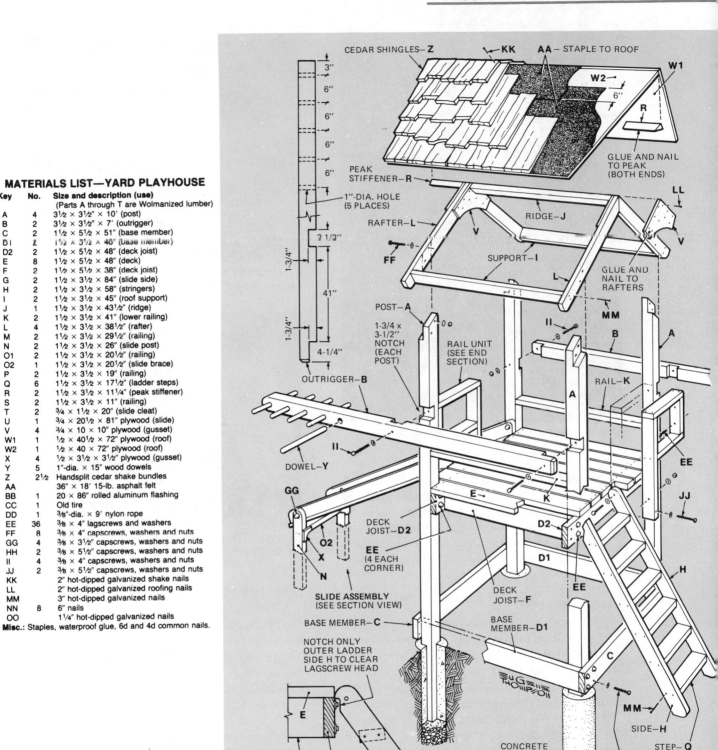

MATERIALS LIST—YARD PLAYHOUSE

Key	No.	Size and description (use)
		(Parts A through T are Wolmanized lumber)
A	4	3½ × 3½ × 10' (post)
B	2	3½ × 3½ × 7' (outrigger)
C	2	1½ × 5½ × 51" (base member)
D1	2	1½ × 3½ × 40" (base member)
D2	2	1½ × 5½ × 48" (deck joist)
E	8	1½ × 5½ × 48" (deck)
F	2	1½ × 5½ × 38" (deck joist)
G	2	1½ × 3½ × 84" (slide side)
H	2	1½ × 3½ × 58" (stringers)
I	2	1½ × 3½ × 45" (roof support)
J	1	1½ × 3½ × 43½" (ridge)
K	2	1½ × 3½ × 41" (lower railing)
L	4	1½ × 3½ × 38½" (rafter)
M	2	1½ × 3½ × 29½" (railing)
N	2	1½ × 3½ × 26" (slide post)
O1	2	1½ × 3½ × 20½" (railing)
O2	1	1½ × 3½ × 20½" (slide brace)
P	2	1½ × 3½ × 19" (railing)
Q	6	1½ × 3½ × 17½" (ladder steps)
R	2	1½ × 3½ × 11¼" (peak stiffener)
S	2	1½ × 3½ × 11" (railing)
T	2	¾ × 1½ × 20" (slide cleat)
U	1	¾ × 20½ × 81" plywood (slide)
V	4	¾ × 10 × 10" plywood (gusset)
W1	1	½ × 40½ × 72" plywood (roof)
W2	1	½ × 40 × 72" plywood (roof)
X	4	½ × 3½ × 3½" plywood (gusset)
Y	5	1"-dia. × 15" wood dowels
Z	2½	Handsplit cedar shake bundles
AA		36" × 18' 15-lb. asphalt felt
BB	1	20 × 86" rolled aluminum flashing
CC	1	Old tire
DD	1	⅜"-dia. × 9' nylon rope
EE	36	⅜ × 4" lagscrews and washers
FF	8	⅜ × 4" capscrews, washers and nuts
GG	4	⅜ × 3½" capscrews, washers and nuts
HH	2	⅜ × 5½" capscrews, washers and nuts
II	4	⅜ × 4" capscrews, washers and nuts
JJ	2	⅜ × 5½" capscrews, washers and nuts
KK		2" hot-dipped galvanized shake nails
LL		2" hot-dipped galvanized roofing nails
MM		3" hot-dipped galvanized nails
NN	8	6" nails
OO		1¼" hot-dipped galvanized nails

Misc.: Staples, waterproof glue, 6d and 4d common nails.

Then flop the post on its side and make the rip cut. By stopping both cuts just short of their mark, and removing the waste by hand, you will get the neatest possible joint. The straight

notches are made in the outriggers with six parallel 1¾-in.-deep kerf cuts. Clean these out with a sharp chisel, keeping in mind that all edges will be exposed.

play tower continued on next page

THE OUTRIGGER is high enough to provide good sport, but low enough to be nonhazardous.

CLAMP POST firmly to sawhorse; keep saw level when making mitered shoulder cut.

STOP CUTS just short of desired depth. Finish the notch with a handsaw or chisel.

Cut all four rafters to length, then cut the tail detail with a sabre saw. Use waterproof glue and 2-in., hot-dipped galvanized nails to attach the plywood gussets to both sides. Because there are no joists or collar beams in this tower, it is extremely important that the joint between the rafters be properly constructed.

framing the tower

Next, working on a flat surface such as your garage floor or driveway, lay the posts down in pairs. After making certain that the paired posts are parallel and square to each other, tack-nail three braces between them, one each at the top, bottom and on the diagonal.

By setting the rafter assemblies into the shoulder cuts and clamping them in place, you can bore the holes for both simultaneously and thereby assure proper alignment. Bolt the rafter assemblies to each pair of posts as shown.

Cut the deck joists and base members next and assemble with lagscrews and washers.

Be sure that you bore pilot holes to prevent splitting. After the joists and deck members are complete, attach them to the four posts and nail the ridge and roof supports between the rafters. Again, check for square and use braces between each pair of posts.

moving the tower

Now, dig four holes for the posts with a clamshell posthole digger. Make certain that the centers of the holes form a square with 44½-in. sides. The postholes should have a diameter of about 8 in. and be 28 in. deep. Pour 6 in. of gravel into each hole.

It is best to move the tower now, before it gets any heavier. Once you stand it in the holes, rock it slightly to seat it in the gravel. If the structure has remained square during the move, all that's needed is to plumb it and hold it that way with several diagonal braces secured to the posts on one end and to the stakes on the other end. Next, pour concrete around all posts.

Cut the roof panels from ½-in. plywood, as in the drawing, and attach them to the rafters and supports with 6d common nails. Because the underside is the visible surface, put the better side of the panels down. Add the peak stiffeners (R) by nailing them from above with 4d common nails.

TO AVOID ERROR, use a felt pen to mark a clear line; the Xs show which side is waste.

HOLD SAW at downward angle and rip slowly. Taking extra time now will pay off later.

MAKE INSIDE notches 1¾-in. deep with repeated saw-kerf cuts spaced ⅜ in. apart.

USE A WIDE CHISEL to remove waste, straighten edges and level the bottom of the notch.

Hold each stiffener securely with one hand while you drive the nails from above with the other.

Next, staple on 15-lb. felt to cover the roof, overlapping the peak. Then apply the hand-split cedar shakes using 4d, hot-dipped galvanized nails. These nails extend through the plywood and *must be clipped flush to the surface with an end nipper.*

The holes for the swing and the dowels can now be bored in the outriggers and the dowels glued in place. Then bolt the outriggers to the posts. Next, preassemble the railing units with nails and glue to assure maximum strength and notch them as shown to fit over the outrigger bolts that extend past the posts.

Bolt the railings to the posts and joists, then cut the lower railings below the outriggers. These are nailed in place from the far side of the post with 6-in. nails. Pilot holes should be bored first to prevent splitting.

The slide is made by stapling 20-in.-wide aluminum flashing to the plywood along the edges; the heads will be covered later by the slide sides. Because aluminum flashing comes in a roll, it tends to curl, so cut it to length and reroll it in the opposite direction to straighten it out. At the top and bottom of the plywood, gently bend the flashing around the edge to avoid creasing and then nail the cleats over the ragged edges as shown.

Complete the slide by sanding all edges and making the slide support. Support holes have to be dug about 1 ft. deep for this. They can be positioned by merely holding the slide in its proper location and marking where the holes should be. No gravel or concrete is needed in these holes, but be sure to tamp down the backfilled dirt.

Finally, attach the slide and the ladder with capscrews as shown and cut and nail the deck boards to the joists.

Dollhouse is a toybox, too

By ROSARIO CAPOTOSTO AND HARRY WICKS

■ BUILD THIS charming dollhouse and you're certain to become the hero father of your block. Its bright, cheerful design will blend well in any little girl's room; the two roomy floors and the spacious toy box are sure to make this a child's favorite toy. Your children will enjoy spending hours playing with it and then put all their toys away neatly when done. (Perhaps!)

Adapted from dollhouse plans offered by Georgia-Pacific Corp., the house is built with conventional building techniques and standard workshop tools. You need neither exotic tools nor any super-sophisticated carpentry knowledge to duplicate the house on these pages. Our goal, when we built the prototype shown, was to simplify construction as much as possible, thus making the house quicker and easier to build.

The windows, door and stairway are integral parts of the hinged front panel, which swings aside readily for access to the dollhouse behind it.

roof-panel safety feature

The hinged roof panel over the toy box is simply lifted for access to the storage space below. There is an important design note regarding the toy box roof that you should consider. We debated whether or not to install permanent hardware to hold the roof in the open position and decided against it, fearing that there is too great a chance of one child releasing the roof while another youngster is leaning into the box.

Similarly, if there is no hinge protection at all, there is a real risk of hinge damage caused by an exuberant child opening the rooftop too enthusiastically. We opted for a length of chain that prevents opening the roof beyond hinge capacity. *But be aware that the chain does not serve as a permanent stop in the open position.* You should instruct your child in the safe use of this roof/lid.

You'll need 1⅓ sheets of ½x48x96-in. fir plywood to build the house. Lay out the parts as shown in the cutting diagrams. Don't forget to allow for saw-kerf waste between the pieces. Since three roof panels require compound angle cuts, you should allow an extra inch or so for those parts to permit resawing after all square cuts have been made.

obtaining straight cuts

Use a smooth-cutting plywood blade to cut out the parts. Work with a straightedge guide and

portable circular saw or, if you can, use a table saw. If necessary, the cutting can be done with a sabre saw and straightedge.

Note that the pointed right-end panel (B) features two pointed fillers (R). You'll find it much simpler to do the cutting if you make straight through cuts along the parallel sides, then add ½x1 in. strips of solid pine to each edge of the top slants. Use glue and masking tape to hold them in place, then mark and cut the panel to the required angle.

Fill all voids and surface blemishes, usually on the C or D side, then sand all parts before assembly. If you mark all of the glue-joint lines and bore undersize pilot holes for the nails, you will ensure a neat, accurate assembly. This will also help prevent splitting of the plywood. Use carpenter's glue and 4d (1½ in.) finishing nails to join all pieces.

order of assembly

The best order of assembly is as follows: Attach the back of the right end, then add the bottom of the storage compartment. Next, add the front (D), then the partition (F). The room ceiling and the floors go on next, followed by the left endpiece. Finally, add the triangular attic front.

The back roof panel (A) requires a 30° bevel cut along its top edge and a compound angle cut along the end abutting the house roof. To make this cut on the table saw, tilt the blade to 13° and set the miter gauge to 25°.

If desired, a beveled cleat (O on the back wall) can be nailed and glued in position on the inside of the roof panel to simplify and strengthen the assembly. This cleat *should not* extend beyond the attic area. Glue and nail the piece in place.

Cut both attic roof panels to size, beveled and mitered as shown. Once again, attach cleats (O). Note that the bottom edge of the right attic roof panel has a beveled setback. It's easier to achieve this notch by making a through bevel cut, then adding a short strip (K) to form the overhang. Also, when the panel is attached, it will project slightly above the peak. After the glue has dried, use a belt sander to true up the joint.

Mark and cut the lid/roof panel to fit and attach it with a 1¹⁄₁₆-in.-wide continuous hinge. Attach a length of chain and two screw eyes to limit the lid's travel.

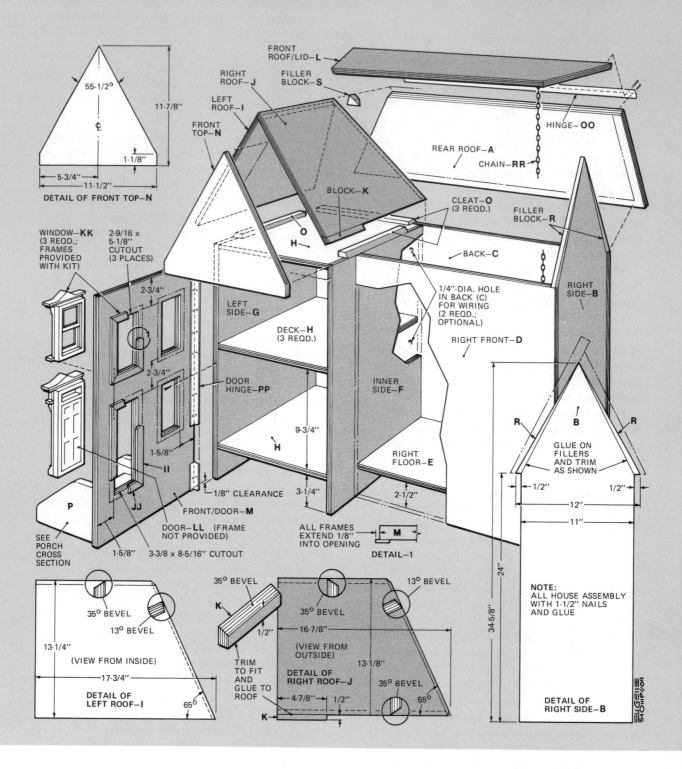

DETAIL OF FRONT TOP–N

55-1/2°
11-7/8″
1-1/8″
5-3/4″
11-1/2″

FRONT ROOF/LID–L
RIGHT ROOF–J
FILLER BLOCK–S
LEFT ROOF–I
FRONT TOP–N
HINGE–OO
REAR ROOF–A
CHAIN–RR
BLOCK–K
CLEAT–O (3 REQD.)
FILLER BLOCK–R
O
H
BACK–C
RIGHT SIDE–B

WINDOW–KK (3 REQD.; FRAMES PROVIDED WITH KIT)
2-9/16 x 5-1/8″ CUTOUT (3 PLACES)
2-3/4″
2-3/4″
LEFT SIDE–G
DECK–H (3 REQD.)
1/4″-DIA. HOLE IN BACK (C) FOR WIRING (2 REQD.; OPTIONAL)
RIGHT FRONT–D
INNER SIDE–F
DOOR HINGE–PP
9-3/4″
H
RIGHT FLOOR–E
1-5/8″
II
3-1/4″
2-1/2″
R
B
R
1/8″ CLEARANCE
GLUE ON FILLERS AND TRIM AS SHOWN
1/2″
1/2″
P
JJ
FRONT/DOOR–M
12″
SEE PORCH CROSS SECTION
1-5/8″
3-3/8 x 8-5/16″ CUTOUT
DOOR–LL (FRAME NOT PROVIDED)
ALL FRAMES EXTEND 1/8″ INTO OPENING
M
DETAIL–1
11″

24″
34-5/8″

NOTE: ALL HOUSE ASSEMBLY WITH 1-1/2″ NAILS AND GLUE

DETAIL OF RIGHT SIDE–B

35° BEVEL
13° BEVEL
35° BEVEL
K
35° BEVEL
13° BEVEL
1/2″
16-7/8″
13-1/4″
(VIEW FROM INSIDE)
(VIEW FROM OUTSIDE)
13-1/8″
17-3/4″
65°
TRIM TO FIT AND GLUE TO ROOF
DETAIL OF RIGHT ROOF–J
35° BEVEL
DETAIL OF LEFT ROOF–I
4-7/8″
1/2″
K
65°

EUGENE THOMPSON

MATERIALS LIST—DOLLHOUSE

Key	No.	Size and description (use) (All parts below are of ½″ plywood)
A	1	13³⁄₈ × 30½″ (roof, rear)
B	1	11 × 34⅝″ (side, right)
C	1	24 × 29⁹⁄₁₆″ (back)
D	1	13¹⁄₁₆ × 24″ (front, right)
E	1	11 × 17⁹⁄₁₆″ (floor, right)
F	1	15 × 24″ (side, inner)
G	1	15 × 24″ (side, left)
H	3	10½ × 15″ (decks)
I	1	13¼ × 17¾″ (roof, left)
J	1	13⅛ × 16⁷⁄₈″ (roof, right)
K	1	1 × 4⁷⁄₈″ (block, right roof; trim to size)
L	1	14⅛ × 24⅜″ (roof/lid, front)
M	1	11½ × 22⅝″ (front/door)
N	1	11½ × 11⁷⁄₈″ (front/top)

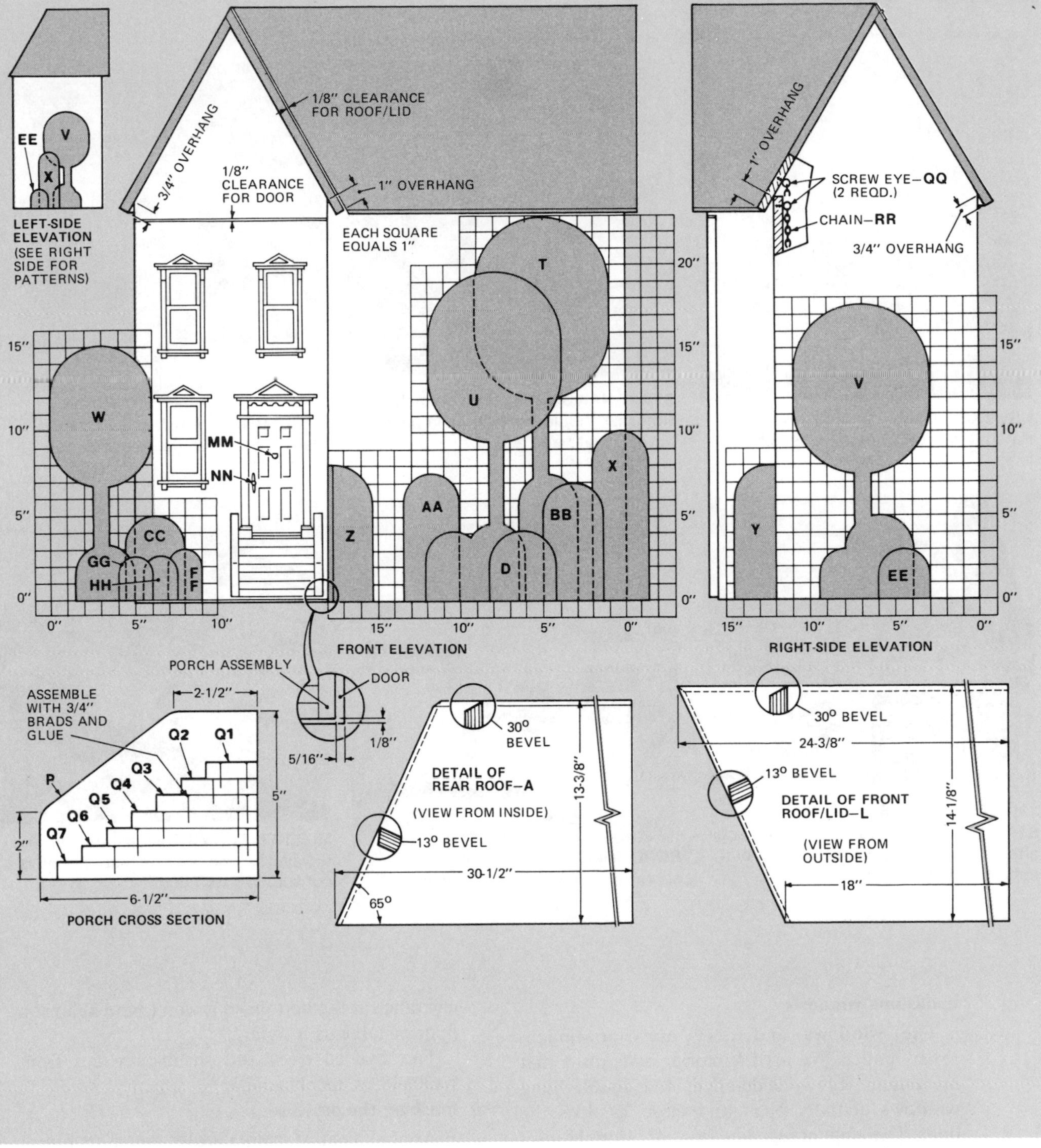

LEFT-SIDE ELEVATION (SEE RIGHT SIDE FOR PATTERNS)
EE
V
X
3/4" OVERHANG
1/8" CLEARANCE FOR DOOR
1/8" CLEARANCE FOR ROOF/LID
1" OVERHANG
EACH SQUARE EQUALS 1"
MM
NN
W
CC
GG
HH
F
F
T
U
AA
Z
D
BB
X
0"
5"
10"
15"
20"
FRONT ELEVATION
1" OVERHANG
SCREW EYE—QQ (2 REQD.)
CHAIN—RR
3/4" OVERHANG
V
Y
EE
RIGHT-SIDE ELEVATION
PORCH ASSEMBLY
DOOR
1/8"
5/16"
ASSEMBLE WITH 3/4" BRADS AND GLUE
2-1/2"
P
Q1
Q2
Q3
Q4
Q5
Q6
Q7
2"
5"
6-1/2"
PORCH CROSS SECTION
30° BEVEL
DETAIL OF REAR ROOF—A
(VIEW FROM INSIDE)
13° BEVEL
13-3/8"
30-1/2"
65°
24-3/8"
DETAIL OF FRONT ROOF/LID—L
(VIEW FROM OUTSIDE)
14-1/8"
18"

Key	No.	Size and description (use)
O	3	1 × 10" (cleats; trim to fit)
P	2	5 × 6 1/2" (porch side)
		(All parts below are of 1/2" pine)
Q-1	1	1 1/2 × 4 1/2" (porch step)
Q-2	1	2 1/4 × 4 1/2" (porch step)
Q-3	1	3 × 4 1/2" (porch step)
Q-4	1	3 3/4 × 4 1/2" (porch step)
Q-5	1	4 1/2 × 4 1/2" (porch step)
Q-6	1	4 1/2 × 5 1/4" (porch step)
Q-7	1	4 1/2 × 6" (porch step)
R	2	1 × 15" (filler, right side; trim as shown)
S	1	2 × 2" (filler block; trim to fit)
		(All parts below are of 1/4" plywood)
T	1	8 × 22"
U	1	8 × 18"

Key	No.	Size and description (use)
V	3	8 × 17"
W	1	5 × 16"
X	2	3 1/2 × 10"
Y	1	2 1/2 × 7 1/2"
Z	1	2 1/4 × 7 1/2"
AA	1	2 1/4 × 7"
BB	1	3 7/8 × 7"
CC	1	3 1/2 × 5"
DD	1	3 3/4 × 4"
EE	2	2 1/4 × 3"
FF	1	2 × 3"
GG	1	1 3/4 × 2 1/2"
HH	1	2 1/4 × 2 1/4"
II	1	1/8 × 1/2 × 9 1/16" pine
JJ	1	1/8 × 1/2 × 4 1/8" pine
KK	3	Windows (Houseworks No. 5002)
LL	1	Door (Houseworks No. 6013)

Key	No.	Size and description (use)
MM	1	Door knocker (Houseworks No. H07)
NN	1	Doorknob (Houseworks No. 1105)
OO	1	1 1/6 × 24" roof hinge, continuous
PP	1	1 1/16 × 22 1/2" door hinge, continuous
QQ	2	Screw eyes
RR	1	25" chain

Misc.: 3/4" nails, 1 1/2" nails, glue, pigmented shellac sealer, paint, sandpaper.

Dollhouse accessories: Houseworks Ltd., 2388 Pleasantdale Rd. N.E., Atlanta, Ga. 30340. Send $1 for a product catalog. Request the list of retail outlets.

Dollhouse furnishings in color photo were supplied by Tiny Doll House, 231 East 53rd St., New York, N.Y. 10022 Send $3 to the company if you desire its catalog.

dollhouse/toybox, continued

USE COMPOUND such as ZAR Wood Patch to fill voids before assembly.

START NAILS during dry assembly. Note that shoulders (O) on end panel have not yet been added.

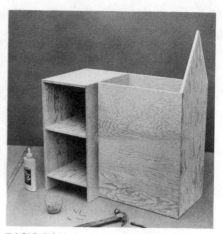

BASIC BOX, ready for roof to be installed, as it's shown in drawings.

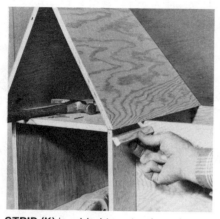

STRIP (K) is added to extend overhang after through bevel cut is made on bottom of roof panel.

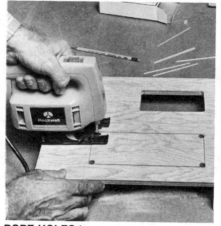

BORE HOLES in corners, then use sabre saw to cut window openings.

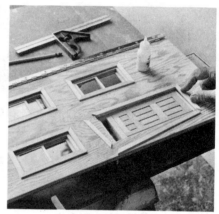

MITERED FRAMING strips are installed for window and door backup. Frame is not supplied with door.

handsome windows

The windows and door are store-bought ready-mades. We used Victorian-style units that are remarkably well detailed: The double-hung windows actually open and close, as does the door. The elegant reproductions are from Houseworks Ltd.; see the materials list for how-to-order information.

Lay out the openings for the windows and door, then bore a small blade-entry hole in each corner; use a sabre saw with a fine-tooth blade to make the cutouts.

The windows come with mitered frame members for use in trimming the back side. Rear frame strips are not supplied with the door, but can be easily made with ⅛x½-in. pine stock.

Build the stairway as a unit and attach it directly to the front panel of the house. Allow clearance at the bottom so it won't bind against a floor or table as it swings.

The stylized trees and shrubs are cut from ¼x36x48-in. fir plywood.

finishing the project

Apply a coat of primer sealer—such as Bin or Enamelac—to all surfaces, but leave small, bare patches of wood where trees and shrubs will be glued. Don't paint the backs of the trees and shrubs.

Trees, windows and front door are attached with glue and ¾-in. brads after *all* painting is done.

The dollhouse shown here was painted with latex interior semigloss enamel. To obtain vari-colored trees and shrubs, we poured some green paint into a separate container and darkened it with burnt umber pigment from a tube.

Build an extension flash bracket

Here's a versatile flash arm you can build that will keep your strobe light high above the lens no matter how you twist or turn the camera

By FRANK LaMANNA

Measure 1½ inches from one end of the tubing and position the hinge pin there. Mark locations of the screw holes and remove the hinge.

Cut a 4-in length of the ¾-inch wood stock and insert it into the aluminum tubing. Using a ³/₃₂-inch bit, drill the holes marked on the aluminum so the bit slightly penetrates the wood. Trim the ends of the hinge leaves to allow clearance for the elbow catches. Attach the hinge to the aluminum, making sure the screws are seated in the wood. The screws will form threads in the soft aluminum, and thread into the wood for added strength.

Cut a second piece of aluminum tubing approximately 3 inches long. Cut a ³/₈x³/₈-inch notch into one end to provide clearance for the hinge pin. Fit the hinge pin in this notch and mark locations of the remaining screw holes. Cut a 2¾-inch length of the wood stock and insert it into the tubing. Drill holes and attach the hinge, driving screws all the way into the wood.

Cut a 6-inch piece of ⅛x1-inch flat steel-bar stock and place it on top of the 3-inch length of tubing as shown. Drill a ³/₃₂-inch hole about ⅜ to

■ THE FLASH BRACKET shown here holds the strobe high above the camera and swings to keep it over the lens whether the camera is vertical or horizontal. The lightweight bracket design is easily customized to suit your needs. The center post adjusts to raise the light even higher. Since the post is removable, the flash can be switched to a similar bracket on another camera without removing the whole mount.

A bracket like this one will help you avoid a red-eye effect in slides and prints where the pupils of the eye seem to be red dots. The bracket prevents the bounce-back reflections causing the problem.

Our bracket also prevents harsh shadows caused by turning the camera vertically and having your strobe off to the side.

Begin by measuring how high above the camera you wish the flash to be. Allow about 8 inches above the lens plus enough more to let the lower end of the flash arm extend 2½ inches below the base of the camera. Mark this length on the square aluminum tubing. Use a hacksaw to cut the tubing.

DUAL-PURPOSE strobe bracket helps eliminate "red-eye" effect and provides more pleasing, shadowless lighting. Its hinged arm flips to best position no matter which way you hold camera.

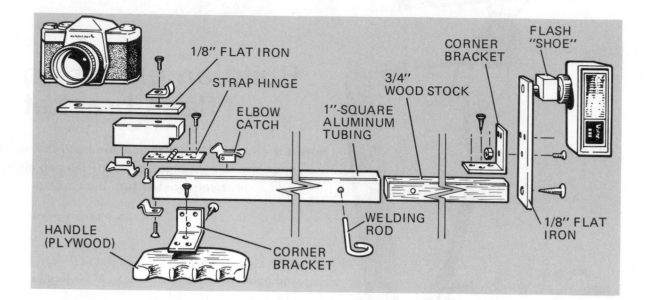

½ inch from the end nearest the flash arm. This hole should go through the steel and aluminum into the wood. Enlarge the hole in the steel using a ⅛-inch bit. Attach the steel to the aluminum tubing.

Test-position the striker and elbow catch so they will hold the flash arm properly in the up position. Mark the hole in the striker plate on the steel bar. Drill a hole through to the wood with a ³⁄₃₂-inch bit, then enlarge the hole in the steel to ⅛ inch. Use a screw to hold the striker plate in place. Place the catch, drill the necessary ³⁄₃₂-inch holes and attach with the screws provided. Adjust with washers if needed. File all edges smooth. Carefully drill a ¼-inch hole in the steel bar about 2 inches in from the opposite end. This is for attaching the flash bracket to your camera using a ¼-20 thumbscrew in the tripod socket. Attach the second striker and catch in the same way as the first.

Insert the remainder of the ¾-inch wood stock into the top of the vertical flash arm and cut it off so it protrudes about 1½ inches above the tubing. To this protruding end, attach the 1½-inch corner bracket as shown, using wood screws. Position a second 6-inch length of ⅛x1-inch bar stock over this bracket, allowing a ¾-inch overlap so that the bar can be screwed to the top of the flash post.

Drill out all of the necessary holes and assemble the bar and bracket to the post. Drill a ¼-inch hole in the opposite end of the bar to line up with the mounting hole in the lower bar.

With the square stock in the tubing, drill a ⅛-inch hole as shown. Raise the post 1 inch and repeat. Continue at one-inch intervals as far as you wish. These holes allow the height of the flash arm to be adjusted.

Next, insert a piece of welding rod into the desired hole and kink it slightly to keep it from falling out. (A rubber band will also help to hold it in place.)

Mount a flash shoe on the upper steel bar using a ¼-20 machine screw. For further flash adjustment, especially important in closeups, you may wish to add a ball-and-socket swivel between the shoe and your camera. These are available to fit a standard flash shoe and will accept the shoe on your strobe.

Shape the ¾-inch plywood with a coping saw to make a comfortable grip for your hand. Sand the edges smooth. Fasten the grip to the side of the vertical flash post using a right-angle bracket or a length of ⅛-inch bar stock bent to an angle.

Finish by gluing a rubber strip to the base plate and spraying the unit black. Attach your camera to the bracket, slip your flash in the shoe, and connect the strobe to the camera with an accessory coil cord. You should be cautious about using this bracket with wide-angle lenses as the angle of the flash may not be sufficient to cover the entire angle of the lens.

MATERIALS LIST—FLASH BRACKET

No.	Size and description
1	2″ strap hinge
2	Elbow catches
1	½″-sq. aluminum tubing
1	1½″ corner bracket
1	¾ × ¾ × 24″ pine or hardwood
1	¾ × 5 × 7″ plywood
1	6 × 1″ rubber strip

Misc.: Roundhead No. 6 ¾″ wood screws, ⅛ × ³⁄₄″ roundhead bolts with lock washers and nuts, flash shoe threaded ¼″-20, short piece of welding rod.

Ten big cameras you can hide in your hand

**New miniaturization doesn't mean you have to forfeit the big camera features:
Here you will find SLR or rangefinder, 35 mm or 110 and manual or fully automated
to fit all your needs**

By BOB BERGER

■ MOST COMPACT cameras are small enough to nestle in your palm. But modest size and weight are not their only virtues. Some boast features that would be hard to find in larger, more costly cameras. (Note: Prices listed here were in effect when this article was written.)

Pentax Auto 110

The tiniest of our compacts, the Pentax, at a mere 6.1 ounces and less than 4 inches long, is almost toylike in appearance. But it's a high-precision, single-lens reflex, and offers a unique feature for a compact—interchangeable lenses.

The lenses are featherweights. A film winder is an option, as is a set of closeup lenses. Film loading is a cinch—the Pentax takes 110 cartridges.

Even with wide-angle and telephoto, the whole Pentax outfit remains pocketable. The Pentax list price is about $250. Telephoto and wide-angle list for about $80 each.

Minolta 110 Zoom Mark II

A lot of photographers like the Minolta, and what they like best is its 25-67-mm zoom lens. In its macro mode, the lens focuses down to 7.7 inches. The shutter, like that on the Pentax, is electronic, but instead of the Pentax fully automated exposure, the Minolta requires that the lens aperture be set manually. The built-in meter then automatically selects the appropriate shutter speed.

A fine feature on the Minolta is a switch just above the eyepiece that adjusts the viewfinder to suit your vision. The Minolta holds a 110 cartridge firmly in place. Included in its $342 list price are a detachable grip and lens hood.

Chinon 110

A simple camera, the Chinon 110 is strictly for snapshooting, but has such amenities as built-in

MINIATURIZED CAMERAS offer both standard and unique features made tiny. Switch on lens of Minolta 110 (top) lets you focus to 7.7 inches. Wheels on Rollei 35SE (above) have been placed on the front of the case instead of on the top surface.

THESE CARRY-ALONGS can go anywhere, so their lenses could get into trouble. Olympus XA (above) uses a sliding front to protect its lens. Two barn-door-style arrangements are used on Chinon Bellami camera (top) to keep lens clean—and unbroken.

A WIDE CHOICE in system designs is offered by various manufacturers. Real pros will appreciate interchangeable lenses on Pentax 110 (top). Snapshooters might be happier with automation of Chinon 110 (below). Flash unit is built in on this one.

MINOX GL

CANON AF 35M

CHINON BELLAMI

RICOH FF-1S

power winder and built-in flash. The fixed-focus lens is designed to keep things sharp from 3.3 feet to infinity. Its shutter is mechanical, with two speeds. Suggested retail price is $74.95.

Olympus XA

Like others in the Olympus lineup, the XA is a design tour de force. The lens is actually shorter than its focal length, by some 4 mm.

Other XA innovations include rangefinder windows and a sliding cover. The latter is an integral part of the camera that switches off the electronics when closed—and effectively protects the lens and viewfinder.

That's right—despite its 4-inch length and a weight of only 7.9 ounces, the XA has a coupled rangefinder. And the electromagnetic shutter release is marvelous. The XA uses 35-mm film, as

do the remainder of the cameras in our story. List price, including electronic flash, is $233.

Minox GL

The lightest 35-mm of the group, the Minox has a folding front cover to guard the lens and viewfinder. When it's closed, the cover also shuts off the electronics and locks the shutter. The electronic shutter, just as on the Olympus, automatically sets the proper speed for any aperture selected. List price: $330.

Chinon Bellami

Though a bit heavier than some of its rivals, the Bellami, at 8.8 ounces, is a trim little package. Actuating the film-advance lever opens two dust-cover doors that seal the lens. After you set the desired ASA rating, the Bellami's automatic ex-

MINOLTA 110 ZOOM MARK II

ROLLEIMAT AF

CHINON 110

OLYMPUS XA

ROLLEI 35SE

PENTAX AUTO 110

posure system does the rest of the work. Suggested retail is $185.

Ricoh FF-1s

The Ricoh weighs in at just under 8 ounces. It offers fully automated exposure. A feature that may be helpful to snapshooters is an LED warning signal in the viewfinder. When the shutter is set slower than 1/60 second, the LED comes on as a reminder to hold the camera extra steady. Suggested list is $219.50.

Rollei 35SE

With its left-handed advance lever, Leica-style collapsible lens mount, baseplate-mounted rewind crank and flash shoe, the Rollei is a true oddity. In this new version, three stacked LEDs in the viewfinder indicate overexposure, correct exposure and underexposure. Weight is 11.2 ounces. A black SE lists for $292; chrome is $277.

Rolleimat AF

It weighs almost 14 ounces and measures more than 5 inches long, but the Rolleimat features automatic focus, automatic exposure and built-in flash. The autofocus operates from 4 feet to infinity. Suggested retail is $159.95.

Canon AF 35M

Another compact on the hefty side, the Canon weighs 14.2 ounces. But it may not be so weighty if you consider that it has everything you can think of: autofocus, autoexposure, built-in, pop-up flash, and built-in motorized film advance and rewind. The cost of absolute automation: $240 list.

Build a power meter and stylus timer

By JEFF SANDLER

These two handy electronic devices measure wear and tear on your stereo system. One checks on power to the speakers and the other monitors stylus wear

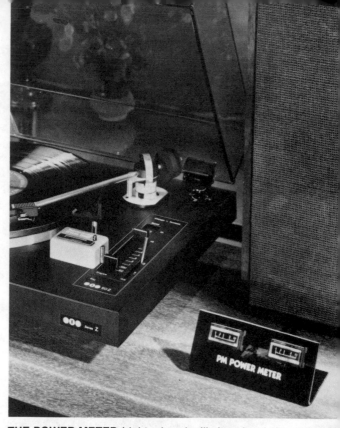

THE POWER METER (right, above) will show just how many watts are getting to your speakers. The stylus timer (pictured atop the turntable) will meter out the hours your stylus has been tracking the grooves so that you will know when to replace it.

■ IF YOU HAVE an expensive stereo set, the most crucial and easily damaged components are the largest and the smallest—your speakers and your stylus. Here are two projects, a power meter and a stylus timer, that can be added to most stereo systems.

the power meter

A power meter, even a three-range one like ours, is a very simple circuit. Essentially, it's a resistor, a diode and a meter in a series circuit. Its function is to measure the voltage going into the speakers. The more voltage, the more power the speakers use. The nonlinear meter scale converts this into the customary units of power—watts.

In the circuit, each resistor limits the voltage going into the sensitive meter and also determines the range of 1, 10 or 100 watts. Since there are three ranges, you need three resistors and a switch to select the desired range. The diode rectifies the a.c. voltage to the speakers into d.c. voltage that the meter can display.

But you need two independent meters, one for each stereo channel. The solution is to duplicate the circuit—so that you have six resistors, two diodes and one double-pole, double-throw switch.

In the construction, you solder these parts onto a printed-circuit board, along with the clips that will hold the speaker leads, or use point-to-point wiring. We supply a plastic holder (see parts list on page 183) or you can use your own design. Using hookup wire, connect the M1+ pad on the circuit board to the plus meter terminal. Likewise, the M1− pad goes to the minus meter terminal. This is repeated for the second meter,

using the M2+ and M2− pads on the circuit board.

Next, glue the circuit board to the clear-plastic support rails. Set the board so you get a good view of it through the smoked plastic. Finally, connect the speaker wires to the circuit-board clips. One channel goes to the two clips on one side of the circuit board and the other channel goes to the other side.

Now you can test your system. On the 1-watt scale, even at very low volume, the meters will bounce in synchronization with the loudness. Of course, as you increase the volume, the deflection becomes greater.

You should switch over to the 10- or 100-watt range when the meter needles reach the end of the lower scale.

As you move up to the higher wattage scales, you may be surprised that the sound level you hear doesn't seem to increase nearly as fast as the meters indicate. In other words, 100 watts doesn't sound 10 times louder than 10 watts, but perhaps only twice as loud.

There's nothing wrong with the meters—your own ears' logarithmic response cuts down loud sounds and builds up soft ones. It's the only way you can make sense of the range of sound levels you hear in a typical day—where the loudest can be a billion times stronger than the softest.

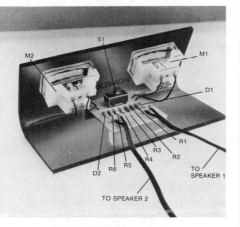

POWER METER contains two circuits that are mirror images of each other—one power-measuring circuit with two meters, one for each of your speakers.

STYLUS TIMER uses a unique mecury-plating device to measure the passage of time. When "used up," just reverse contacts and the meter is reusable.

THESE FOIL and component-side views show how to make the printed circuits for both projects. Alternatively, you can use the schematics above to do your own layout.

PM's STYLUSE TIMER

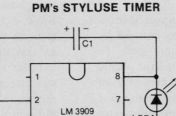

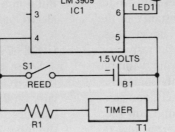

FOIL SIDE

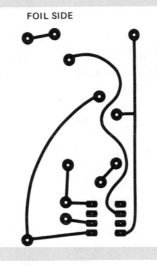

COMPONENT SIDE

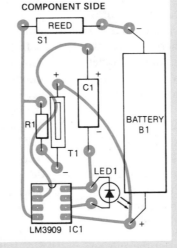

PM's POWER METER

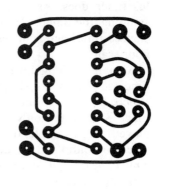

SWT DPDT

FOIL SIDE

COMPONENT SIDE

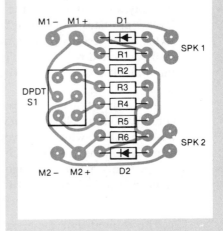

PARTS LIST—STYLUS TIMER

B1: AA-size battery, 1.5 v.
IC1: LM3909 LED flasher integrated circuit
LED1: Light-emitting diode
R1: 430K carbon resistor
S1: Reed switch
T1: Mercury tube timer (Curtis Instruments)
PCB: Drilled, etched and labeled printed-circuit board.
Misc.: Drilled and machined aluminum case, small bar magnet.

PARTS LIST—POWER METER

D1, D2: Germanium diodes (LN34A or equivalent)
M1, M2: Meter with power scale
R1, R6: 56K carbon resistors, ¼ w.
R2, R3: 24K carbon resistors, ¼ w.
R4, R5: 5.1K carbon resistors, ¼ w.
S1: d.p.d.t. slide switch
PCB: Drilled, etched and labeled printed-circuit board.
Misc.: Formed, machined, smoked Plexiglas holder, wire, solder, printed-circuit-board connection clips.

the stylus timer

The stylus tip on your record player leads a very harsh life indeed. While being crushed by up to 33 tons of pressure per square inch, it's dragged over two-thirds of a mile of hard plastic per hour. If that's not enough, it's whipped from side to side in the groove with accelerations of more than 100 Gs, up to 20,000 times per second!

Even a diamond, the hardest substance in the world, can't hold up indefinitely under these conditions. The result—a chipped, raspy tip abrading two-thirds of a mile of your valuable record groove per hour—is certainly something you would like to avoid. Unfortunately, you can't stop the steady erosion of the tip, but if you keep track of playing time, you can insert a new tip before your record player turns into a record shredder.

And keeping track of time is just what the stylus timer does. As soon as your records start spinning, the timer's LED starts to flash, and the elapsed-time meter moves down its 0 to 1,000-hour scale.

Actually, nailing down the exact stylus playing time isn't quite as simple as it first appears. Where do you tap into your system so that the timer is activated only when records are being played? For example, the ON-OFF switch is "on" when the radio or tape deck is used—neither of which wears out styluses. Applying the same logic eliminates such tie-in points as speaker outputs, switched outlets, preamp outputs and so forth.

But every time you play a record, you move the play lever, and when the record is done, the lever snaps back on its own. So here is where the stylus timer records playing time with a magnetically activated reed switch. This way, you avoid the difficult task of "hard-wiring" into your system.

Inside the stylus timer case is an interesting combination of old and new technology. The flashing LED, which lets you know the stylus timer is "timing," is driven by a modern IC developed only a few years ago. This IC is so efficient, it can flash the LED for more than 3,000 hours on a single alkaline penlight cell.

The elapsed-time meter relies on the old and seemingly inappropriate technology of electroplating—plating one metal on another using electric current. During electroplating, the amount of metal which is plated is only a function of the current multiplied by the time the current is flowing. If you keep the current constant, then the plating becomes only a function of

time, which is the variable we want to determine. But to determine the actual time, you have to determine the exact amount of metal plated—not an easy task.

Enter a clever idea—so clever, in fact, that it was patented recently. Instead of plating solid metals, why not use a liquid metal—mercury? Put it in a small-diameter glass tube with a liquid electrolyte "gap" in the mercury column.

changing sides

When the current is passed through the tube, the mercury on one side is plated onto the mercury on the other side of the gap. As the mercury changes sides, so to speak, the gap travels down the tube. The elapsed time is shown by the location of the gap on the printed time scale next to the tube.

In the circuit—as you might expect—the tube current starts when the reed switch closes (play lever on). The 430K (430,000-ohm) resistor sets the current so the gap takes 1,000 hours to go down the scale. Different resistors give other scales.

And the stylus timer can be reused. When the gap reaches the end of the scale, you reset it to zero by reversing the tube holder.

The function of the LM3909 IC and the capacitor is to flash the LED. They are powered through the reed switch to give you a fail-safe indication that the timer is operating.

To use the stylus timer effectively, check how long the manufacturer recommends you should go between stylus changes. Typically, for diamond styluses, it's 800 hours.

But deviations from ideal playing conditions can cut this time considerably. Dirty records can knock 30 percent off the figure. Even more critical is the tracking force—the weight that holds the needle in the groove. The ideal force for good systems is around 1¼ grams. Up at 3 grams, stylus life can be cut in half. Too little tracking force, however, is worse than too much: An underweight stylus "chatters" and chews out the sides of the groove.

WHERE TO BUY PARTS

The following are available from Circuit Craft Inc., 10 Idell Rd., Valley Stream, N.Y. 11580. Prices include postage and handling.

Power meter:
$9.95—kit of power meter parts (less case).
$16.95—kit of power meter parts including machined, formed, smoked Plexiglas case.
$19.95—completely assembled, ready-to-use power meter.

Stylus Timer:
$19.95—kit of stylus timer parts, including case.
$24.95—completely assembled stylus timer.

OHM N2 SUBWOOFER (left) has two 8-inch woofers which reach down to bone- thumping 30 Hz. Ohm minispeakers (right) handle the high notes in the $950 set.

Subwoofers reach for the bass-ment

■ AFTER YEARS of trying to reach the upper limits of the audible range, speaker designers now seem to be going the other way. Suddenly, they are delving for the depths.

One reason for this turnabout is that the heights have been conquered. The latest tweeters have no trouble reaching all the way to the top, so attention now shifts.

Designers used to be quite complacent about response below 40 Hz. They figured that only rarely did musical notes fall below that pitch. But that's no longer so. The advent of digitally recorded master tapes (from which so-called digital records are produced) has made it easier to capture the bottom lows on record.

In response to this challenge, a number of companies are now producing subwoofers—special, low-frequency speakers that take over where "normal" speakers leave off.

It is *not* necessary to have separate left and right subwoofers for stereo. Rather, the bass from both stereo channels can be pooled in a single subwoofer. That's because the lower frequencies are inherently nondirectional, and in the bass range, the distinction between left and right is lost.

An extra subwoofer in the system particularly complements the newly popular minispeakers, which are inherently bass-shy. One subwoofer especially designed as a bass extender for small speakers is the Ohm N2 for $385. It's an unusually compact, almost cube-shaped box (15x15 x16 inches), containing two 8-inch woofers which reach all the way down to 30 Hz. Unlike

most subwoofers, the Ohm N2 is not greedy for power; 10 watts suffice for its needs. Yet it will handle up to 100 watts easily.

Instead of two full-range speakers, it is now possible to use so-called satellite speakers—small speakers handling only the upper range—and combine them with a subwoofer to handle the bottom.

The advantage is that the small satellites (left and right) can easily be put on shelves or hung on the wall—thereby saving floor space—while the subwoofer itself can be used as a coffee table (if you don't mind occasionally rattling your cups). Such an arrangement takes up less space than two conventional, full size speakers. Ohm also offers its subwoofer as part of such a complete three-part system, with their Model M minispeakers serving as satellites. The total system price is a hefty $950, but the sound is splendid.

The most awesome bass to be heard from any of the new subwoofers comes from a contraption called the Contre-Bombarde, named after the deepest of all organ pipes. Produced by Shahinian Acoustics of Selden, N.Y., this massive (35x27x18 inch) unit aims not to save space, but to render the utmost lows of the audible spectrum down to 16 Hz. The horn-shaped, 20-foot-long sound path inside the box enables the Contre-Bombarde to emit ultradeep sounds. These are not so much heard through the ears as they are felt through vibrations of the body. When driven by a suitably powerful amplifier, this unique $850 device moves the air enough to blow out matches.

This may look like a record being eaten by a shark, but it's really the Vacorec from Vor Industries in operation, whisking dust away from a disc.

Manual antistatic generators look like futuristic ray guns and work as the trigger is pumped back and forth. But they do carry a good charge; so don't point them at anyone. The ones we show are: 1. Robins' Rob-O-Stat; 2. Discwasher's Zerostat; 3. Empire from Audio Groome.

The Kilavolt antistatic generator from Nagoka (left) works off battery with just the push of a button.

Placed on center of record, a heavy stabilizer, such as this one from Nagoka, will help stop warping.

Record-care hardware, such as the "Scotch" system from 3M, will help you protect your records from damaging static and oils.

The PDQII system from Audio-Technica will guard both your records and your turntable's stylus. Parts are also available separately.

Keep your records sounding new

By BILL KANNER

■ RECORD CARE has grown, from a small industry selling mainly treated cloths, to giant companies using space-age technology to guard discs against nicks, scratches and static. Along with the new ways to take care of records has come quite a bit of confusion over which method is best for which problem. There's even some question about how some of the more esoteric products work. You'll have to make your own judgment as to which system works best for your own particular situation.

Perhaps the best known device is the Disc-

washer, which has spawned many variations. The Discwasher is a directionally textured, plush pad mounted on a handsome wood handle. The pad is wetted with Discwasher's D3 solution and drawn around the record, tracking the grooves. As you brush the record, dust is swept up into the soft pad.

The variations include the liquid used to loosen the dirt, which can range from water to multichemical and antistatic formulas. Among the companies that produce this type of preener device, you'll find Watts, Recoton (whose Clean

Sound II has replaceable pads) and Audio-Technica (whose Sonic Broom has a brush cleaner). Robins' Whiskee and Sound Saver's Classic I have a cavity in the handle for the cleaning solution, as does the Discwasher.

sprays

While most of these devices have some sort of fluid to aid them, the basic item is really the wiper or brush. However, there is a group of products for which the reverse is true. You still squirt or spray a product onto a record or pad, but you *huff in* the substance rather than wipe up the dirt. The application is more important than the applicator.

Sound Guard is probably the most widely known of these products. It is a lubricant product of space-age technology. Its major feature is that it forms a chemical bond with the vinyl record groove and locks out dirt and grit; it also acts as a lubricant to reduce the friction of the stylus in the groove.

Audio-Technica's Lifesaver is a similar pump-spray product. However, it contains not only a record preservative/lubricant, but a cleaner, as well. The same can be said for Stanton's Permostat. If you prefer a full spray, Quietone, from Hammond Industries, is one that has a preservative/lubricant and antistatic agent.

ionic neutralizers

If you find you have lots of pops and clicks, symptomatic of static electricity, on your discs, you may want to try one of the solely antistatic products on the market. Again, the best known is probably from Discwasher, the Zerostat. There are a number of versions of this pistol-shaped device on the market. A slow squeeze of the trigger over the disc and static-neutralizing ions are released over the record. Empire and Robins have similar items. However, these products do produce a voltage and carry warnings not to aim at people and to keep out of the reach of children. Watts has a device that operates on the same principle, but is shaped like an oversized cigaret lighter instead of a gun. Osawa's Kilavolt is another ionic antistatic product. It is shaped something like a paint scraper and, unlike the other products mentioned, requires a "C" battery.

antistatic sleeves and mats

Once you've taken the trouble to remove static from your disc's surface, you will want to keep the static charge down. Empire and Discwasher are among the companies that produce antistatic, felt-type mats.

Since a static charge can be created simply by removing a disc from its sleeve, Discwasher and Empire, among other companies, have developed antistatic record jackets. Discwasher's VRPs are just the plastic-type sleeve, while Empire's is a paper sleeve with the plastic inner lining. Both come in packages of 10.

facials and vacuums

Empire's Disc-O-Film is a facial for records. While it contains an antistatic ingredient, its primary function is deep cleaning of record surfaces and grooves the same way a standard facial removes dirt and oil from the skin. The application is similar, too. Just squirt the goo on the record and wait (usually 45 minutes to an hour) and then just peel the hardened film from the disc. Along with the preparation should come all of the dust, dirt and grime you've let accumulate.

If the hour wait is too long for you, try vacuum-cleaning your records before you play them. Vacorec (now part of Robins) has two models on the market that do just that. The Model 100 first appeared a few years ago. It's a device that looks a little like a shark's jaw. You place the record in the groove (the shark's mouth), turn on the machine and the record is rotated and both sides are vacuumed clean.

cleaning the needle

Your stylus should be kept clean and your turntable level. A clean stylus will not push and grind dirt into the grooves of a clean record and a level turntable won't turn your diamond stylus into a Grade-A cutting tool. Stylus cleaners are also widely available now. Watts, Discwasher and Robins among the companies marketing devices to clean your diamond. The Watts stylus cleaner is a soft pad mounted on clear plastic. Discwasher's SC-1 is a brush on one side and a magnifying mirror on the other, all encased in a walnut handle. The SC-1 is designed to be used with Discwasher's D3 solution. Robins offers an entire kit including a brush, small screwdriver (for cartridge hardware), stylus microscope and stylus cleaning fluid.

The newest and most unusual set of devices are the stabilizers. Available from several companies, these heavy weights are designed to fit over the label area of your record and on the spindle. Many records arrive already warped, and the heavy weight will tend to flatten them for the time they are on the turntable.

HERE'S A STRAIGHT-LINE turntable that won't play your records lying down. It's the LT 5V from Mitsubishi, and it must stand vertically during operation. A pressure pad on the spindle holds records in place, while arm and stylus track in a straight line along a recessed worm gear.

Turntables that play it straight

By FRED PETRAS

EASY-ON-THE-FINGERS controls set functions of the LT 5V, including lifting the tone arm.

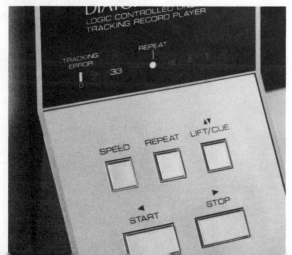

■ SHORTLY AFTER celebrating the phonograph's 100th anniversary, the audio industry is rediscovering Thomas Edison's approach to the phonographic art. Edison believed that the radial-drive, straight-line, tangential tracking method was the best way to move a pickup and its "needle" to extract all the nuances of sound in the record groove.

The audio industry is taking a new look at Edison's tangential tracking method—relative to today's state-of-the-art records that impose stiff demands on the equipment meant to play them.

REVOX MODEL B795 sells for $599. Stylus is carried, not by a tone arm, but by a "trolley" arrangement. The system, called Linatrack, is one of the most novel. It's explained at the right.

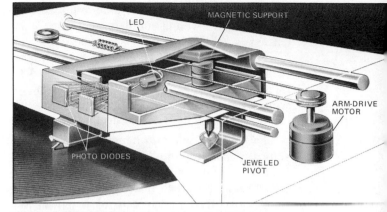

REVOX'S LINATRACK system moves the stylus across the record much as an industrial crane moves along its tracks. Photodiodes watch upcoming grooves and keep the stylus angle properly adjusted.

stylus moves in straight line

In some forms, a tangential tracking system dispenses with tone-arms; in others, it utilizes an abbreviated tone arm. But in all systems, the stylus moves in a straight line across the record surface, as opposed to moving in an arc, as on a pivoted tone arm. This arc skews the position at the outside grooves of a record, causing improper groove tracking and distortion that's greatest at the inside grooves of the record. While this distortion, even in high-quality, well-engineered turntables, may not be noticeable to many buffs, it is there.

Following is a rundown on how seven manufacturers achieve proper tracking. We describe nine current turntables with unusual tone-arm drive mechanisms. All prices were in effect at the time this was written.

Yamaha PX-2

In *Yamaha's Model PX-2* ($900), the tone arm is driven across the record by a precision-engineered, high-torque coreless motor coupled to the tone-arm carriage via a gear system and noise-damping belt. The motor is encased in neoprene and supported on a butyl base to minimize transmission of mechanical noise. The belt further dampens mechanical noise to transmit only smooth power to the tone-arm carriage. All these design details contribute to the PX-2's fine 80-decibel signal-to-noise ratio. Tone-arm position is controlled by a highly sensitive, dual-CDS opto-electronic tracking sensor.

Mitsubishi LT 5V

Mitsubishi Model LT 5V ($450) is a vertical "stand-up" radial-drive turntable. A high-pre-

THE MOST UNUSUAL feature of the Aiwa LP-3000 is that the tone arm is powered by two separate motors—one drives the arm, the other lifts and cues it.

PHOTODIODES are also in the Yamaha PX-2 table (below) and they continually adjust the angle.

cision servomotor drives the tone arm assembly via a specially wound stainless-steel wire. Wire tension is kept constant by spring loading, and servomotor rotation is applied by a worm-type reduction gear. This system holds the tone-arm assembly firmly in position. The tone-arm assembly rides on a mirror-finished, high-precision rod of nonmagnetic stainless steel.

The 8¾-inch tone arm hangs down vertically, statically balanced in all three directions for stable and accurate tracking of the grooves. It's even able to follow warped discs—and handle vibrations—with less tendency to skip out of the groove.

A spring-loaded clamp anchors the disc to the vertical platter. It hinges out of the way for convenience. Vertical operation offers a major benefit: virtually dustproof operation for "cleaner" sound.

The LT 5V accepts both moving-coil and moving-magnet cartridges mounted in "universal" headshells.

Mitsubishi LT 30

Mitsubishi Model LT 30 ($690) is a lay-down table with an 8⅞-inch tone arm. It uses two sensitive, optical sensors to maintain perfect tracking. Any departure from the tangent position detected by the sensors activates a servomotor that immediately moves the tone-arm base the correct amount to restore exact tangential tracking.

Revox B790 and B795

Revox Models B790 ($899) and *B795* ($599) appeal to two budget levels.

Both models feature Linatrack straight-line tracking. With Linatrack, the 1½-inch servo-controlled tone arm moves across the record on a carriage mounted on guide rails, traveling much like the trolley on an industrial crane. Variations in groove spacing can't surprise the tone arm. A photosensor scans the light from two LEDs, and it reports tracking contour to a computer.

built-in minicomputer

The computer generates the appropriate signals required by the servomotor, which alters the speed of the tone-arm carriage accordingly. Result: The tracking position of the pickup system is optimized.

Technics Model SL-10 ($600), with a moving-coil cartridge (and required head amp), is unusually compact for a turntable: Its top measures a mere 12½ inches square. The tone arm is 4⅛ inches long. Instead of conventional ball bearings

or rollers, the arm uses a slide bearing with a very low friction coefficient to avoid undesirable vibrations, allow silent, smooth operation and provide precise tone-arm transport. Gimbal suspension and dynamic balance allow the SL-10 to function standing up, angled at 45°, or in any other position, without loss of proper tracking.

The SL-10 is unique. It's a two-piece system joined in the middle. The top half has the linear-tracking tone arm, the drive system, and a microcomputer electronic control block. The lower half has an integral direct-drive turntable and motor with their driving and quartz-phase-locked control circuit.

Bang & Olufsen's Beogram 4004 ($850), with installed moving-magnet cartridge, uses a 6¾-inch low-mass tone arm. The tone-arm assembly is electronically controlled and driven by its own d.c. motor which moves the entire system toward the center of the record with constant accuracy. Ultralow-friction bearings reduce horizontal and vertical friction to a minimum. Riding tandem with the tone arm is a detector arm that includes an optical scanner to sense the pressure or absence of a record.

A 7½-inch tone arm is used in *Aiwa Model LP-3000* ($1000). The arm is transported by a precision-machined, single-support, rack-screw drive mechanism turned by its own coreless motor. It's said to minimize torque fluctuations and vibrations to the arm. Also, to assure stable lifting and lowering of the arm mechanism, Aiwa eliminated the traditional hydraulic damping mechanism and gave the arm an independent coreless motor, instead.

preselection feature offered

You can preselect up to 15 musical passages in any order, including multiple plays of the same passage. The selected program can be set to play up to 24 times or until halted manually.

Phase Linear Model 8000 ($750) has a direct-induction linear motor that moves in a straight line. The motor is essentially a permanent magnet, moved by an electromagnet. The 8000's tone-arm base is a permanently magnetized armature that glides along guide bars above the coil. When the current flows through the coil, the tone arm travels along a straight path. Current fluctuations instantly alter the tone arm's movement.

Inside the tone-arm base is an opto-electronic detector cell that senses the slightest tracking error, and instantly sends correcting signals to the differential amplifier that powers the coils.

Index

The page number refers to the first page on which specific information can be found.

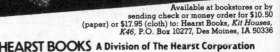

METRIC CONVERSION

Conversion factors can be carried so far they become impractical. In cases below where an entry is exact it is followed by an asterisk (*). Where considerable rounding off has taken place, the entry is followed by a + or a – sign.

CUSTOMARY TO METRIC

Linear Measure

inches	millimeters
1/16	1.5875*
1/8	3.2
3/16	4.8
1/4	6.35*
5/16	7.9
3/8	9.5
7/16	11.1
1/2	12.7*
9/16	14.3
5/8	15.9
11/16	17.5
3/4	19.05*
13/16	20.6
7/8	22.2
15/16	23.8
1	25.4*

inches	centimeters
1	2.54*
2	5.1
3	7.6
4	10.2
5	12.7*
6	15.2
7	17.8
8	20.3
9	22.9
10	25.4*
11	27.9
12	30.5

feet	centimeters	meters
1	30.48*	.3048*
2	61	.61
3	91	.91
4	122	1.22
5	152	1.52
6	183	1.83
7	213	2.13
8	244	2.44
9	274	2.74
10	305	3.05
50	1524*	15.24*
100	3048*	30.48*

1 yard =
 .9144* meters
1 rod =
 5.0292* meters
1 mile =
 1.6 kilometers
1 nautical mile =
 1.852* kilometers

Fluid Measure

(Milliliters [ml] and cubic centimeters [cc or cu cm] are equivalent, but it is customary to use milliliters for liquids.)

1 cu in = 16.39 ml
1 fl oz = 29.6 ml
1 cup = 237 ml
1 pint = 473 ml
1 quart = 946 ml
 = .946 liters
1 gallon = 3785 ml
 = 3.785 liters
Formula (exact):
fluid ounces × 29.573 529 562 5*
 = milliliters

Weights

ounces	grams
1	28.3
2	56.7
3	85
4	113
5	142
6	170
7	198
8	227
9	255
10	283
11	312
12	340
13	369
14	397
15	425
16	454

Formula (exact):
 ounces × 28.349 523 125* =
 grams

pounds	kilograms
1	.45
2	.9
3	1.4
4	1.8
5	2.3
6	2.7
7	3.2
8	3.6
9	4.1
10	4.5

1 short ton (2000 lbs) =
 907 kilograms (kg)
Formula (exact):
 pounds × .453 592 37* =
 kilograms

Volume

1 cu in = 16.39 cubic
 centimeters (cc)
1 cu ft = 28 316.7 cc
1 bushel = 35 239.1 cc
1 peck = 8 809.8 cc

Area

1 sq in = 6.45 sq cm
1 sq ft = 929 sq cm
 = .093 sq meters
1 sq yd = .84 sq meters
1 acre = 4 046.9 sq meters
 = .404 7 hectares
1 sq mile = 2 589 988 sq meters
 = 259 hectares
 = 2.589 9 sq
 kilometers

Kitchen Measure

1 teaspoon = 4.93 milliliters (ml)
1 Tablespoon = 14.79
 milliliters (ml)

Miscellaneous

1 British thermal unit (Btu) (mean)
 = 1 055.9 joules
1 calorie (mean) = 4.19 joules
1 horsepower = 745.7 watts
 = .75 kilowatts
caliber (diameter of a firearm's
 bore in hundredths of an inch)
 = .254 millimeters (mm)
1 atmosphere pressure = 101 325*
 pascals (newtons per sq meter)
1 pound per square inch (psi) =
 6 895 pascals
1 pound per square foot =
 47.9 pascals
1 knot = 1.85 kilometers per hour
25 miles per hour = 40.2
 kilometers per hour
50 miles per hour = 80.5
 kilometers per hour
75 miles per hour = 120.7
 kilometers per hour